ROUTLEDGE
GENERAL EDITOR · JOHN DRAKAKIS

9.50

The Importance of
Being Earnest
and
Related Writings

Oscar Wilde

ROUTLEDGE · ENGLISH · TEXTS
GENERAL EDITOR · JOHN DRAKAKIS

The Importance of
Being Earnest
and
Related Writings

Oscar Wilde

Edited by Joseph Bristow

LONDON AND NEW YORK

First published 1992 by
Routledge
11 New Fetter Lane,
London EC4P 4EE

Simultaneously published in the USA
and Canada by
Routledge
29 West 35th Street, New York,
NY 10001

© 1992 Joseph Bristow:
Introduction, Critical Commentary
and Notes

Typeset by Hewer Text
Composition Services Edinburgh
Printed in Great Britain by Clays Ltd,
St Ives plc

British Library Cataloguing in
Publication Data

The importance of being earnest and
related writings: Oscar Wilde
I. Title II. Bristow, Joseph
822.8

Library of Congress Cataloging in
Publication Data
The importance of being earnest and
related writings: Oscar Wilde /
edited by Joseph Bristow.
        p.   cm.   (Routledge English texts)
Includes bibliographical reference
    I. Bristow, Joseph.   II. Title.   III. Series.
PR5818.14   1992b
822'.8 — dc20   91–33612

ISBN 0–415–04368–9

To Frances Dann
for help, support, and friendship
Sheffield 1986–1991

friends was Lord Alfred Douglas, his lover and almost constant companion for several years. Wilde openly consorted with male homosexuals, although he did not enjoy an openly gay identity – that is, the type of sexual identity many men have adopted since the partial legalization of homosexual acts in Britain in 1967. Wilde strolled around the most fashionable quarters of London leading the kind of 'double life' noted in a playful allusion in *The Importance of Being Earnest*. Such activities would lead him into a sexual underworld whose extraordinary goings-on would burst upon late Victorian society when he was imprisoned for committing acts of 'gross indecency' in 1895.

It was the persistent importunities of Douglas's father, the irascible Marquess of Queensberry, that finally provoked Wilde into the disastrous court proceedings that excited the press for weeks. An impetuous man, remembered then as now for inventing the modern rules of boxing, Queensberry had left a visiting card at Wilde's club accusing the author of posing, in an infamous misspelling, as a 'somdomite'. In what turned out to be an ill-timed piece of litigation, the case taken against Queensberry tragically turned back on Wilde. As evidence from witnesses mounted against the author, Queensberry's insulting remark was vindicated by the courts. After confessions had been heard from young men who claimed to have performed sexual favours for Wilde, this highly regarded playwright was sentenced to two years in solitary confinement with hard labour. Most of this demoralizing period was spent in Reading Gaol, an experience which led to Wilde's two well-known prison writings: his long, open, and often recriminatory letter to Douglas, *De Profundis* (written 1897, but not published in full until much later), and his celebrated poem, *The Ballad of Reading Gaol* (published in 1898). Three and a half years after his release, with both his health and spirit broken, Wilde died in Paris, converting to Roman Catholicism in his final hours. Indeed, many homosexual men and women in Britain at this time turned to Roman Catholicism as a form of spiritual succour. The Catholic, as opposed to the Anglican, church seems to have represented a refuge for many sexual outsiders.

The three humiliating trials that took place during April and May 1895 occurred when two of Wilde's successful dramas were playing to packed houses in the West End of London. Shortly

Introduction

Oscar Fingal O'Flahertie Wills Wilde (as he first signed himself) was a highly controversial figure who for nearly twenty years thrived in the most fashionable circles of literary London. Achieving a considerable reputation as a man of many parts – as society wit, outlandish dresser, amusing public speaker, skilled dramatist, and writer of both adult and children's fiction – Wilde stood in forceful and often dangerous opposition to the reigning morality of late Victorian Britain. A socialist, an Anglo-Irishman, and a homosexual, Wilde in both his lifestyle and his writing managed to do two contradictory things at once: to entertain the most cultured ranks of society and yet mock many of the values cherished by that highly educated elite. It was a precarious situation, even for so talented a writer as Wilde. Much of his essays, drama, and fiction took great risks with affronting his often appreciative audiences. To note one well-known example: his only full-length fictional narrative, *The Picture of Dorian Gray*, was quickly withdrawn from sale in 1890 when suspicions were raised about the immorality of its contents. Reviewers saw that homosexual desire lay at its core (and they were quite correct to identify this carefully veiled aspect of Wilde's novel). Indeed, sexual scandal and gossip about Wilde's extra-marital private life continually circulated around him, particularly as he enjoyed the public company of handsome young men. The most notable of Wilde's male

1

Acknowledgements

Anyone working on Wilde these days is obliged to make an acknowledgement to the late Richard Ellmann, whose definitive biography of Wilde is now an indispensable tool of research. This edition would not have been completed without the help of the staff of the Mary Badland Library, Sheffield City Polytechnic, who obtained several important inter-library loans. My thanks to Lionel Pilkington for comments on the Introduction, and to Frances Dann, Judith Still, and the series editor, John Drakakis, for advice on some of the notes.

Joseph Bristow
Sheffield, 1991

Contents

after the first trial had begun, both plays, *An Ideal Husband* and *The Importance of Being Earnest*, were quickly shut down. Likewise, Wilde's name was promptly removed from hoardings and bill posters. Since Wilde had by then become a focus of public outrage and contempt, it was not until 1902 that *Earnest* was put back on stage. Fortunately, *Earnest* has been a standard part of repertory theatre ever since, and it is upon this comedy that Wilde's high standing as a writer mainly rests.

The sad ending to Wilde's life is at a far remove from his auspicious beginnings. He wrote regretfully from prison:

> [My mother] and my father bequeathed a name they had made noble and honoured not merely in Literature, Art, Archaeology and Science, but in the public history of my own country in its evolution as a nation. I had disgraced that name eternally. I had made it a byword among low people.[1]

Wilde was born on 16 October 1854 into an Anglo-Irish family of distinction. His parents were respected figures in the fields of medicine and politics. Lady Wilde, who wrote under the pseudonym 'Speranza', was a leading voice in the Irish nationalist cause. Sir William was appointed Surgeon Oculist to the Queen in Ireland in 1863. Both had wider interests. Sir William engaged in ethnographic researches, producing a book on Irish folklore that, in later years, the Irish poet, W.B. Yeats, would use as a resource. 'Speranza' published two volumes of poetry in the 1860s. These diverse activities show that the Wilde family was a creative, intellectual, and politically forthright one. Growing up in this erudite and artistically accomplished environment, Wilde received an excellent formal education. At Portora Royal School, he first developed his love of Ancient Greece, its literature and its culture, and proceeded to excel in classics at both Trinity College, Dublin and Magdalen College, Oxford. Wilde was a first-rate classics scholar. His detailed knowledge of classical writing informs practically every aspect of his work. He never missed an opportunity to exploit his considerable academic skills, often to criticize the most learned members of his own class.

During his time at Oxford (1874–8), Wilde came into contact with several other areas of intellectual inquiry that would leave their impression on the whole shape of his career. At Oxford Wilde went to hear John Ruskin, the greatest art critic of the era. In his lectures on 'The Aesthetic and Mathematical Schools of Art in Florence', delivered in November and December 1874, Ruskin expounded his long-held views on the evolution of the aesthetic sense: that is, the faculty of mind which discerns beauty from ugliness. The aesthetic sense had been a central concern of European philosophy from the mid-eighteenth century onwards. For Ruskin, the work of Florentine painters such as Cimabue and Giotto proved there was a racially inherited aesthetic sense that passed from one generation to another, and that successive centuries of art bore witness to the modifications and increasing improvement of that heritage. As the editors of Wilde's *Oxford Notebooks* point out, this particular attitude to art was central to Wilde's own aesthetics, especially in the essays he published in the 1880s.[2] The most significant of these articles, 'The Critic as Artist', is reprinted in the present edition, and should be seen as a critical complement to *Earnest*. Ruskin's lectures encouraged Wilde towards the idea that art-works are not produced with the same aims in mind from one period to another. Instead, for Ruskin, as for Wilde, art is forever changing, if bounded, within an identifiable cultural (European) tradition. Moreover, for Wilde, this type of developmental thinking led him to conclude that there was no fixed and timeless interpretation applicable to any art-work. In other words, he believed that western art was always subject to the differing perceptions, desires, and tastes of succeeding generations. All of Wilde's work is marked by a strenuous resistance to fixed interpretations, since he felt that each and every one of them would inevitably alter with time. His writing revels in ambiguity and contradiction. For him, no one meaning will do – hence the pun on E(a)rnest, about which a great deal more needs to be said.

At Oxford, Wilde was not only listening to Ruskin's lectures, he was also reading the newly translated works of the German philosopher, G.W.F. Hegel. Hegelian philosophy also created great shifts in Victorian intellectual life – if somewhat belatedly, since Hegel had died in 1831. Wilde adapted Hegelian theories of art and history into a model of cultural and historical development. Taken together, Ruskin's and Hegel's works provided Wilde with a theory of art as testimony to the enduring labours of ancient and modern cultures trying to perfect the representation of beauty. He could see a clear movement from classical (or ancient) to modern (or Victorian) painting and sculpture. Centuries of differing kinds of painting and sculpture bore witness to this struggle to breathe life into art, to make it appear as if it were alive, and so to go beyond the artistic endeavours of earlier societies. Wilde's earliest full-length essay, 'The Rise of Historical Criticism' (1878–9) – which he entered for a prize at Oxford – clearly indicates his Hegelian interest in history as the continual unfolding towards 'the far-off divine event of the attainment of perfect truth'.[3]

Wilde's appreciation of Ruskin's developmental theories of art, and his understanding of Hegel's *Aesthetics*, joined with an altogether larger conception of evolutionary thinking first initiated with the publication of Charles Darwin's *The Origin of Species* in 1859. This was not a conventional convergence of interests. But Wilde drew on the work of both thinkers to create a dynamic theory of cultural interaction – one that stressed the mutability and gradual growth of artistic forms. After Darwin's pathbreaking theory of 'natural selection', intellectual thought in Britain took a predominantly evolutionist turn. In addition, Darwin's book proved to be the ultimate scientific challenge to Christian belief since it contributed to a large body of scientific research that deemed that the world was far older than the Bible would lead people to believe. Thereafter, Darwin's work proved to be the main reference point for how and why Victorian Britain was becoming transformed from a religious into a secular society. That said, Christianity still held sway over the Victorians' official view of God's earth. But these typically high-minded people – especially the educated middle classes – frequently failed to practise what they preached. It was a culture of contrasts. Public displays of religious piety were set against private indulgences of pleasure. Wilde never hesitated to attack such double standards, as *Earnest* brilliantly shows. Following Ruskin in the pursuit of beauty, and drawing on aspects of German philosophy to tease out the contradictions in the Victorian world, Wilde added his own, often punishing, wit. It is important to bear in mind, then, that the seemingly superficial glitter of his phrasing has a firm intellectual basis in significant currents of Victorian thought.

Avant-garde beliefs about cultural development were prevalent in many spheres of knowledge at Oxford. Notable examples would include inquiries into the history of language (the work of F. Max Müller) and in the natural sciences (notably, the lectures of William Kingdon Clifford). Indeed, Wilde's understanding of historical and artistic progress expanded at a time when the evolutionist writings of Herbert Spencer and T.H. Huxley came into their own. In a very general sense, this lively climate of learning made Wilde into a progressive, even radical, writer. Wilde, therefore, was a man exploring ideas that often went against conventional modes of thought but were gaining increasing respect in scholarly circles. His philosophy of life and art was structured by a restless and contentious principle of change, always aiming at aesthetic perfection. And his memorable style finds its basis, in part, in the dialectical theory he would first have encountered in Aristotle and then seen remodelled by Hegel.

Dialectic defines a dynamic process of argumentation. At the most simple level, it means the progression of argument based on a system of opposites. First, a thesis is put forward, which is countered by its antithesis. And from this conflict of interests a hypothesis – or third stage of argument – may be inferred. Dialectic, therefore, generates debate through a system of radical modification between opposing viewpoints. A great number of Wilde's wittiest phrases turn conventional wisdom on its head, as if by dialectic. Take this one, for example: 'Wickedness is a myth invented by good people to account for the curious attractiveness of others.' Or this: 'If one tells a truth, one is sure, sooner or later, to be found out.' Or, finally: 'Industry is the root of all ugliness.' These rather mischievous aphorisms, which breathe new life into commonplace proverbs, are taken from 'Phrases and Philosophies for the Use of the Young', all of which are reprinted in this edition. Each axiomatic phrase inverts the original wise saying upon which it is based. And these parodic aphorisms, which recur time and again in Wilde's work, would count among those of his provocative writings that finally landed him in trouble. Such sayings were cited as evidence against him in court, and so, in a sense, they were partly responsible for sending him to gaol. Yet being clever in print was not Wilde's only means of shocking as well as entertaining the public. Wilde, notoriously, also practised his wit in person.

In fact, Wilde made his interests in aesthetics into a whole way of life. His decision to move in this direction undoubtedly owed much to another Oxford thinker. The figure in question is Walter Pater, a reclusive man who had no formal contact with Wilde during 1874–8 but who remained exceptionally influential among progressively minded undergraduates there. Pater, if quiet and introspective in person, was in many ways the instigator of the Aesthetic Movement, a loosely defined group of artists in favour of 'art for art's sake', which proved to be a focus of fascination and derision to the largely conservative British public. His lectures on Plato and, in particular, on Renaissance painters were put in the service of the belief that the study and practice of art necessarily challenged traditional views of the world. It was in the controversial Conclusion to *Studies in the History of the Renaissance* (1873) that Pater upheld his commitment to 'testing opinions and courting new impressions, never acquiescing in a facile orthodoxy'.[4] Several of Pater's critics thought beliefs of this kind were tantamount to revolution. Enthusiasm for purely sensuous pleasures seemed all too likely to corrupt innocent young people. Pater's critics certainly felt his Conclusion was sponsoring sexual indulgence. Wilde took it upon himself to put Pater's theory into action, and thus became an embodiment of the aesthetic sensibility, which meant taking risks with public opinion. At Oxford, in the midst of reading classical literature and analysing modern evolutionist thinking, Wilde drew attention to himself with his unconventional forms of dress and his affected taste for idiosyncratic types of decoration. Posing as an aesthete, Wilde deliberately affronted dominant ideals of manliness and upright moral behaviour. He exhibited a combination of qualities that alarmed many people. He was both artistic and effeminate, making himself into a glorious spectacle that maintained a powerful hold over the Victorians' prurient gaze. Wilde did not set himself up as an object of ridicule. Rather, his ambition was to turn the public's laughter back on itself, and his extraordinary manipulation of visual and verbal effects saw to that.

Wilde's interest in costume began with a coat tailored in the shape of a violincello, which he wore to the opening of the new Grosvenor Gallery in April 1877. He was the main attraction at this social gathering, enhancing his unusual attire with his splendid turn of phrase. Richard Ellmann points out that it is at this celebrated event that Wilde became a self-appointed critic of art.[5] It was a perfectly timed entrance into the most fashionable company. Very rapidly, Wilde took every opportunity to dress more and more outrageously. One of his most startling entrances on to the public stage was at a fancy-dress ball in May 1878, where he appeared as Prince Rupert. He liked the outfit so much that he bought what had been a hired costume. An equally noteworthy interest in ceramics had started a little earlier. Wilde's rooms in Magdalen College were decorated with vases and other pottery, about which he made another of his infamous and well-publicized remarks: 'How often I feel how hard it is to live up to my blue china.' (The blue and white china Wilde was talking about had been made fashionable by the poet and painter, Dante Gabriel Rossetti, and the painter, James Abbott McNeill Whistler. Blue china was thus a symbol of the aesthetic sensibility.) Declarations like these were felt to be so irresponsible in their frivolity that they moved one preacher to condemn them as 'heathenism'.[6] But Wilde's time did not go purely into living an aesthetic life of self-advertisement. His exhibitionism in no respect impaired his remarkable examination performance, in which he achieved first-class honours in classics.

Later, after leaving Oxford, when undertaking his highly praised lecture tours of North America during the 1880s, Wilde became more adventurous with *haute couture*. Tricked out in velvet breeches and silk hose, quilted jackets and flowing locks of hair, he was sporting a blatantly effeminate manner of dress, which was as spectacular as it was offensive to those middle-class observers who eyed his movements closely. By 1881, Wilde's reputation was so well known – especially through the offices of the satirical magazine *Punch* – that a parody of his ostentatious style became a major subject of comment in an operetta. The popular librettist of the day, W.S. Gilbert, included the following refrain in the second act of *Patience* (1881):

> A most intense young man,
> A soulful-eyed young man,
> An ultra-poetical, super-aesthetical,
> Out-of-the-way young man!

The send-ups of Wilde's aestheticism did not stop here. Wilde and his operatic persona in *Patience*, Bunthorne, provided the design for a Royal Worcester teapot – with the spout and handle affecting an appropriately 'aesthetic' and languorous pose. (This teapot – designed by Richard Binns and modelled by James Hadley, both celebrated for their vases – is now a collector's item.) Wilde certainly aroused enormous social excitement, just as the painter James Abbott McNeill Whistler had, on whom Bunthorne is also partly based. This very 'out-of-the-way young man' knew how and why he was much more shocking than the type of 'Beau Brummell' dandy who had preceded him many years before, during the time of the Regency. In Wilde, as he understood only too well, the late Victorians could see a reflection of their own fears and fascinations about gender and art.

By the 1880s the cultural meanings of both sexuality and artistic practices had begun to appear dangerously unstable, especially for the supposedly respectable bourgeoisie. Art, as the humorous illustrations of George du Maurier in *Punch* plainly show, had become associated with effeminacy, limp-wristedness and, by extension, homosexuality. Wilde became an icon of the artist as a lover of feminine things, such as the sunflowers that would adorn so many interior and architectural designs emanating from the Aesthetic Movement of the 1880s. As his fame grew, theatrical people were quick to invite this spectacular young aesthete to their parties. By this time, at the age of twenty-four, he was very much a society man-about-town. He mixed with celebrities of the day, such as the actress Lillie Langtry. He also made friends with another star performer, Ellen Terry. Apart from contributing a few reviews to journals (such as the distinguished literary periodical, the *Athenaeum*), Wilde remained a socialite, perfecting his charm, and sharpening the edge of his wit.

At that time lecturing was his forte. All across America, Wilde drew enormous crowds. In one famous instance, a group of Harvard undergraduates turned up for one of his performances dressed as Bunthorne look-alikes. The ploy had been leaked to Wilde, who chose that evening not to wear his velvet, silk, and lace, but a sober dinner suit instead. And so those who had tried to upstage him were humiliatingly upstaged themselves. Reports of Wilde's lectures are full of incidents such as this. Facing his American audience, Wilde advised them on points of dress, favouring knickerbockers over trousers. (In fact, dress reform was a widely debated topic during the 1880s. Wilde was a leading member of the Rational Dress Society.) Travelling from New York to San Francisco and thence to the Canadian eastern seaboard, Wilde pronounced his celebrated judgements on art and life to an ever-attentive America. Songs and poems mockingly publicized his name. In one city after another, he made much of the need for craft in design rather than industrially manufactured wares. In this respect, Wilde was adhering to the principles of a fellow socialist, William Morris, whose commitment to designs drawn directly from nature gave much of the impetus to eighties aestheticism. If seemingly trivial in intent, many of Wilde's 'aesthetical' views were in keeping with his lifelong criticism of the brutalities of consumer capitalism, and the alienation of working people from life. These points are drawn out in political form in 'The Soul of Man under Socialism', which accompanies *Earnest*, 'The Critic as Artist', and 'Phrases and Philosophies' in this edition.

For the remainder of the eighties, Wilde's time was taken up with several preoccupations: his marriage to Constance Lloyd in 1884, and the birth of their two children; his lecture-tour of Britain (1884–5); and his editorial work on a magazine, *The Woman's World* (1887–9). It was only towards the end of this decade, after gaining a reputation as an editor and journalist, that Wilde produced his major critical essays. He was, as the nineties approached, still a relatively young man with fine career prospects ahead of him. 'The Critic as Artist' first appeared in the liberal periodical, the *Nineteenth Century*, in July and September 1890; and 'The Soul of Man under Socialism' was published in another of the liberal journals, the *Fortnightly Review*, in February the following year. His other major essays, such 'The Portrait of Mr W.H.', date from this time. 'The Critic as Artist' is Wilde's most sustained contemplation of the relations between life and art, and its significance for the development of literary modernism in the early twentieth century is inestimable.

The main event that spurred Wilde into writing 'The Critic as Artist' occurred in 1885–6. A dreadful row with the well-known and innovative American painter, Whistler, had exploded in print. Wilde had known the easily offended Whistler for nearly a decade, and to some degree Wilde's style was also Whistler's. During Wilde's years at Oxford, Whistler had come to the fore of the public mind with his infamous lawsuit against Ruskin. Whistler was angered by Ruskin's adverse criticism, and sued him for substantial damages. (In *Fors Clavigera* [published in parts, 1871–8], Ruskin said that Whistler's 'Nocturne in Black and Gold: The Falling Rocket' had insultingly flung 'a pot of paint in the public's face'.[7] Ruskin was certainly not alone in his indignant response to Whistler's highly experimental 'nocturnes', which were repeatedly made fun of in the press. Whistler's painting was exceptionally innovative, and closely resembled the use of tone and colour by the French Impressionists.) In 1878 Whistler won his well-publicized case against Ruskin. However, the courts belittlingly awarded Whistler only a farthing's compensation, so he had to bear the brunt of tremendous legal costs. Whistler, much to his chagrin, went bankrupt. Little did Wilde realize that Whistler, a close neighbour of his, would turn against him too in 1886. Their own particular conflict of views about art illuminates key points in Wilde's aesthetics.

Whistler was by far the older of the two men, and he always insisted on holding the upper hand over Wilde. His wit could be as incisive as Wilde's, and he used it to try to keep Wilde in a subservient position. By 1885, Whistler believed that many of his own ideas about art and life were being plagiarized by Wilde. So in February that year, Whistler decided to engage in his own piece of self-publicity and give a lecture at an unheard-of time. 'The Ten O'Clock Lecture' was filled out with scurrilous remarks that implicitly referred to Wilde. The gist of this lecture was that inspired artists, rather than mere critics (like Wilde), are the sole arbiters of the value and meaning of art. 'For some time past,' wrote Whistler, 'the unattached writer [the critic such as Wilde] has become the middleman in this matter of art, and his influence, while it has widened the gulf between the people and the painter, has brought about the most complete misunderstanding as to the aim of the picture.'[8] Whistler despised critics because they, and not artists, increasingly controlled public taste. Controversy about the educative role of critics persists in modern debates concerning the study of art and literature. Wilde is among the first of the Victorians to point out that the act of criticism is also an art-form in itself, and that art and criticism are inseparable. Nor does he wish to place them in a hierarchy, with art standing above criticism, or vice versa. Rather, Wilde's essays go so far as to break down the distinction between art and criticism entirely. For him, criticism of an art-work becomes an art-work in itself. Similarly, the art-work is necessarily a criticism of the culture in which it was produced. In this view, Wilde was a much more advanced thinker than Whistler.

Wilde responded promptly to Whistler. Two articles in the *Pall Mall Gazette* (a newspaper noted as a forum for controversial debate) laughingly imitated Whistler's mock-biblical lecturing style (the inflated rhetoric of which Whistler, of course, had adopted as a joke). Wilde's point was that art does not depend upon individual genius alone, it is fostered by the general cultural climate. Art, in other words, is an indicator of social change. Wilde's parodic riposte infuriated Whistler, and a fierce exchange of correspondence followed. But it would take several years for Wilde to compose a long and serious meditation on the artistic impulse motivating criticism; 'The Critic as Artist' in many ways is the culmination of Wilde's ongoing dissatisfaction with Whistler's views. Its other main target is Matthew Arnold, one of the most distinguished Victorian men of letters. Many of the arguments advanced by Wilde's speaker, Gilbert, rub against the critical prescriptions laid down by Arnold in 'The Function of Criticism at the Present Time' (1864), where, according to Wilde, Arnold devalues the critical spirit at the expense of the creative faculty. It would seem, then, that Wilde saw Arnold and Whistler as sharing similar prejudices.

Yet, if serious in intent, 'The Critic as Artist' is hardly free from wit. In its erudition and pointedness of phrase, which implicitly send up Arnold's wide range of classical and modern reference, this essay is far more intellectually adept than Whistler's eccentrically timed lecture – which is one of its chief quarries. 'The Critic as Artist' is not the only of Wilde's works to engage in an attack on Whistler. Ellmann, very suggestively, remarks that the death of the painter Basil Hallward in *The Picture of Dorian Gray* (1890–1), Wilde's only novel, also discloses Wilde's vengeance on Whistler – an artist who wanted to keep a firm grip on his audience and control its understanding of his paintings. In *Dorian Gray*, Wilde's hero swaps identities with the portrait Hallward has produced of him. In Wilde's dialectical aesthetics, where criticism can become art, so too a person like Dorian Gray can become his own portrait. As Wilde moved into the 1890s, a powerful social critique was emerging from this tendency to turn identities upside-down and inside-out. By breaking down distinctions between life and art, and so making his life into a form of art, Wilde brought into perspective ideas and questions that society would prefer not to have to consider.

POLITICS

Wilde is rarely thought of as an overtly political writer. But as all his dramas show, he was highly critical of the double standards that operated in the largely upper-class world he chose to depict. Apart from his well-known and somewhat unorthodox essay on socialism, there are no other works of his which profess explicitly political opinions. His letters make scattered statements about his Celtic background, and his pride in his Irish identity, yet his creative work is not directly addressed to Irish nationalism. Wilde, however, wrote a highly significant review of a novel by J.A. Froude, whom he despised for maintaining a longstanding English 'race-hatred' towards the Irish.[9] And the transcript of one of his American lectures, on 'The Irish Poets of '48', ends with these words: 'I do not know anything more wonderful, or more characteristic of the Celtic genius, than the quick artistic spirit in which we adapted ourselves to the English tongue. The Saxon took our lands from us and left us desolate. We took their language and added new beauties to it.'[10] Similarly, in the second part of 'The Critic as Artist', Wilde's speaker, Gilbert, declares that 'aesthetic criticism' should emulate the achievements of the Celts:

We have now to make what is beautiful. And though the mission of the Aesthetic Movement is to lure people to contemplate, not to lead them to create, yet, as the creative instinct is strong in the Celt, and it is the Celt who leads in art, there is no reason why in future years this strange Renaissance should not become almost as mighty in its way as that new birth of Art that woke many centuries ago in the cities of Italy. (p. 148)

In making this claim, Wilde is addressing himself to the Anglo-Saxon prejudices against Celtic art laid out in Arnold's controversial and high-handed essay, *On the Study of Celtic Literature* (1867). A short extract will indicate Arnold's singularly intolerant attitude towards Celtic culture:

To know the Celtic case thoroughly, one must know the Celtic people; and to know them one must know that by which a people best express themselves, – their literature. Few of us have any notion what a mass of Celtic literature is really yet extant and accessible. One constantly finds even very accomplished people, who fancy that the remains of Welsh and Irish literature are as inconsiderable by their volume, as, in their opinion, they are by their intrinsic merit; that these remains consist of a few prose stories, in great part borrowed from the literature of nations more civilized than the Welsh or Irish nation, and of some unintelligible poetry.[11]

No doubt such sentiments exasperated Wilde. Irish culture guided Wilde's aesthetic and political choices as well. Terry Eagleton emphasizes how Wilde 'inherits a form of Anglo-Irish writing which is ironic about realism, sportive, satirical and fantastic, ecstatically comic with a dark, sobering subtext, and, in its contradictions and subversive wit, deeply perverse'.[12] In other words, it is Wilde's Irishness that shapes the oppositional energies of his writing, and which thereby refuses to take the English language literally. Wilde may well be seen to be turning English against itself, using an Irish style to subvert English imperialism from within.

Wilde's politics can be understood more generally in his theories of art. He saw art as a potentially revolutionary force.

The pursuit of aesthetic perfection was the pursuit of a better world. As a largely utopian thinker, he had no clear programme about exactly how to proceed from the class-divided society of late Victorian Britain to a classless socialist future. Although Wilde was not involved with the emerging Fabian movement of socialists, the Fabians considered reprinting 'The Soul of Man' as one of their pamphlets in 1906.[13] (It also proved popular, much later, in the Soviet Union.) Yet the essay was not viewed as a document central to the socialist parties that were gaining more and more political power in the 1890s. Wilde's politics was never overtly connected with the Labour movement. His link with Victorian socialism is mainly through the auspices of a particular theory of art which drew, in part, on the work of William Morris and the Pre-Raphaelites, many of whom used painting and poetry as a form of social criticism and as a means of representing new concepts of beauty. However, scattered throughout Wilde's writings are biting criticisms of social injustice, often in the most unexpected places. For example, a children's story, 'The Selfish Giant' (1888), tells a moral tale that is unmistakably an allegory of capitalist greed.

One of the main areas of political debate that relates to Wilde's drama and fiction concerns women's rights. The late 1880s and early 1890s witnessed a new surge in the suffragist cause, and with it came an abundance of stories, poems, and novels celebrating women's independence from patriarchal rule. A whole genre of 'New Woman' fiction gained in popularity. A good example is Sarah Grand's *The Heavenly Twins* (1894). *Earnest* certainly registers the emergence of the 'New Woman' in Cecily. Although she takes ill to political economy and lessons in German, she is a young woman who is well educated, assertive, and uncompromising, one trained for a career, not just marriage. The 'New Woman' proves to be one of the novel and highly contemporary kinds of character that Wilde uses to say the most unforeseen things in the polite world of upper-class decorum. However, the question of characterization in Wilde's drama is an exceptionally difficult one, and it would be a mistake to argue that his work was explicitly pro-feminist. Cecily, after all, presents a very odd mixture of qualities. On the one hand keenly intelligent, she is, on the other, prone to stereotypically girlish fancies. The point is that female characters are prominent in all of Wilde's dramas. And women are given as many powerful lines as men.

Apart from *Earnest*, Wilde's other successes on the London stage – *Lady Windermere's Fan* (1892), *A Woman of No Importance* (1893), and *An Ideal Husband* (1895) – all examine the plight of women caught between conflicting desires about marriage and extra-marital relationships. These dramas are largely about the abuses and deceptions done by husbands to their wives, and vice versa. They are not polemical since they elegantly harmonize the domestic problems they have raised. But whereas in the three society comedies just mentioned these abuses are treated with quiet resolve, in *Earnest* they raise riotous laughter. For the moment, it is more appropriate to say that Wilde's plays, if not exactly pro-feminist, represent new types of female identity.

That his women and, indeed, his men so often seem surprisingly out of character is, in *Earnest*, part of an extremely involved plot that makes a mockery of conventional attitudes to courtship and marriage, and the class system as a whole. The play, after all, is subtitled 'A Trivial Comedy for Serious People'. It uses pointed humour as a tool for social satire. The satire runs very deep, so deep perhaps that it is, on occasions, almost obscure. There are some jokes in this drama that many people in Wilde's audiences may have been unable to grasp because they alluded, altogether covertly, to homosexuality. In a sense, it could be said that *Earnest* contains the beginnings of a homosexual politics. Had this aspect of the drama been comprehended by the majority of Wilde's audience, the play would never have been produced. Yet a small minority would have understood the joke about living a life of deception referred to in a number of carefully coded allusions. A play about deception, therefore, has within it a highly deceptive subtext.

DEGENERATION

Late nineteenth-century homosexuality emerged in an atmosphere where an anxious society feared more and more the threat of 'degeneration'. The idea of 'degeneration' brought together a cluster of ideas about moral corruption, racial impurity, lack of sanitation among the working classes, and, most controversially of all, homosexuality. All sorts of books pertaining to 'degeneration' were published from the 1880s onwards. Concerns about the spread of this nebulous social and physical disease were accentuated by the publication of the English translation of Max Nordau's book, *Degeneration*, in 1895. The Wilde trials took place in a climate when nearly every periodical carried an article on Nordau's opinions, discussing how 'degeneration' could be found in many novels of the day. Reviewers were concerned about the increasingly distasteful representation of sexuality in modern fiction. One comment, from the *Fortnightly Review*, is typical: 'The end of an established order, a contempt for inherited views of custom and morality – that is what Dr Max Nordau finds to be the essence of the much-abused *fin de siècle*.'[14] The controversy that preoccupied the periodicals in 1895 had largely been stirred up by an indignant article in the *Westminster Review* signed 'A Philistine'. This adamant 'philistine' deplored the upsurge of 'Sex in Fiction'. That such an article could put novelists and intellectuals so briskly on the defensive indicates just how tense feelings had grown between an upstanding Victorian morality and a more modern permissiveness. It was certainly on the issue of sex that much twentieth-century writing would stake its identity. One only has to look at the most famous modernist authors – T.S. Eliot, James Joyce, and Virginia Woolf – to see this.

These journal articles from the mid-1890s frequently referred to 'morbid' sexuality, by which they probably meant homosexuality. It is worth bearing in mind that at this time 'homosexuality' was not known by that name. Historians have shown how the idea of the homosexual as a particular type of person was not established until the débâcle of the Wilde trials. It was the Criminal Law Amendment Act of 1885 that first legislated against acts of 'gross indecency' between men (even in private), and under which Wilde was tried. Prior to that, homosexuality was understood only in terms of the sexual act. Men were hanged for committing buggery or sodomy, rather than for being homosexuals, until 1836. Wilde's own homosexual liaisons probably began in the late 1880s but it is unlikely that he referred to himself as a homosexual. The word, in any case, was a pathological definition, very far removed from Wilde's celebratory attitude to male same-sex love. By 1890 his writing was already examining sexual desire between men, and it was for this reason that *Dorian Gray* incensed some reviewers. One of them, Charles Whibley, wrote in the Tory *Scots Observer*: 'if he [Wilde] can write for none but outlawed noblemen and perverted telegraph-boys, the sooner he takes to tailoring (or some other decent trade) the better for his own reputation and public morals'.[15] Whibley was alluding to the major homosexual scandals of the 1880s, notably the Cleveland Street affair where wealthy men employed the sexual services of young post office workers. The sexual subtext of *Dorian Gray* goes against such middle-class virtues as 'self-help' (to be noted in the idea of the 'decent' tailor working at an honest trade). It was Walter Pater who advised Wilde on how to revise the novel, which went on sale in an emended version in 1891. Certainly, Pater could see just as clearly as Wilde how Victorian society would be offended by the sexual interests of this novel.

Wilde moved in homosexual circles with literary ambitions. The poet, Lionel Johnson, was one of his main admirers. Johnson wrote a poem in Latin celebrating *Dorian Gray*. It was through Johnson that Wilde met Alfred Douglas, and it was within this network of contacts that the implicit homosexual allusions of *Earnest* would have been understood. Part of the origins of *Earnest* lie in an Oxford undergraduate magazine, the *Chameleon*, published in 1894, and which, for reasons that shall become obvious, ran to only one number. Wilde contributed his 'Phrases and Philosophies for the Use of the Young' to the *Chameleon*. These 'Phrases' were juxtaposed with Douglas's two poems on same-sex desire, 'The Love that Dare Not Speak Its Name' and 'In Praise of Shame'. Each of these works was brought up by Queensberry's counsel during the court proceedings of 1895. Amid the contents were items by two 'Uranian' (or boy-loving) writers. One was a story, 'The Priest and the Acolyte', by the editor, Jack Bloxam; the other was 'The Shadow of the End', a poem by John Gambril Nicholson. Two years earlier, in 1892, Nicholson had published a short collection of poems, *Love in Earnest*, which contained a homoerotic ballad entitled 'Of Boys' Names'. This is the closing quatrain:

> My little Prince, Love's mystic spell
> Lights all the letters of your name,
>   And you, if no one else, can tell
> Why Ernest sets my heart a-flame.

Timothy d'Arch Smith suggests that 'Ernest' is a carefully coded word for homosexual desire.[16] Certainly, Wilde's play makes the notion of being earnest into its complete opposite. He also makes a hilarious joke about the identity of 'Ernest'. Both the leading male characters pretend to be 'Ernest' at different points of the action, as they struggle to maintain their lives of deception. Since *Earnest* refers to living a 'double life' at key moments, it is possible to glimpse how the comedy addresses issues that only those closest to Wilde would comprehend. In any case, *Earnest* is full of private allusions. The editor of the *Chameleon* turns up in the name of Lady Bloxham (p. 41); Lady Bracknell has the honour of naming the town where Douglas's mother lived; Jack Worthing (who really is Ernest at the end of the third act) has a surname referring to the town where Wilde wrote the play; and Jack's address, the Albany, was the residence of the homosexual emancipationist, George Ives.

Earnest, then, is a privately coded as well as publicly entertaining play. It is probable that most people in Wilde's audience saw the use of the name Ernest as a simple inversion of terms. Samuel Butler, who also engaged in an untiring attack on Victorian values, gave the same name to the hero of his novel, *The Way of All Flesh* (1903). Here Butler's narrator comments on the popularity of the name Ernest in the 1830s: 'The word "earnest" was just beginning to come into fashion, and he [Ernest's father] thought the possession of such a name might, like his having been baptised in water from the Jordan, have a permanent effect upon the boy's character.'[17] Ernest, then, meant moral earnestness. The sexual joke that Wilde, not Butler, was making therefore had all the more force. This rather daring play on the meaning of being Ernest had already occurred in 'The Critic as Artist', where Ernest is the name of the younger man in the Socratic dialogue that structures the essay. There are further connections between the play and the essay. 'The Critic as Artist' is subtitled 'With some remarks upon the importance of doing nothing'. It was not uncommon for Wilde to take his

19

choicest phrasing from one work and then implant it in another. Most of his writings are, to varying degrees, verbally entwined.

The pun on Ernest was not the only private joke about homosexuality that Wilde relished at the expense of the unknowing majority of theatre-goers. At the première of *Lady Windermere's Fan*, he went up on stage donning a green carnation as a buttonhole. Before the performance, these unnaturally coloured flowers were distributed to all the men in the audience: it was a typically Wildean piece of frivolity. And yet, once again, the green carnation could only be appreciated by the homosexual coterie, since this flower was used in Paris as a means of making sexual contact between men. It is likely that many of Wilde's audience thought this affected use of flowers was simply a continuation of an eighties fad where aesthetic men and women would don a lily or a sunflower at fashionable gatherings. (There is a well-known painting by William Powell Frith that features Wilde, among many other artists and Society figures, at the Royal Academy opening in 1881. A large lily graces Wilde's lapel.) Wilde's somewhat outré adoption of the green carnation would be sent up by one of the many writers who chose to celebrate his aestheticism. Robert Hichens's novel, named after the flower, was published in 1894. Hichens had shown Wilde and Douglas the manuscript, and they found it amusing. Queensberry, predictably, was utterly outraged by the book. By that time, it seems, a small if growing number of people were becoming irritated with the increasing celebrity of Wilde's homosexual identity. The aesthete who had been fun in the 1880s was transmogrifying into the monstrous degenerate of the 1890s, which is precisely how Wilde would be seen in the courtroom in 1895.

EARNEST AND THE THEATRE

At the time of *Earnest*'s revival in 1902, the much-admired satirist Max Beerbohm commented: 'In kind the play always was unlike any other, and in its kind it still seems perfect.'[18] (Beerbohm, too, turns up in the final act of *Earnest*. He is referred to as 'Maxbohm' when names are read out loud from the Army Lists.) If a source for the plot of this comedy is to be found, it would be in Gilbert's *Engaged* (1877), although the resemblances are slight.

There are altogether stronger affinities between Wilde's Society comedies – such as *An Ideal Husband* – and the popular successes of the day, notably Arthur Wing Pinero's sensational drama of the 'woman with a past', *The Second Mrs Tanqueray* (1893). The 'woman with a past' would become something of a stock figure in society drama at this time. Both Wilde and Pinero enjoyed the upper middle-class audience attending the Haymarket and the St James's theatres, but Wilde is far less Victorian in his emotional range and tastes. He spared his audience Pinero's variety of retributive and dramatically very powerful moralizing. Where, for example, Pinero's second Mrs Tanqueray finally kills herself after her shameful history has been revealed, Wilde makes Sir Robert Chiltern of *An Ideal Husband* into a 'man with a past', and gives the play a happy ending. Once again, it was Wilde's instinct to run against established principles, this time theatrical ones.

In broad terms, Wilde's interest in the drama of class differences links him with wider developments in theatre history. Tom Robertson's well-known melodrama, *Caste* (1867) is often seen as the play which marks a new focus on class. Yet again Wilde's comedies are not in the same mould as Robertson's agonized depiction of how one man's high social standing (or 'caste') promises to prevent him from marrying a woman from an insufficiently respectable background. Wilde's concern, in any case, is with making jokes about the pretensions of upper-class propriety. *Earnest*, as a comedy, is a class-conscious drama that appeals not to melodrama but to farce, manipulating all sorts of coincidences of plot, rapid escapes and embarrassing entrances. But if farcical in stretching the plausibility of action to extremes, *Earnest* was unlike the kinds of French boulevard farce where characters made ridiculous pratfalls and had doors slammed in their faces. This type of frenetic action took place in a manic plot woven into a tale of actual or near adultery. With their exaggerated gesticulations and reliance on physical effects, farces like Brandon Thomas's *Charley's Aunt* (1892) counted among the most popular plays of their day. In terms of its rhetoric of gestures, *Earnest* is relatively tame by comparison. Indeed, the surface of the play is exquisitely polite, although points of etiquette and behaving properly are constantly made to look silly. *Earnest* suggests a lot about how the upper classes policed the boundaries of good taste, and how such a strict moral world could lead a couple of young men into a life of deception.

Wilde spent August to October of 1894 in the seaside town of Worthing, Sussex to write *Earnest*. In its earliest conception, the play was to have had four acts. For technical and perhaps legal reasons, Wilde excised a scene concerning debt-collectors. This was another private joke, since the solicitors in this omitted act bore strong resemblances to the bailiffs who had been pursuing Wilde for outstanding monies; Wilde was often in debt, largely because of the luxurious lifestyle he chose to lead, and also because of the funds he spent on entertaining Douglas. This deleted scene, known as the 'Gribsby episode', is printed separately in the present book (pp. 88–94). Wilde reduced the play from four to three acts under the recommendation of the actor and producer, George Alexander, who, on first seeing the script, felt the comedy was not for him. Wilde subsequently sent *Earnest* to another theatre manager for consideration. But after Henry James's play, *Guy Domville*, failed miserably at the St James's Theatre in January 1895, Alexander asked for the manuscript back, negotiated some changes with Wilde, and opened the play the following month. So in early 1895 *Earnest* went quickly into rehearsals, and on 14 February Wilde turned up to the opening night sporting, once more, a green carnation. Prevented from entering the theatre, where he planned to demonstrate against Wilde, Queensberry left a bouquet not of flowers but vegetables, eager to incense the playwright. Queensberry's anger with Wilde was no doubt compounded by the fact that the Marquess's eldest son, Viscount Drumlanrig, had committed suicide in 1894, and a homosexual liaison with the then Foreign Secretary, Lord Rosebery, was suspected. Within days, Queensberry's abusive correspondence with Wilde began, which finally reached its climax with the offensive visiting card that precipitated the author's perilous litigation. *Earnest*, in the mean time, was performing well, even if critics found their patience tried by the display of verbal pyrotechnics that untiringly set every scene ablaze. Since *Earnest* only ran to sixty-six performances on its first run, it lost money for Alexander (the deficit was nearly £300). But when he revived it in 1902 it ran for eleven months, netting well over £20,000. By then, Wilde's name was recovering some of its one-time respectability.

In 1895 critical responses to *Earnest* were, on the whole, grudgingly sympathetic. Wilde's relentless wit, if amusing, was taken to such extremes that it frustrated and annoyed most reviewers. The comedy seemed irritatingly clever. The earliest reviews are consistently marked by complaints about the 'affectation' and 'mannerism' of his style, and the 'exaggerated' nature of his characters and action. Some made pointed references to its 'extravagance'. Others disdained the 'frivolity' of the drama.[19] It was the 'contrivance' of *Earnest* that managed to impress as well as disconcert different sections of the reviewing public. And it is this sense of artifice or artificiality that is worth pausing over for a moment. Clearly, several of Wilde's critics were disturbed by the unnaturalness of his characters. Every single person in this comedy seems to lack either an authentic voice or an authentic persona. It is as if each voice is Wilde's own, since all of the characters speak in clever phrases: they are more like mouthpieces. 'All talk exactly alike,' as one reviewer put it, and 'it must be admitted their talk is extremely entertaining, until through the monotony of its strain it becomes just a trifle wearisome'.[20]

One hostile critic, writing in the *Theatre*, felt it was difficult to distinguish between 'the tinsel glitter of sham epigram and the authentic sheen of true wit', adding that 'there can be no doubt' that 'its audacity – we had almost said impertinence – will not fail to attract votaries of a society which enjoys nothing more keenly than an exhibition of its own weaknesses'.[21] Again, Wilde's flamboyant writing challenged conventional distinctions – here between art and artifice. Every scene in *Earnest* thrives on a humorously mannered way of speaking. It is as if the comedy had a grammar of its own, which all the characters share, and which makes them all 'talk alike'. The play confronts the audience with a sparring match between the most verbally agile of partners, each possessing similar verbal skills. The point is, in this ethos of rhetorical one-upmanship, there is no pretence to realism. Plot and language have full rein instead. Wilde's comedy marks a radical departure from earlier forms of drama. In fact, in *Earnest* – where everything is exceptionally artificial – there are the beginnings of a theatre of 'alienation' or 'estrangement', which would become a cornerstone of European modernism, especially in the dramas of Bertolt Brecht. *Earnest*, as its first reviewers noted, has the effect of distancing the audience from its furious turns of phrase.

With their trenchantly witty remarks, delivered in the fast timing of farce, these characters are, as characters, superficial. The fact that both men are, at different points of the action, the same person, 'Ernest', neatly underlines this point. What they say, and the way they say it, is far more important than who or what they really are. These characters have no psychological depth, no place in a world of human sympathies. When they cry or feel anger, or even practise deception, their every action seems a contrivance. Time and again, they are devices voicing eminently quotable phrases. *Earnest*, with its relentless punning and gamesome banter, suggests that human beings are made up of many contradictory linguistic elements. The play implies that human character is subject to the slips and slides of language. When is Ernest truly in 'e(a)rnest'? It might be said that language, which quickly changes costume here, holds the stage.

Yet, for all the wild antics and verbal fireworks that animate the comedy, there is a serious criticism of modern life present in *Earnest*, already signalled in its thought-provoking subtitle. Trivial comedy can put people into a serious frame of mind. And so, once more, Wilde is challenging conventional expectations about what a farce is capable of doing. *Earnest* certainly has the potential to make an audience reflect on how and why certain things in life are worth laughing at. It can amuse, charm, exasperate, even alienate its spectators and readers. And it is with *Earnest* that Wilde's most important artistic accomplishments begin and end.

NOTE ON THE TEXTS

The text of *Earnest* reproduced here follows that of the first published edition of 1899; this is the three-act version usually performed on stage. The text of 'The Critic as Artist' and that of 'The Soul of Man under Socialism' are reprinted from *Intentions* (1891). 'A Few Maxims for the Instruction of the Over-Educated' appeared in the *Saturday Review* in 1890. 'Phrases and Philosophies for the Use of the Young' was first published in the *Chameleon* in 1894.

1 *De Profundis*, in *The Complete Works of Oscar Wilde*, ed. J.B. Foreman (London: Collins, 1966), p. 905.

2 See 'The Context of the Text' and 'The Text as Context', in Philip E. Smith II and Michael S. Helfand (eds), *Oscar Wilde's Oxford Notebooks: A Portrait of Mind in the Making* (New York: Oxford University Press, 1989), pp. 5–106.

3 'The Rise of Historical Criticism', in *The Complete Works of Oscar Wilde*, p. 1049.

4 Walter Pater, *The Renaissance: Studies in Art and Poetry*, ed. Donald L. Hill (Berkeley: University of California Press, 1980), p. 190. This is one of the best-known quotations from Pater's works.

5 Richard Ellmann, *Oscar Wilde* (London: Hamish Hamilton, 1987), pp. 75–6.

6 ibid., p. 44.

7 John Ruskin, *The Works of John Ruskin*, ed. E.T. Cook and Alexander Wedderburn (London: Allen, 1903–12), vol. 29, p. 160.

8 James McNeill Whistler, *Ten O'Clock Lecture* (London, 1885), p. 17. Irritation with Whistler can be detected elsewhere in Wilde's work: see, for example, the children's story, 'The Remarkable Rocket' (1888), where the vain rocket strongly resembles Whistler. Ellmann draws attention to this parallel (*Oscar Wilde*, p. 279).

9 'Mr Froude's Blue Book [on Ireland]', *Pall Mall Gazette* 49: 7511, 13 April 1889, p. 3 reprinted in Richard Ellmann (ed.), *The Artist as Critic: Critical Writings of Oscar Wilde* (London: W.H. Allen, 1970), p. 136.

10 'The Irish Poets of '48', delivered 5 April 1882, Platt's Hall, San Francisco, in *The Annotated Oscar Wilde*, ed. H. Montgomery Hyde (London: Orbis Publishing, 1982), p. 378.

11 Matthew Arnold, 'On the Study of Celtic Literature' (1866), in *Lectures and Essays in Criticism*, ed. R.H. Super and Sister Thomas Marion Hoctor (Ann Arbor: University of Michigan Press, 1962), p. 303.

12 Terry Eagleton, 'Foreword' to *Saint Oscar* (Derry: Field Day, 1989), p. ix.

13 On the marginal place of Wilde's socialism in Fabian thought, see Ian Britain, *Fabianism and Culture: A Study in British Socialism and the Arts 1884–1918* (Cambridge: Cambridge University Press, 1982), pp. 7–8.

14 Janet E. Hogarth, 'Literary Degenerates', *The Fortnightly Review*, NS 51 (1895), p. 586.

15 Charles Whibley, Review of *The Picture of Dorian Gray*, 5 July 1890, *Scots Observer*, reprinted in *Selected Letters of Oscar Wilde*, ed. Rupert Hart-Davis (Oxford: Oxford University Press, 1979), p. 81. Wilde made a spirited response to Whibley's attack.

16 Timothy d'Arch Smith, *Love in Earnest: Some Notes on the Lives and Writings of English 'Uranian' Poets from 1889 to 1930* (London: Routledge & Kegan Paul, 1970), p. viii.

17 Samuel Butler, *The Way of All Flesh* (1903: Harmondsworth: Penguin Books, 1966), p. 106.

18 Max Beerbohm, *Around Theatres* (London: Rupert Hart-Davis, 1953), p. 189.

19 A useful short selection of reviews is reprinted in William Tydeman (ed.), *Wilde: Comedies*, 'Casebook' series (London: Macmillan, 1982), pp. 62–6. For a further selection of reviews, see Karl Beckson (ed.), *Oscar Wilde: The Critical Heritage* (London: Routledge & Kegan Paul, 1970), pp. 187–200.

20 Unsigned review, *Observer*, 17 February 1895, p. 6, reprinted in Tydeman, *Wilde: Comedies*, p. 65.

21 Unsigned review, *Theatre*, 20 February 1895, p. 170.

The Importance of Being Earnest

The Persons of the Play

JOHN WORTHING, J.P.
ALGERNON MONCRIEFF
REV. CANON CHASUBLE, D.D.
MERRIMAN, BUTLER
LANE, MANSERVANT
LADY BRACKNELL
HON. GWENDOLEN FAIRFAX
CECILY CARDEW
MISS PRISM, GOVERNESS

The Scenes of the Play

ACT I   *Algernon Moncrieff's flat in Half-Moon Street, W.*
ACT II   *The Garden at the Manor House, Woolton.*
ACT III   *Drawing-Room at the Manor House, Woolton.*

FIRST ACT

Scene. Morning-room in ALGERNON's flat in Half-Moon Street. The room is luxuriously and artistically furnished. The sound of a piano is heard in the adjoining room.
(LANE is arranging afternoon tea on the table, and after the music has ceased, ALGERNON enters.)

ALGERNON.   Did you hear what I was playing, Lane?

LANE.   I didn't think it polite to listen, sir.

ALGERNON.   I'm sorry for that, for your sake. I don't play accurately – anyone can play accurately – but I play with wonderful expression. As far as the piano is concerned, sentiment is my forte. I keep science for life.

LANE.   Yes, sir.

ALGERNON.   And, speaking of the science of life, have you got the cucumber sandwiches out for Lady Bracknell?

LANE.   Yes, sir. (*Hands them on a salver.*)

ALGERNON.   (*Inspects them, takes two, and sits down on the sofa.*) Oh! . . . by the way, Lane, I see from your book that on Thursday night, when Lord Shoreman and Mr Worthing were dining with me, eight bottles of champagne are entered as having been consumed.

LANE.   Yes, sir; eight bottles and a pint.

ALGERNON.   Why is it that at a bachelor's establishment the servants invariably drink the champagne? I ask merely for information.

LANE.   I attribute it to the superior quality of the wine, sir. I have often observed that in married households the champagne is rarely of a first-rate brand.

ALGERNON.   Good Heavens! Is marriage so demoralizing as that?

LANE.   I believe it *is* a very pleasant state, sir. I have had very little experience of it myself up to the present. I have only been married once. That was in consequence of a misunderstanding between myself and a young person.

ALGERNON.   (*Languidly.*) I don't know that I am much interested in your family life, Lane.

LANE.   No, sir; it is not a very interesting subject. I never think of it myself.

ALGERNON.   Very natural, I am sure. That will do, Lane, thank you.

LANE.   Thank you, sir.   (LANE *goes out.*)

ALGERNON.   Lane's views on marriage seem somewhat lax. Really, if the lower orders don't set us a good example, what on earth is the use of them? They seem, as a class, to have absolutely no sense of moral responsibility.

(*Enter* LANE.)

LANE.   Mr Ernest Worthing.

(*Enter* JACK.) (LANE *goes out*)

ALGERNON.   How are you, my dear Ernest? What brings you up to town?

JACK.   Oh, pleasure, pleasure! What else should bring one anywhere? Eating as usual, I see, Algy!

ALGERNON.   (*Stiffly.*) I believe it is customary in good society to take some slight refreshment at five o'clock. Where have you been since last Thursday?

JACK.   (*Sitting down on the sofa.*) In the country.

ALGERNON.   What on earth do you do there?

JACK.   (*Pulling off his gloves.*) When one is in town one amuses oneself. When one is in the country one amuses other people. It is excessively boring.

ALGERNON.   And who are the people you amuse?

JACK.   (*Airily*) Oh, neighbours, neighbours.

ALGERNON.   Got nice neighbours in your part of Shropshire?

JACK.   Perfectly horrid! Never speak to one of them.

ALGERNON.   How immensely you must amuse them! (*Goes over and takes sandwich.*) By the way, Shropshire is your county, is it not?

JACK.   Eh? Shropshire? Yes, of course. Hallo! Why all these cups? Why cucumber sandwiches? Why such reckless extravagance in one so young? Who is coming to tea?

ALGERNON.   Oh! merely Aunt Augusta and Gwendolen.

JACK.   How perfectly delightful!

ALGERNON.   Yes, that is all very well; but I am afraid Aunt Augusta won't quite approve of your being here.

JACK.   May I ask why?

ALGERNON.   My dear fellow, the way you flirt with Gwendolen is perfectly disgraceful. It is almost as bad as the way Gwendolen flirts with you.

JACK.   I am in love with Gwendolen. I have come up to town expressly to propose to her.

ALGERNON.   I thought you had come up for pleasure? . . . I call that business.

JACK   How utterly unromantic you are!

ALGERNON.   I really don't see anything romantic in proposing. It is very romantic to be in love. But there is nothing romantic about a definite proposal. Why, one may be accepted. One usually is, I believe. Then the excitement.

29

If ever I get married, I'll certainly try to forget the fact.

JACK.   I have no doubt about that, dear Algy. The Divorce Court was specially invented for people whose memories are so curiously constituted.

ALGERNON.   Oh! there is no use speculating on that subject. Divorces are made in Heaven – (JACK *puts out his hand to take a sandwich.* ALGERNON *at once interferes.*) Please don't touch the cucumber sandwiches. They are ordered specially for Aunt Augusta. (*Takes one and eats it.*)

JACK.   Well, you have been eating them all the time.

ALGERNON.   That it quite a different matter. She is my aunt. (*Takes plate from below.*) Have some bread and butter. The bread and butter is for Gwendolen. Gwendolen is devoted to bread and butter.

JACK.   (*Advancing to table and helping himself.*) And very good bread and butter it is too.

ALGERNON.   Well, my dear fellow, you need not eat as if you were going to eat it all. You behave as if you were married to her already. You are not married to her already, and I don't think you ever will be.

JACK.   Why on earth do you say that?

ALGERNON.   Well, in the first place girls never marry the men they flirt with. Girls don't think it right.

JACK.   Oh, that is nonsense!

ALGERNON.   It isn't. It is a great truth. It accounts for the extraordinary number of bachelors that one sees all over the place. In the second place, I don't give my consent.

JACK.   Your consent!

ALGERNON.   My dear fellow. Gwendolen is my first cousin. And before I allow you to marry her, your will have to clear up the whole question of Cecily. (*Rings bell.*)

JACK.   Cecily! What on earth do you mean? What do you mean, Algy, by Cecily? I don't know anyone of the name of Cecily.

(*Enter* LANE.)

ALGERNON.   Bring me that cigarette case Mr Worthing left in the smoking-room the last time he dined here.

LANE.   Yes, sir.   (LANE *goes out.*)

JACK.   Do you mean to say you have had my cigarette case all this time? I wish to goodness you had let me know. I have been writing frantic letters to Scotland Yard about it. I was very nearly offering a large reward.

ALGERNON.   Well, I wish you would offer one. I happen to be more than usually hard up.

JACK.   There is no good offering a large reward now that the thing is found.

(*Enter* LANE *with the cigarette case on a salver.* ALGERNON *takes it at once.* LANE *goes out.*)

ALGERNON.   I think that is rather mean of you, Ernest, I must say. (*Opens case and examines it.*) However, it makes no matter, for, now that I look at the inscription inside, I find that the thing isn't yours after all.

JACK.   Of course it's mine. (*Moving to him.*) You have seen me with it a hundred times, and you have no right whatsoever to read what is written inside. It is a very ungentlemanly thing to read a private cigarette case.

ALGERNON.   Oh! it is absurd to have a hard-and-fast rule about what one should read and what one shouldn't. More than half of modern culture depends on what one shouldn't read.

JACK.   I am quite aware of the fact, and I don't propose to discuss modern culture. It isn't the sort of thing one should talk of in private. I simply want my cigarette case back.

ALGERNON.   Yes; but this isn't your cigarette case. This cigarette case is a present from someone of the name of Cecily, and you said you didn't know anyone of that name.

JACK.   Well, if you want to know, Cecily happens to be my aunt.

ALGERNON.   Your aunt!

JACK.   Yes. Charming old lady she is, too, Lives at Tunbridge Wells. Just give it back to me, Algy.

ALGERNON.   (*Retreating to back of sofa.*) But why does she call herself little Cecily if she is your aunt and lives at Tunbridge Wells? (*Reading.*) 'From little Cecily with her fondest love.'

JACK.   (*Moving to sofa and kneeling upon it.*) My dear fellow, what on earth is there in that? Some aunts are tall, some aunts are not tall. That is a matter that surely an aunt may be allowed to decide for herself. You seem to think that every aunt should be exactly like your aunt! That is absurd! For Heaven's sake give me back my cigarette case. (*Follows* ALGERNON *round the room.*)

ALGERNON.   Yes. But why does your aunt call you her uncle? 'From little Cecily, with her fondest love to her dear Uncle Jack.' There is no objection, I admit, to an aunt being a small aunt, but why an aunt, no matter what her size may be, should call her own nephew her uncle, I can't quite make out. Besides, your name isn't Jack at all; it is Ernest.

JACK.   It isn't Ernest; it's Jack.

ALGERNON.   You have always told me it was Ernest. I have introduced you to everyone as Ernest. You answer to the name of Ernest. You look as if your name was Ernest. You are the most earnest looking person I ever saw in my life. It is perfectly absurd your saying that your name isn't Ernest. It's on your cards. Here is one of them. (*Taking it from case.*) 'Mr Ernest Worthing, B. 4, The Albany.' I'll keep this as a proof that your name is Ernest if ever you attempt to deny it to me, or to Gwendolen, or to anyone else. (*Puts the card in his pocket.*)

JACK.   Well, my name is Ernest in town and Jack in the country, and the cigarette case was given to me in the country.

ALGERNON.   Yes, but that does not account for the fact that your small Aunt Cecily, who lives at Tunbridge Wells, calls you her dear uncle. Come, old boy, you had much better have the thing out at once.

JACK.   My dear Algy, you talk exactly as if you were a dentist. It is very vulgar to talk like a dentist when one isn't a dentist. It produces a false impression.

ALGERNON.   Well, that is exactly what dentists always do. Now, go on! Tell me the whole thing. I may mention I have always suspected you of being a confirmed and secret Bunburyist; and I am quite sure of it now.

JACK.   Bunburyist? What on earth do you mean by a Bunburyist?

ALGERNON.   I'll reveal to you the meaning of that incomparable expression as soon as you are kind enough to inform me why you are Ernest in town and Jack in the country.

JACK.   Well, produce my cigarette case first.

ALGERNON.   Here it is. (*Hands cigarette case.*) Now produce your explanation, and pray make it improbable. (*Sits on sofa.*)

JACK. My dear fellow, there is nothing improbable about my explanation at all. In fact it's perfectly ordinary. Old Mr Thomas Cardew, who adopted me when I was a little boy, made me in his will guardian to his granddaughter, Miss Cecily Cardew. Cecily, who addresses me as her uncle from motives or respect that you could not possibly appreciate, lives at my place in the country under the charge of her admirable governess, Miss Prism.

ALGERNON. Where is that place in the country, by the way?

JACK. That is nothing to you, dear boy. You are not going to be invited. . . . I may tell you candidly that the place is not in Shropshire.

ALGERNON. I suspected that, my dear fellow! I have Bunburyed all over Shropshire on two separate occasions. Now, go on. Why are you Ernest in town and Jack in the country?

JACK. My dear Algy, I don't know whether you will be able to understand my real motives. You are hardly serious enough. When one is placed in the position of guardian, one has to adopt a very high moral tone on all subjects. It's one's duty to do so. And as a high moral tone can hardly be said to conduce very much to either one's health or one's happiness, in order to get up to town I have always pretended to have a younger brother of the name of Ernest, who lives in the Albany, and gets into the most dreadful scrapes. That, my dear Algy, is the whole truth pure and simple.

ALGERNON. The truth is rarely pure and never simple. Modern life would be very tedious if it were either, and modern literature a complete impossibility!

JACK. That wouldn't be at all a bad thing.

ALGERNON. Literary criticism is not your forte, my dear fellow. Don't try it. You should leave that to people who haven't been at a University. They do it so well in the daily papers. What you really are is a Bunburyist. I was right in saying you were a Bunburyist. You are one of the most advanced Bunburyists I know.

JACK. What on earth do you mean?

ALGERNON. You have invented a very useful young brother called Ernest, in order that you may be able to come up to town as often as you like. I have invented an invaluable permanent invalid called Bunbury, in order that I may be

33

able to go down into the country whenever I choose. Bunbury is perfectly invaluable. If it wasn't for Bunbury's extraordinary bad health, for instance, I wouldn't be able to dine with you at Willis's tonight, for I have been really engaged to Aunt Augusta for more than a week.

JACK.   I haven't asked you to dine with me anywhere tonight.

ALGERNON.   I know. You are absurdly careless about sending out invitations. It is very foolish of you. Nothing annoys people so much as not receiving invitations.

JACK.   You had much better dine with your Aunt Augusta.

ALGERNON.   I haven't the smallest intention of doing anything of the kind. To begin with, I dined there on Monday, and once a week is quite enough to dine with one's own relations. In the second place, whenever I do dine there I am always treated as a member of the family, and sent down with either no woman at all, or two. In the third place, I know perfectly well whom she will place me next to, tonight. She will place me next Mary Farquhar, who always flirts with her own husband across the dinner-table. That is not very pleasant. Indeed, it is not even decent . . . and that sort of thing is enormously on the increase. The amount of women in London who flirt with their own husbands is perfectly scandalous. It looks so bad. It is simply washing one's clean linen in public. Besides, now that I know you to be a confirmed Bunburyist, I naturally want to talk to you about Bunburying. I want to tell you the rules.

JACK.   I'm not a Bunburyist at all. If Gwendolen accepts me, I am going to kill my brother, indeed I think I'll kill him in any case. Cecily is a little too much interested in him. It is rather a bore. So I am going to get rid of Ernest. And I strongly advise you to do the same with Mr . . . with your invalid friend who has the absurd name.

ALGERNON.   Nothing will induce me to part with Bunbury, and if you ever get married, which seems to me extremely problematic, you will be very glad to know Bunbury. A man who marries without knowing Bunbury has a very tedious time of it.

JACK.   That is nonsense. If I marry a charming girl like Gwendolen, and she is the only girl I ever saw in my life that I would marry, I certainly won't want to know Bunbury.

ALGERNON.   Then your wife will. You don't seem to realize,
that in married life three is company and two is none.

JACK.   (*Sententiously*) That, my dear young friend, is the theory
that the corrupt French Drama has been propounding for
the last fifty years.

ALGERNON.   Yes; and that the happy English home has proved
in half the time.

JACK.   For Heaven's sake, don't try to be cynical. It's perfectly
easy to be cynical.

ALGERNON.   My dear fellow, it isn't easy to be anything
nowadays. There's such a lot of beastly competition about.
(*The sound of an electric bell is heard.*) Ah! that must be Aunt
Augusta. Only relatives, or creditors, ever ring in that
Wagnerian manner. Now, if I get her out of the way for ten
minutes, so that you can have an opportunity for proposing
to Gwendolen, may I dine with you tonight at Willis's?

JACK.   I suppose so, if you want to.

ALGERNON.   Yes, but you must be serious about it. I hate
people who are not serious about meals. It is so shallow
of them.

(*Enter* LANE.)

LANE.   Lady Bracknell and Miss Fairfax.

(ALGERNON *goes forward to meet them. Enter* LADY BRACKNELL
and GWENDOLEN.)

LADY BRACKNELL.   Good afternoon, dear Algernon, I hope you
are behaving very well.

ALGERNON.   I'm feeling very well, Aunt Augusta.

LADY BRACKNELL.   That's not quite the same thing. In fact the
two things rarely go together. (*Sees* JACK *and bows to him with
icy coldness.*)

ALGERNON.   (*To* GWENDOLEN) Dear me, you are smart!

GWENDOLEN.   I am always smart! Aren't I, Mr Worthing?

JACK.   You're quite perfect, Miss Fairfax.

GWENDOLEN.   Oh! I hope I am not that. It would leave
no room for developments, and I intend to develop in
many directions. (GWENDOLEN *and* JACK *sit down together in
the corner.*)

LADY BRACKNELL.   I'm sorry if we are a little late, Algernon,
but I was obliged to call on dear Lady Harbury. I hadn't
been there since her poor husband's death. I never saw a

35

woman so altered; she looks quite twenty years younger. And now I'll have a cup of tea, and one of those nice cucumber sandwiches you promised me.

ALGERNON.   Certainly, Aunt Augusta. (*Goes over to tea-table.*)

LADY BRACKNELL.   Won't you come and sit here, Gwendolen?

GWENDOLEN.   Thanks, Mamma, I'm quite comfortable where I am.

ALGERNON.   (*Picking up empty plate in horror.*) Good heavens! Lane! Why are there no cucumber sandwiches? I ordered them specially.

LANE.   (*Gravely.*) There were no cucumbers in the market this morning, sir. I went down twice.

ALGERNON.   No cucumbers!

LANE.   No, sir. Not even for ready money.

ALGERNON.   That will do, Lane, thank you.

LANE.   Thank you, sir.

ALGERNON.   I am greatly distressed, Aunt Augusta, about there being no cucumbers, not even for ready money.

LADY BRACKNELL.   It really makes no matter, Algernon. I had some crumpets with Lady Harbury, who seems to me to be living entirely for pleasure now.

ALGERNON.   I hear her hair has turned quite gold from grief.

LADY BRACKNELL.   It certainly has changed its colour. From what cause I, of course, cannot say. (ALGERNON *crosses and hands tea.*) Thank you. I've quite a treat for you tonight, Algernon. I am going to send you down with Mary Farquhar. She is such a nice woman, and so attentive to her husband. It's delightful to watch them.

ALGERNON.   I am afraid, Aunt Augusta, I shall have to give up the pleasure of dining with you tonight after all.

LADY BRACKNELL.   (*Frowning*) I hope not, Algernon. It would put my table completely out. Your uncle would have to dine upstairs. Fortunately he is accustomed to that.

ALGERNON.   It is a great bore, and, I need hardly say, a terrible disappointment to me, but the fact is I have just had a telegram to say that my poor friend Bunbury is very ill again. (*Exchanges glances with* JACK.) They seem to think I should be with him.

LADY BRACKNELL.   It is very strange. This Mr Bunbury seems to suffer from curiously bad health.

ALGERNON.   Yes; poor Bunbury is a dreadful invalid.

LADY BRACKNELL.   Well, I must say, Algernon, that I think it is high time that Mr Bunbury made up his mind whether he was going to live or to die. This shilly-shallying with the question is absurd. Nor do I in any way approve of the modern sympathy with invalids. I consider it morbid. Illness of any kind is hardly a thing to be encouraged in others. Health is the primary duty of life. I am always telling that to your poor uncle, but he never seems to take much notice . . . as far as any improvement in his ailments goes. I should be obliged if you would ask Mr Bunbury, from me, to be kind enough not to have a relapse on Saturday, for I rely on you to arrange my music for me. It is my last reception, and one wants something that will encourage conversation, particularly at the end of the season when everyone has practically said whatever they had to say, which, in most cases, was probably not much.

ALGERNON.   I'll speak to Bunbury, Aunt Augusta, if he is still conscious, and I think I can promise you he'll be all right by Saturday. Of course the music is a great difficulty. You see, if one plays good music, people don't listen, and if one plays bad music, people don't talk. But I'll run over the programme I've drawn out, if you will kindly come into the next room for a moment.

LADY BRACKNELL.   Thank you, Algernon. It is very thoughtful of you. (*Rising, and following* ALGERNON.) I'm sure the programme will be delightful, after a few expurgations. French songs I cannot possibly allow. People always seem to think that they are improper, and either look shocked, which is vulgar, or laugh, which is worse. But German sounds a thoroughly respectable language, and indeed, I believe is so. Gwendolen, you will accompany me.

GWENDOLEN.   Certainly, Mamma.

(LADY BRACKNELL *and* ALGERNON *go into the music-room,* GWENDOLEN *remains behind.*)

JACK.   Charming day it has been, Miss Fairfax.

GWENDOLEN.   Pray don't talk to me about the weather, Mr Worthing. Whenever people talk to me about the weather, I always feel quite certain that they mean something else. And that makes me so nervous.

JACK.   I do mean something else.

GWENDOLEN.   I thought so. In fact, I am never wrong.

JACK.   And I would like to be allowed to take advantage of
Lady Bracknell's temporary absence. . . .

GWENDOLEN.   I would certainly advise you to do so. Mamma
has a way of coming back suddenly into a room that I have
often had to speak to her about.

JACK.   (*Nervously.*) Miss Fairfax, ever since I met you I have
admired you more than any girl . . . I have ever met since
. . . I met you.

GWENDOLEN.   Yes, I am quite aware of the fact. And I often
wish that in public, at any rate, you had been more
demonstrative. For me you have always had an irresistible
fascination. Even before I met you I was far from indifferent
to you. (JACK *looks at her in amazement.*) We live, as I hope
you know, Mr Worthing, in an age of ideals. The fact
is constantly mentioned in the more expensive monthly
magazines, and has reached the provincial pulpits I am told:
and my ideal has always been to love someone of the name of
Ernest. There is something in that name that inspires absolute
confidence. The moment Algernon first mentioned to me
that he had a friend called Ernest, I knew I was destined to
love you.

JACK.   You really love me, Gwendolen?

GWENDOLEN.   Passionately!

JACK.   Darling! You don't know how happy you've made
me.

GWENDOLEN.   My own Ernest!

JACK.   But you don't really mean to say that you couldn't love
me if my name wasn't Ernest?

GWENDOLEN.   But your name is Ernest.

JACK.   Yes, I know it is. But supposing it was something else?
Do you mean to say you couldn't love me then?

GWENDOLEN.   (*Glibly.*) Ah! that is clearly a metaphysical
speculation, and like most metaphysical speculations has
very little reference at all to the actual facts of real life, as
we know them.

JACK.   Personally, darling, to speak quite candidly, I don't much
care about the name of Ernest . . . I don't think the name
suits me at all.

GWENDOLEN.   It suits you perfectly. It is a divine name. It has
a music of its own. It produces vibrations.

JACK.   Well, really, Gwendolen, I must say that I think there
are lots of other much nicer names. I think Jack, for instance,
a charming name.

GWENDOLEN.   Jack? . . . No, there is very little music in the
name Jack, if any at all, indeed. It does not thrill. It produces
absolutely no vibrations. . . . I have known several Jacks, and
they all, without exception, were more than usually plain.
Besides, Jack is a notorious domesticity for John! And I
pity any woman who is married to a man called John. She
would probably never be allowed to know the entrancing
pleasure of a single moment's solitude. The only really safe
name is Ernest.

JACK.   Gwendolen, I must get christened at once – I mean
we must get married at once. There is no time to be
lost.

GWENDOLEN.   Married, Mr Worthing?

JACK.   (*Astounded.*) Well . . . surely. You know that I love you,
and you led me to believe, Miss Fairfax, that you were not
absolutely indifferent to me.

GWENDOLEN.   I adore you. But you haven't proposed to me
yet. Nothing has been said at all about marriage. The subject
has not even been touched on.

JACK.   Well . . . may I propose to you now?

GWENDOLEN.   I think it would be an admirable opportunity.
And to spare you any possible disappointment, Mr Worthing,
I think it only fair to tell you quite frankly beforehand that
I am fully determined to accept you.

JACK.   Gwendolen!

GWENDOLEN.   Yes, Mr Worthing, what have you got to say to
me?

JACK.   You know what I have got to say to you.

GWENDOLEN.   Yes, but you don't say it.

JACK.   Gwendolen, will you marry me? (*Goes on his knees.*)

GWENDOLEN.   Of course I will, darling. How long you have
been about it! I am afraid you have had very little experience
in how to propose.

JACK.   My own one, I have never loved anyone in the world
but you.

GWENDOLEN.   Yes, but men often propose for practice. I know
my brother Gerald does. All my girl-friends tell me so. What
wonderfully blue eyes you have, Ernest! They are quite,
quite blue. I hope you will always look at me just like that,
especially when there are other people present.

(*Enter* LADY BRACKNELL.)

LADY BRACKNELL.   Mr Worthing! Rise, sir, from this semi-
recumbent posture. It is most indecorous.

GWENDOLEN.   Mamma! (*He tries to rise; she restrains him.*) I
must beg you to retire. This is no place for you. Besides,
Mr Worthing has not quite finished yet.

LADY BRACKNELL.   Finished what, may I ask?

GWENDOLEN.   I am engaged to Mr Worthing, Mamma. (*They
rise together.*)

LADY BRACKNELL.   Pardon me, you are not engaged to anyone.
When you do become engaged to someone, I, or your
father, should his health permit him, will inform you of
the fact. An engagement should come on a young girl as
a surprise, pleasant or unpleasant, as the case may be. It
is hardly a matter that she could be allowed to arrange
for herself. . . . And now I have a few questions to put to
you, Mr Worthing. While I am making these inquiries, you,
Gwendolen, will wait for me below in the carriage.

GWENDOLEN.   (*Reproachfully.*) Mamma!

LADY BRACKNELL.   In the carriage, Gwendolen!

(GWENDOLEN *goes to the door. She and* JACK *blow kisses to each
other behind* LADY BRACKNELL's *back.* LADY BRACKNELL
*looks vaguely about as if she could not understand what the
noise was. Finally turns round.*) Gwendolen, the carriage!

GWENDOLEN.   Yes, Mamma. (*Goes out, looking back at* JACK.)

LADY BRACKNELL.   (*Sitting down.*) You can take a seat, Mr
Worthing. (*Looks in her pocket for note-book and pencil.*)

JACK.   Thank you, Lady Bracknell, I prefer standing.

LADY BRACKNELL.   (*Pencil and note-book in hand.*) I feel bound to
tell you that you are not down on my list of eligible young
men, although I have the same list as the dear Duchess of
Bolton has. We work together, in fact. However, I am quite
ready to enter your name, should your answers be what a
really affectionate mother requires. Do you smoke?

JACK.   Well, yes, I must admit I smoke.

LADY BRACKNELL.   I am glad to hear it. A man should always have an occupation of some kind. There are far too many idle men in London as it is. How old are you?

JACK.   Twenty-nine.

LADY BRACKNELL.   A very good age to be married at. I have always been of opinion that a man who desires to get married should know either everything or nothing. Which do you know?

JACK.   (*After some hesitation.*) I know nothing, Lady Bracknell.

LADY BRACKNELL.   I am pleased to hear it. I do not approve of anything that tampers with natural ignorance. Ignorance is like a delicate exotic fruit; touch it and the bloom is gone. The whole theory of modern education is radically unsound. Fortunately in England, at any rate, education produces no effect whatsoever. If it did, it would prove a serious danger to the upper classes, and probably lead to acts of violence in Grosvenor Square. What is your income?

JACK.   Between seven and eight thousand a year.

LADY BRACKNELL.   (*Makes a note in her book.*) In land, or in *investments*?

JACK.   In investments, chiefly.

LADY BRACKNELL.   That is satisfactory. What between the duties expected of one during one's lifetime, and the duties exacted from one after one's death, land has ceased to be either a profit or a pleasure. It gives one position, and prevents one from keeping it up. That's all that can be said about land.

JACK.   I have a country house with some land, of course, attached to it, about fifteen hundred acres, I believe; but I don't depend on that for my real income. In fact, as far as I can make out, the poachers are the only people who make anything out of it.

LADY BRACKNELL.   A country house! How many bedrooms? Well, that point can be cleared up afterwards. You have a town house, I hope? A girl with a simple, unspoiled nature, like Gwendolen, could hardly be expected to reside in the country.

JACK.   Well, I own a house in Belgrave Square, but it is let by the year to Lady Bloxham. Of course, I can get it back whenever I like, at six months' notice.

LADY BRACKNELL.   Lady Bloxham? I don't know her.

JACK.   Oh, she goes about very little. She is a lady considerably advanced in years.

LADY BRACKNELL.   Ah, nowadays that is no guarantee of respectability of character. What number in Belgrave Square?

JACK.   149.

LADY BRACKNELL.   (*Shaking her head.*) The unfashionable side. I thought there was something. However, that could easily be altered.

JACK.   Do you mean the fashion, or the side?

LADY BRACKNELL.   (*Sternly.*) Both, if necessary, I presume. What are your politics?

JACK.   Well, I am afraid I really have none. I am a Liberal Unionist.

LADY BRACKNELL.   Oh, they count as Tories. They dine with us. Or come in the evening, at any rate. Now to minor matters. Are your parents living?

JACK.   I have lost both my parents.

LADY BRACKNELL.   Both?. . . That seems like carelessness. Who was your father? He was evidently a man of some wealth. Was he born in what the Radical papers call the purple of commerce, or did he rise from the ranks of aristocracy?

JACK.   I am afraid I really don't know. The fact is, Lady Bracknell, I said I had lost my parents. It would be nearer the truth to say that my parents seem to have lost me. . . . I don't actually know who I am by birth. I was . . . well, I was found.

LADY BRACKNELL.   Found!

JACK.   The late Mr Thomas Cardew, an old gentleman of a very charitable and kindly disposition, found me, and gave me the name of Worthing, because he happened to have a first-class ticket for Worthing in his pocket at the time. Worthing is a place in Sussex. It is a seaside resort.

LADY BRACKNELL.   Where did the charitable gentleman who had a first-class ticket for this seaside resort find you?

JACK.   (*Gravely.*) In a handbag.

LADY BRACKNELL.   A handbag?

JACK.   (*Very seriously.*) Yes, Lady Bracknell. I was in a handbag – a somewhat large, black leather handbag, with handles to it – an ordinary handbag, in fact.

LADY BRACKNELL. In what locality did this Mr James, or Thomas, Cardew come across this ordinary handbag?

JACK. In the cloakroom at Victoria Station. It was given to him in mistake for his own.

LADY BRACKNELL. The cloakroom at Victoria Station?

JACK. Yes. The Brighton line.

LADY BRACKNELL. The line is immaterial. Mr Worthing, I confess I feel somewhat bewildered by what you have just told me. To be born, or at any rate, bred in a handbag, whether it had handles or not, seems to me to display a contempt for the ordinary decencies of family life that remind one of the worst excesses of the French Revolution. And I presume you know what that unfortunate movement led to? As for the particular locality in which the handbag was found, a cloakroom at a railway station might serve to conceal a social indiscretion – has probably, indeed, been used for that purpose before now – but it could hardly be regarded as an assured basis for a recognized position in good society.

JACK. May I ask you then what you would advise me to do? I need hardly say I would do anything in the world to ensure Gwendolen's happiness.

LADY BRACKNELL. I would strongly advise you, Mr Worthing, to try and acquire some relations as soon as possible, and to make a definite effort to produce at any rate one parent, of either sex, before the season is quite over.

JACK. Well, I don't see how I could possibly manage to do that. I can produce the handbag at any moment. It is in my dressing-room at home. I really think that should satisfy you, Lady Bracknell.

LADY BRACKNELL. Me, sir! What has it to do with me? You can hardly imagine that I and Lord Bracknell would dream of allowing our only daughter – a girl brought up with the utmost care – to marry into a cloakroom, and form an alliance with a parcel? Good morning, Mr Worthing!

(LADY BRACKNELL *sweeps out in majestic indignation.*)

JACK. Good morning! (ALGERNON, *from the other room, strikes up the* Wedding March. JACK *looks perfectly furious, and goes to the door.*) For goodness' sake don't play that ghastly tune, Algy! How idiotic you are!

(*The music stops, and* ALGERNON *enters cheerily.*)

ALGERNON.   Didn't it go off all right, old boy? You don't
mean to say Gwendolen refused you? I know it is a way
she has. She is always refusing people. I think it is most
ill-natured of her.

JACK.   Oh, Gwendolen is as right as a trivet. As far as she
is concerned, we are engaged. Her mother is perfectly
unbearable. Never met such a gorgon . . . I don't really
know what a gorgon is like, but I am quite sure that Lady
Bracknell is one. In any case, she is a monster, without being
a myth, which is rather unfair . . . I beg your pardon, Algy,
I suppose I shouldn't talk about your own aunt in that way
before you.

ALGERNON.   My dear boy, I love hearing my relations abused.
It is the only thing that makes me put up with them at all.
Relations are simply a tedious pack of people who haven't
got the remotest knowledge of how to live, nor the smallest
instinct about when to die.

JACK.   Oh, that is nonsense!

ALGERNON.   It isn't!

JACK.   Well, I won't argue about the matter. You always want
to argue about things.

ALGERNON.   That is exactly what things were originally made
for.

JACK.   Upon my word, if I thought that, I'd shoot myself. . . .
(*A pause.*) You don't think there is any chance of Gwendolen
becoming like her mother in about a hundred and fifty years,
do you, Algy?

ALGERNON.   All women become like their mothers. That is
their tragedy. No man does. That's his.

JACK.   Is that clever?

ALGERNON.   It is perfectly phrased! and quite as true as any
observation in civilized life should be.

JACK.   I am sick to death of cleverness. Everybody is clever
nowadays. You can't go anywhere without meeting clever
people. The thing has become an absolute public nuisance.
I wish to goodness we had a few fools left.

ALGERNON.   We have.

JACK.   I should extremely like to meet them. What do they
talk about?

ALGERNON. The fools! Oh! about the clever people, of course.

JACK. What fools!

ALGERNON. By the way, did you tell Gwendolen the truth about your being Ernest in town, and Jack in the country?

JACK. (*In a very patronizing manner.*) My dear fellow, the truth isn't quite the sort of thing one tells to a nice sweet refined girl. What extraordinary ideas you have about the way to behave to a woman!

ALGERNON. The only way to behave to a woman is to make love to her, if she is pretty, and to someone else if she is plain.

JACK. Oh, that is nonsense.

ALGERNON. What about your brother? What about the profligate Ernest?

JACK. Oh, before the end of the week I shall have got rid of him. I'll say he died in Paris of apoplexy. Lots of people die of apoplexy, quite suddenly, don't they?

ALGERNON. Yes, but it's hereditary, my dear fellow. It's a sort of thing that runs in families. You had much better say a severe chill.

JACK. You are sure a severe chill isn't hereditary, or anything of that kind?

ALGERNON. Of course it isn't!

JACK. Very well, then. My poor brother Ernest is carried off suddenly in Paris, by a severe chill. That gets rid of him.

ALGERNON. But I thought you said that . . . Miss Cardew was a little too much interested in your poor brother Ernest? Won't she feel his loss a good deal?

JACK. Oh, that is all right. Cecily is not a silly romantic girl, I am glad to say. She has got a capital appetite, goes long walks, and pays no attention at all to her lessons.

ALGERNON. I would rather like to see Cecily.

JACK. I will take very good care you never do. She is excessively pretty, and she is only just eighteen.

ALGERNON. Have you told Gwendolen yet that you have an excessively pretty ward who is only just eighteen?

JACK. Oh! one doesn't blurt these things out to people. Cecily and Gwendolen are perfectly certain to be extremely great friends. I'll bet you anything you like that half an hour after they have met, they will be calling each other sister.

ALGERNON.   Women only do that when they have called each
  other a lot of other things first. Now, my dear boy, if we
  want to get a good table at Willis's, we really must go and
  dress. Do you know it is nearly seven?

JACK.   (*Irritably*) Oh! it always is nearly seven.

ALGERNON.   Well, I'm hungry.

JACK.   I never knew you when you weren't. . . .

ALGERNON.   What shall we do after dinner? Go to the theatre?

JACK.   Oh no! I loathe listening.

ALGERNON.   Well, let us go to the club?

JACK.   Oh, no! I hate talking.

ALGERNON.   Well, we might trot round to the Empire at ten?

JACK.   Oh no! I can't bear looking at things. It is so silly.

ALGERNON.   Well, what shall we do?

JACK.   Nothing!

ALGERNON.   It is awfully hard work doing nothing. However,
  I don't mind hard work where there is no definite object of
  any kind.

(*Enter* LANE).

LANE.   Miss Fairfax.

(*Enter* GWENDOLEN. LANE *goes out.*)

ALGERNON.   Gwendolen, upon my word!

GWENDOLEN.   Algy, kindly turn your back. I have something
  very particular to say to Mr Worthing.

ALGERNON.   Really, Gwendolen, I don't think I can allow
  this at all.

GWENDOLEN.   Algy, you always adopt a strictly immoral
  attitude towards life. You are not quite old enough to do
  that. (ALGERNON *retires to the fireplace.*)

JACK.   My own darling!

GWENDOLEN.   Ernest, we may never be married. From the
  expression on Mamma's face I fear we never shall. Few
  parents nowadays pay any regard to what their children
  say to them. The old-fashioned respect for the young is fast
  dying out. Whatever influence I ever had over Mamma, I
  lost at the age of three. But although she may prevent us
  from becoming man and wife, and I may marry someone
  else, and marry often, nothing that she can possibly do can
  alter my eternal devotion to you.

JACK.   Dear Gwendolen!

GWENDOLEN.   The story of your romantic origin, as related to me by Mamma, with unpleasing comments, has naturally stirred the deeper fibres of my nature. Your Christian name has an irresistible fascination. The simplicity of your character makes you exquisitely incomprehensible to me. Your town address at the Albany I have. What is your address in the country?

JACK.   The Manor House, Woolton, Hertfordshire.

(ALGERNON, *who has been carefully listening, smiles to himself, and writes the address on his shirt-cuff. Then picks up the Railway Guide.*)

GWENDOLEN.   There is a good postal service, I suppose? It may be necessary to do something desperate. That of course will require serious consideration. I will communicate with you daily.

JACK.   My own one!

GWENDOLEN.   How long do you remain in town?

JACK.   Till Monday.

GWENDOLEN.   Good! Algy, you may turn round now.

ALGERNON.   Thanks, I've turned round already.

GWENDOLEN.   You may also ring the bell.

JACK.   You will let me see you to your carriage, my own darling?

GWENDOLEN.   Certainly.

JACK.   (*To* LANE, *who now enters.*) I will see Miss Fairfax out.

LANE.   Yes, sir. (JACK *and* GWENDOLEN *go off.*)

(LANE *presents several letters on a salver to* ALGERNON. *It is to be surmised that they are bills, as* ALGERNON *after looking at the envelopes, tears them up.*)

ALGERNON.   A glass of sherry, Lane.

LANE.   Yes, sir.

ALGERNON.   Tomorrow, Lane, I'm going Bunburying.

LANE.   Yes, sir.

ALGERNON.   I shall probably not be back till Monday. You can put up my dress clothes, my smoking jacket, and all the Bunbury suits. . . .

LANE.   Yes, sir. (*Handing sherry.*)

ALGERNON.   I hope tomorrow will be a fine day. Lane.

LANE.   It never is, sir.

ALGERNON.   Lane, you're a perfect pessimist.

LANE.   I do my best to give satisfaction, sir.

(*Enter* JACK. LANE *goes off*.)

JACK.   There's a sensible, intellectual girl! The only girl I ever
   cared for in my life. (ALGERNON *is laughing immoderately*.)
   What on earth are you so amused at?

ALGERNON.   Oh, I'm a little anxious about poor Bunbury,
   that is all.

JACK.   If you don't take care, your friend Bunbury will get you
   into a serious scrape some day.

ALGERNON.   I love scrapes. They are the only things that are
   never serious.

JACK.   Oh, that's nonsense, Algy. You never talk anything but
   nonsense.

ALGERNON.   Nobody ever does.

(JACK *looks indignantly at him, and leaves the room*. ALGERNON *lights
   a cigarette, reads his shirt-cuff, and smiles*.)

ACT-DROP.

SECOND ACT

Scene. Garden at the Manor House. A flight of grey stone steps
   leads up to the house. The garden, an old-fashioned one, full
   of roses. Time of year, July. Basket chairs, and a table covered
   with books, are set under a large yew tree.

(MISS PRISM discovered seated at the table. CECILY is at the back
   watering flowers.)

MISS PRISM.   (*Calling*) Cecily, Cecily! Surely such a utilitarian
   occupation as the watering of flowers is rather Moulton's
   duty than yours? Especially at a moment when intellectual
   pleasures await you. Your German grammar is on the table.
   Pray open it at page fifteen. We will repeat yesterday's
   lesson.

CECILY.   (*Coming over very slowly*.) But I don't like German. It
   isn't at all a becoming language. I know perfectly well that I
   look quite plain after my German lesson.

MISS PRISM.   Child, you know how anxious your guardian is
   that you should improve yourself in every way. He laid
   particular stress on your German, as he was leaving for town
   yesterday. Indeed, he always lays stress on your German

when he is leaving for town.

CECILY. Dear Uncle Jack is so very serious! Sometimes he is so serious that I think he cannot be quite well.

MISS PRISM. (*Drawing herself up.*) Your guardian enjoys the best of health, and his gravity of demeanour is especially to be commended in one so comparatively young as he is. I know no one who has a higher sense of duty and responsibility.

CECILY. I suppose that is why he often looks a little bored when we three are together.

MISS PRISM. Cecily! I am surprised at you. Mr Worthing has many troubles in his life. Idle merriment and triviality would be out of place in his conversation. You must remember his constant anxiety about that unfortunate young man his brother.

CECILY. I wish Uncle Jack would allow that unfortunate young man, his brother, to come down here sometimes. We might have a good influence over him, Miss Prism. I am sure you certainly would. You know German, and Geology, and things of that kind influence a man very much. (CECILY *begins to write in her diary.*)

MISS PRISM. (*Shaking her head.*) I do not think that even I could produce any effect on a character that according to his own brother's admission is irretrievably weak and vacillating. Indeed I am not sure that I would desire to reclaim him. I am not in favour of this modern mania for turning bad people into good people at a moment's notice. As a man sows so let him reap. You must put away your diary, Cecily. I really don't see why you should keep a diary at all.

CECILY. I keep a diary in order to enter the wonderful secrets of my life. If I didn't write them down I should probably forget all about them.

MISS PRISM. Memory, my dear Cecily, is the diary that we all carry about with us.

CECILY. Yes, but it usually chronicles the things that have never happened, and couldn't possibly have happened. I believe that memory is responsible for nearly all the three-volume novels that Mudie sends us.

MISS PRISM. Do not speak slightingly of the three-volume novel, Cecily. I wrote one myself in earlier days.

49

CECILY.   Did you really, Miss Prism? How wonderfully clever you are! I hope it did not end happily? I don't like novels that end happily. They depress me so much.

MISS PRISM.   The good ended happily, and the bad unhappily. That is what fiction means.

CECILY.   I suppose so. But it seems very unfair. And was your novel ever published?

MISS PRISM.   Alas! no. The manuscript unfortunately was abandoned. I use the word in the sense of lost or mislaid. To your work, child, these speculations are profitless.

CECILY.   (*Smiling.*) But I see dear Dr Chasuble coming up through the garden.

MISS PRISM.   (*Rising and advancing.*) Dr Chasuble! This is indeed a pleasure.

(*Enter* CANON CHASUBLE.)

CHASUBLE.   And how are we this morning? Miss Prism, you are, I trust, well?

CECILY.   Miss Prism has just been complaining of a slight headache. I think it would do her so much good to have a short stroll with you in the Park, Dr Chasuble.

MISS PRISM.   Cecily, I have not mentioned anything about a headache.

CECILY.   No, dear Miss Prism, I know that, but I felt instinctively that you had a headache. Indeed I was thinking about that, and not about my German lesson, when the Rector came in.

CHASUBLE.   I hope, Cecily, you are not inattentive.

CECILY.   Oh, I am afraid I am.

CHASUBLE.   That is strange. Were I fortunate enough to be Miss Prism's pupil, I would hang upon her lips. (MISS PRISM *glares.*) I spoke metaphorically. – My metaphor was drawn from bees. Ahem! Mr Worthing, I suppose, has not returned from town yet?

MISS PRISM.   We do not expect him till Monday afternoon.

CHASUBLE.   Ah yes, he usually likes to spend his Sunday in London. He is not one of those whose sole aim is enjoyment, as, by all accounts, that unfortunate young man his brother seems to be. But I must not disturb Egeria and her pupil any longer.

MISS PRISM.   Egeria? My name is Lætitia, Doctor.

CHASUBLE.   (*Bowing.*) A classical allusion merely, drawn from the pagan authors. I shall see you both no doubt at Evensong?

MISS PRISM.   I think, dear Doctor, I will have a stroll with you. I find I have a headache after all, and a walk might do it good.

CHASUBLE.   With pleasure, Miss Prism, with pleasure. We might go as far as the schools and back.

MISS PRISM.   That would be delightful. Cecily, you will read your Political Economy in my absence. The chapter on the Fall of the Rupee you may omit. It is somewhat too sensational. Even these metallic problems have their melodramatic side.

(*Goes down the garden with* DR CHASUBLE.)

CECILY.   (*Picks up books and throws them back on table.*) Horrid Political Economy! Horrid Geography! Horrid, horrid German!

(*Enter* MERRIMAN *with a card on a salver.*)

MERRIMAN.   Mr Ernest Worthing has just driven over from the station. He has brought his luggage with him.

CECILY.   (*Takes the card and reads it.*) 'Mr Ernest Worthing, B. 4 The Albany, W.' Uncle Jack's brother! Did you tell him Mr Worthing was in town?

MERRIMAN.   Yes, Miss. He seemed very much disappointed. I mentioned that you and Miss Prism were in the garden. He said he was anxious to speak to you privately for a moment.

CECILY.   Ask Mr Ernest Worthing to come here. I suppose you had better talk to the housekeeper about a room for him.

MERRIMAN.   Yes, Miss.   (MERRIMAN *goes off.*)

CECILY.   I have never met any really wicked person before. I feel rather frightened. I am so afraid he will look just like everyone else.

(*Enter* ALGERNON, *very gay and debonair.*)

He does!

ALGERNON.   (*Raising his hat.*) You are my little cousin Cecily, I'm sure.

CECILY.   You are under some strange mistake. I am not little. In fact, I believe I am more than usually tall for my age.

(ALGERNON *is rather taken aback.*) But I am your cousin Cecily. You, I see from your card, are Uncle Jack's brother, my cousin Ernest, my wicked cousin Ernest.

ALGERNON.   Oh! I am not really wicked at all, cousin Cecily. You mustn't think that I am wicked.

CECILY.   If you are not, then you have certainly been deceiving us all in a very inexcusable manner. I hope you have not been leading a double life, pretending to be wicked and being really good all the time. That would be hypocrisy.

ALGERNON.   (*Looks at her in amazement.*) Oh! Of course I have been rather reckless.

CECILY.   I am glad to hear it.

ALGERNON.   In fact, now you mention the subject, I have been very bad in my own small way.

CECILY.   I don't think you should be so proud of that, though I am sure it must have been very pleasant.

ALGERNON.   It is much pleasanter being here with you.

CECILY.   I can't understand how you are here at all. Uncle Jack won't be back till Monday afternoon.

ALGERNON.   That is a great disappointment. I am obliged to go up by the first train on Monday morning. I have a business appointment that I am anxious . . . to miss.

CECILY.   Couldn't you miss it anywhere but in London?

ALGERNON.   No; the appointment is in London.

CECILY.   Well, I know, of course, how important it is not to keep a business engagement, if one wants to retain any sense of the beauty of life, but still I think you had better wait till Uncle Jack arrives. I know he wants to speak to you about your emigrating.

ALGERNON.   About my what?

CECILY.   Your emigrating. He has gone up to buy your outfit.

ALGERNON.   I certainly wouldn't let Jack buy my outfit. He has no taste in neckties at all.

CECILY.   I don't think you will require neckties. Uncle Jack is sending you to Australia.

ALGERNON.   Australia? I'd sooner die.

CECILY.   Well, he said at dinner on Wednesday night, that you would have to choose between this world, the next world, and Australia.

ALGERNON.   Oh, well! The accounts I have received of

Australia and the next world are not particularly encouraging. This world is good enough for me, cousin Cecily.

CECILY.   Yes, but are you good enough for it?

ALGERNON.   I'm afraid I'm not that. That is why I want you to reform me. You might make that your mission, if you don't mind, cousin Cecily.

CECILY.   I'm afraid I've no time, this afternoon.

ALGERNON.   Well, would you mind my reforming myself this afternoon?

CECILY.   It is rather quixotic of you. But I think you should try.

ALGERNON.   I will. I feel better already.

CECILY.   You are looking a little worse.

ALGERNON.   That is because I am hungry.

CECILY.   How thoughtless of me. I should have remembered that when one is going to lead an entirely new life, one requires regular and wholesome meals. Won't you come in?

ALGERNON.   Thank you. Might I have a button-hole first? I never have any appetite unless I have a button-hole first.

CECILY.   A Maréchal Niel? (*Picks up scissors.*)

ALGERNON.   No, I'd sooner have a pink rose.

CECILY.   Why? (*Cuts a flower.*)

ALGERNON.   Because you are like a pink rose, cousin Cecily.

CECILY.   I don't think it can be right for you to talk to me like that. Miss Prism never says such things to me.

ALGERNON.   Then Miss Prism is a short-sighted old lady. (CECILY *puts the rose in his button-hole.*) You are the prettiest girl I ever saw.

CECILY.   Miss Prism says that all good looks are a snare.

ALGERNON.   They are a snare that every sensible man would like to be caught in.

CECILY.   Oh! I don't think I would care to catch a sensible man. I shouldn't know what to talk to him about.

(*They pass into the house.* MISS PRISM *and* DR CHASUBLE *return.*)

MISS PRISM.   You are too much alone, dear Dr Chasuble. You should get married. A misanthrope I can understand – a womanthrope, never!

CHASUBLE.   (*With a scholar's shudder.*) Believe me, I do not deserve so neologistic a phrase. The precept as well as

53

the practice of the Primitive Church was distinctly against matrimony.

MISS PRISM.   (*Sententiously.*) That is obviously the reason why the Primitive Church has not lasted up to the present day. And you do not seem to realize, dear Doctor, that by persistently remaining single, a man converts himself into a permanent public temptation. Men should be more careful; this very celibacy leads weaker vessels astray.

CHASUBLE.   But is a man not equally attractive when married?

MISS PRISM.   No married man is ever attractive except to his wife.

CHASUBLE.   And often, I've been told, not even to her.

MISS PRISM.   That depends on the intellectual sympathies of the woman. Maturity can always be depended on. Ripeness can be trusted. Young women are green. (DR CHASUBLE *starts.*) I spoke horticulturally. My metaphor was drawn from fruits. But where is Cecily?

CHASUBLE.   Perhaps she followed us to the schools.

(*Enter* JACK *slowly from the back of the garden. He is dressed in the deepest mourning, with crape hatband and black gloves.*)

MISS PRISM.   Mr Worthing!

CHASUBLE.   Mr Worthing?

MISS PRISM.   This is indeed a surprise. We did not look for you till Monday afternoon.

JACK.   (*Shakes* MISS PRISM's *hand in a tragic manner.*) I have returned sooner than I expected. Dr Chasuble, I hope you are well?

CHASUBLE.   Dear Mr Worthing, I trust this garb of woe does not betoken some terrible calamity?

JACK.   My brother.

MISS PRISM.   More shameful debts and extravagance?

CHASUBLE.   Still leading his life of pleasure?

JACK.   (*Shaking his head.*) Dead!

CHASUBLE.   Your brother Ernest dead?

JACK.   Quite dead.

MISS PRISM.   What a lesson for him! I trust he will profit by it.

CHASUBLE.   Mr Worthing, I offer you my sincere condolence. You have at least the consolation of knowing that you were always the most generous and forgiving of brothers.

JACK. Poor Ernest! He had many faults, but it is a sad, sad blow.

CHASUBLE. Very sad indeed. Were you with him at the end?

JACK. No. He died abroad; in Paris, in fact. I had a telegram last night from the manager of the Grand Hotel.

CHASUBLE. Was the cause of death mentioned?

JACK. A severe chill, it seems.

MISS PRISM. As a man sows, so shall he reap.

CHASUBLE. (*Raising his hand.*) Charity, dear Miss Prism, charity! None of us are perfect. I myself am peculiarly susceptible to draughts. Will the interment take place here?

JACK. No. He seemed to have expressed a desire to be buried in Paris.

CHASUBLE. In Paris! (*Shakes his head.*) I fear that hardly points to any very serious state of mind at the last. You would no doubt wish me to make some slight allusion to this tragic domestic affliction next Sunday. (JACK *presses his hand convulsively.*) My sermon on the meaning of the manna in the wilderness can be adapted to almost any occasion, joyful, or, as in the present case, distressing. (*All sigh.*) I have preached it at harvest celebrations, christenings, confirmations, on days of humiliation and festal days. The last time I delivered it was in the Cathedral, as a charity sermon on behalf of the Society for the Prevention of Discontent among the Upper Orders. The Bishop, who was present, was much struck by some of the analogies I drew.

JACK. Ah! that reminds me, you mentioned christenings, I think, Dr Chasuble? I suppose you know how to christen all right? (DR CHASUBLE *looks astounded.*) I mean, of course, you are continually christening, aren't you?

MISS PRISM. It is, I regret to say, one of the Rector's most constant duties in this parish. I have often spoken to the poorer classes on the subject. But they don't seem to know what thrift is.

CHASUBLE. But is there any particular infant in whom you are interested, Mr Worthing? Your brother was, I believe, unmarried, was he not?

JACK. Oh, yes.

MISS PRISM. (*Bitterly.*) People who live entirely for pleasure usually are.

JACK.   But it is not for any child, dear Doctor. I am very fond
of children. No! the fact is, I would like to be christened
myself, this afternoon, if you have nothing better to do.

CHASUBLE.   But surely, Mr Worthing, you have been christened
already?

JACK.   I don't remember anything about it.

CHASUBLE.   But have you any grave doubts on the subject?

JACK.   I certainly intend to have. Of course I don't know if the
thing would bother you in any way, or if you think I am a
little too old now.

CHASUBLE.   Not at all. The sprinkling, and, indeed, the
immersion of adults is a perfectly canonical practice.

JACK.   Immersion!

CHASUBLE.   You need have no apprehensions. Sprinkling is all
that is necessary, or indeed I think advisable. Our weather is
so changeable. At what hour would you wish the ceremony
performed?

JACK.   Oh, I might trot round about five if that would
suit you.

CHASUBLE.   Perfectly, perfectly! In fact I have two similar
ceremonies to perform at that time. A case of twins
that occurred recently in one of the outlying cottages
on your own estate. Poor Jenkins the carter, a most
hard-working man.

JACK.   Oh! I don't see much fun in being christened along
with other babies. It would be childish. Would half-past
five do?

CHASUBLE.   Admirably! Admirably! (*Takes out watch.*) And
now, dear Mr Worthing, I will not intrude any longer
into a house of sorrow. I would merely beg you not to
be too much bowed down by grief. What seems to us bitter
trials are often blessings in disguise.

MISS PRISM.   This seems to me a blessing of an extremely
obvious kind.

(*Enter* CECILY *from the house.*)

CECILY.   Uncle Jack! Oh, I am pleased to see you back.
But what horrid clothes you have got on! Do go and
change them.

MISS PRISM.   Cecily!

CHASUBLE.   My child! my child! (CECILY *goes towards* JACK; *he kisses her brow in a melancholy manner.*)

CECILY.   What is the matter, Uncle Jack? Do look happy! You
    look as if you had toothache, and I have got such a surprise
    for you. Who do you think is in the dining-room? Your
    brother!

JACK.   Who?

CECILY.   Your brother Ernest. He arrived about half an hour
    ago.

JACK.   What nonsense! I haven't got a brother!

CECILY.   Oh, don't say that. However badly he may have
    behaved to you in the past he is still your brother. You
    couldn't be so heartless as to disown him. I'll tell him to
    come out. And you will shake hands with him, won't you,
    Uncle Jack? (*Runs back into the house.*)

CHASUBLE.   These are very joyful tidings.

MISS PRISM.   After we had all been resigned to his loss, his
    sudden return seems to me peculiarly distressing.

JACK.   My brother is in the dining-room? I don't know what
    it all means. I think it is perfectly absurd.

(*Enter* ALGERNON *and* CECILY *hand in hand. They come slowly up
to* JACK.)

JACK.   Good heavens! (*Motions* ALGERNON *away.*)

ALGERNON.   Brother John, I have come down from town to
    tell you that I am very sorry for all the trouble I have given
    you, and that I intend to lead a better life in the future. (JACK
    glares at him and does not take his hand.)

CECILY.   Uncle Jack, you are not going to refuse your own
    brother's hand?

JACK.   Nothing will induce me to take his hand. I think
    his coming down here disgraceful. He knows perfectly
    well why.

CECILY.   Uncle Jack, do be nice. There is some good in
    everyone. Ernest has just been telling me about his poor
    invalid friend Mr Bunbury whom he goes to visit so often.
    And surely there must be much good in one who is kind to
    an invalid, and leaves the pleasures of London to sit by a bed
    of pain.

JACK.   Oh! he has been talking about Bunbury, has he?

CECILY.   Yes, he has told me all about poor Mr Bunbury, and
    his terrible state of health.

JACK.   Bunbury! Well, I won't have him talk to you about Bunbury or about anything else. It is enough to drive one perfectly frantic.

ALGERNON.   Of course I admit that the faults were all on my side. But I must say that I think that Brother John's coldness to me is peculiarly painful. I expected a more enthusiastic welcome, especially considering it is the first time I have come here.

CECILY.   Uncle Jack, if you don't shake hands with Ernest, I will never forgive you.

JACK.   Never forgive me?

CECILY.   Never, never, never!

JACK.   Well, this is the last time I shall ever do it. (*Shakes hands with* ALGERNON *and glares.*)

CHASUBLE.   It's pleasant, is it not, to see so perfect a reconciliation? I think we might leave the two brothers together.

MISS PRISM.   Cecily, you will come with us.

CECILY.   Certainly, Miss Prism. My little task of reconciliation is over.

CHASUBLE.   You have done a beautiful action today, dear child.

MISS PRISM.   We must not be premature in our judgements.

CECILY.   I feel very happy. (*They all go off.*)

JACK.   You young scoundrel, Algy, you must get out of this place as soon as possible. I don't allow any Bunburying here.

(*Enter* MERRIMAN.)

MERRIMAN.   I have put Mr Ernest's things in the room next to yours, sir. I suppose that is all right?

JACK.   What?

MERRIMAN.   Mr Ernest's luggage, sir. I have unpacked it and put it in the room next to your own.

JACK.   His luggage?

MERRIMAN.   Yes, sir. Three portmanteaus, a dressing-case, two hat boxes, and a large luncheon-basket.

ALGERNON.   I am afraid I can't stay more than a week this time.

JACK.   Merriman, order the dog-cart at once. Mr Ernest has been suddenly called back to town.

MERRIMAN.   Yes, sir. (*Goes back into the house.*)

ALGERNON.   What a fearful liar you are, Jack. I have not been called back to town at all.

JACK.   Yes, you have.

ALGERNON.   I haven't heard anyone call me.

JACK.   Your duty as a gentleman calls you back.

ALGERNON.   My duty as a gentleman has never interfered with my pleasures in the smallest degree.

JACK.   I can quite understand that.

ALGERNON.   Well, Cecily is a darling.

JACK.   You are not to talk of Miss Cardew like that. I don't like it.

ALGERNON.   Well, I don't like your clothes. You look perfectly ridiculous in them. Why on earth don't you go up and change? It is perfectly childish to be in deep mourning for a man who is actually staying for a whole week with you in your house as a guest. I call it grotesque.

JACK.   You are certainly not staying with me for a whole week as a guest or anything else. You have got to leave . . . by the four-five train.

ALGERNON.   I certainly won't leave you so long as you are in mourning. It would be most unfriendly. If I were in mourning you would stay with me, I suppose. I should think it very unkind if you didn't.

JACK.   Well, will you go if I change my clothes?

ALGERNON.   Yes, if you are not too long. I never saw anybody take so long to dress, and with such little result.

JACK.   Well, at any rate, that is better than being always overdressed as you are.

ALGERNON.   If I am occasionally a little overdressed, I make up for it by being always immensely over-educated.

JACK.   Your vanity is ridiculous, your conduct an outrage, and your presence in my garden utterly absurd. However, you have got to catch the four-five, and I hope you will have a pleasant journey back to town. This Bunburying, as you call it, has not been a great success for you.

(*Goes into the house.*)

ALGERNON.   I think it has been a great success. I'm in love with Cecily, and that is everything.

(*Enter* CECILY *at the back of the garden. She picks up the can and begins to water the flowers.*) But I must see her before I go, and make arrangements for another Bunbury. Ah, there she is.

CECILY.   Oh, I merely came back to water the roses. I thought you were with Uncle Jack.

ALGERNON.   He's gone to order the dog-cart for me.

CECILY.   Oh, is he going to take you for a nice drive?

ALGERNON.   He's going to send me away.

CECILY.   Then have we got to part?

ALGERNON.   I am afraid so. It's very painful parting.

CECILY.   It is always painful to part from people whom one has known for a very brief space of time. The absence of old friends one can endure with equanimity. But even a momentary separation from anyone to whom one has just been introduced is almost unbearable.

ALGERNON.   Thank you.

(*Enter* MERRIMAN.)

MERRIMAN.   The dog-cart is at the door, sir. (ALGERNON *looks appealingly at* CECILY.)

CECILY.   It can wait, Merriman . . . for . . . five minutes.

MERRIMAN.   Yes, Miss.   (*Exit* MERRIMAN.)

ALGERNON.   I hope, Cecily, I shall not offend you if I state quite frankly and openly that you seem to me to be in every way the visible personification of absolute perfection.

CECILY.   I think your frankness does you great credit, Ernest. If you will allow me I will copy your remarks into my diary. (*Goes over to table and begins writing in diary.*)

ALGERNON.   Do you really keep a diary? I'd give anything to look at it. May I?

CECILY.   Oh no. (*Puts her hand over it.*) You see, it is simply a very young girl's record of her own thoughts and impressions, and consequently meant for publication. When it appears in volume form I hope you will order a copy. But pray, Ernest, don't stop. I delight in taking down from dictation. I have reached 'absolute perfection.' You can go on. I am quite ready for more.

ALGERNON.   (*Somewhat taken aback.*) Ahem! Ahem!

CECILY.   Oh, don't cough, Ernest. When one is dictating one should speak fluently and not cough. Besides, I don't know how to spell a cough. (*Writes as* ALGERNON *speaks.*)

ALGERNON.   (*Speaking very rapidly.*) Cecily, ever since I first

looked upon your wonderful and incomparable beauty, I
have dared to love you wildly, passionately, devotedly,
hopelessly.

CECILY.   I don't think that you should tell me that you love
me wildly, passionately, devotedly, hopelessly. Hopelessly
doesn't seem to make much sense, does it?

ALGERNON.   Cecily!

(*Enter* MERRIMAN.)

MERRIMAN.   The dog-cart is waiting, sir.

ALGERNON.   Tell it to come round next week, at the same
hour.

MERRIMAN.   (*Looks at* CECILY, *who makes no sign.*) Yes, sir.

(MERRIMAN *retires.*)

CECILY.   Uncle Jack would be very much annoyed if he knew
you were staying on till next week, at the same hour.

ALGERNON.   Oh, I don't care about Jack. I don't care for
anybody in the whole world but you. I love you, Cecily.
You will marry me, won't you?

CECILY.   You silly boy! Of course. Why, we have been engaged
for the last three months.

ALGERNON.   For the last three months?

CECILY.   Yes, it will be exactly three months on Thursday.

ALGERNON.   But how did we become engaged?

CECILY.   Well, ever since dear Uncle Jack first confessed to us
that he had a younger brother who was very wicked and bad,
you of course have formed the chief topic of conversation
between myself and Miss Prism. And of course a man who is
much talked about is always very attractive. One feels there
must be something in him after all. I daresay it was foolish
of me, but I fell in love with you, Ernest.

ALGERNON.   Darling! And when was the engagement actually
settled?

CECILY.   On the 14th of February last. Worn out by your entire
ignorance of my existence, I determined to end the matter
one way or the other, and after a long struggle with myself
I accepted you under this dear old tree here. The next day
I bought this little ring in your name, and this is the little
bangle with the true lovers' knot I promised you always
to wear.

ALGERNON.   Did I give you this? It's very pretty, isn't it?

CECILY.   Yes, you've wonderfully good taste, Ernest. It's the
excuse I've always given for your leading such a bad life. And
this is the box in which I keep all your dear letters. (*Kneels at
table, opens box, and produces letters tied up with blue ribbon.*)

ALGERNON.   My letters! But my own sweet Cecily, I have
never written you any letters.

CECILY.   You need hardly remind me of that, Ernest. I
remember only too well that I was forced to write your
letters for you. I always wrote three times a week, and
sometimes oftener.

ALGERNON.   Oh, do let me read them, Cecily?

CECILY.   Oh, I couldn't possibly. They would make you far too
conceited. (*Replaces box.*) The three you wrote me after I
had broken off the engagement are so beautiful, and so
badly spelled, that even now I can hardly read them without
crying a little.

ALGERNON.   But was our engagement ever broken off?

CECILY.   Of course it was. On the 22nd of last March. You can
see the entry if you like. (*Shows diary.*) 'Today I broke off
my engagement with Ernest. I feel it is better to do so. The
weather still continues charming.'

ALGERNON.   But why on earth did you break it off? What had
I done? I had done nothing at all. Cecily, I am very much
hurt indeed to hear you broke it off. Particularly when the
weather was so charming.

CECILY.   It would hardly have been a really serious engagement
if it hadn't been broken off at least once. But I forgave you
before the week was out.

ALGERNON.   (*Crossing to her, and kneeling.*) What a perfect angel
you are, Cecily.

CECILY.   You dear romantic boy. (*He kisses her, she puts her
fingers through his hair.*) I hope your hair curls naturally, does
it?

ALGERNON.   Yes, darling, with a little help from others.

CECILY.   I am so glad.

ALGERNON.   You'll never break off our engagement again,
Cecily?

CECILY.   I don't think I could break it off now that I have
actually met you. Besides, of course, there is the question
of your name.

ALGERNON.   Yes, of course. (*Nervously.*)

CECILY.   You must not laugh at me, darling, but it had always been a girlish dream of mine to love someone whose name was Ernest. (ALGERNON *rises*, CECILY *also*.) There is something in that name that seems to inspire absolute confidence. I pity any poor married woman whose husband is not called Ernest.

ALGERNON.   But, my dear child, do you mean to say you could not love me if I had some other name?

CECILY.   But what name?

ALGERNON.   Oh, any name you like – Algernon – for instance. . . .

CECILY.   But I don't like the name of Algernon.

ALGERNON.   Well, my own dear, sweet, loving little darling, I really can't see why you should object to the name of Algernon. It is not at all a bad name. In fact, it is rather an aristocratic name. Half of the chaps who get into the Bankruptcy Court are called Algernon. But seriously, Cecily . . . (*Moving to her*) . . . if my name was Algy, couldn't you love me?

CECILY.   (*Rising.*) I might respect you, Ernest, I might admire your character, but I fear that I should not be able to give you my undivided attention.

ALGERNON.   Ahem! Cecily! (*Picking up hat.*) Your Rector here is, I suppose, thoroughly experienced in the practice of all the rites and ceremonials of the Church?

CECILY.   Oh, yes. Dr Chasuble is a most learned man. He has never written a single book, so you can imagine how much he knows.

ALGERNON.   I must see him at once on a most important christening – I mean on most important business.

CECILY.   Oh!

ALGERNON.   I shan't be away more than half an hour.

CECILY.   Considering that we have been engaged since February the 14th, and that I only met you today for the first time, I think it is rather hard that you should leave me for so long a period as half an hour. Couldn't you make it twenty minutes?

ALGERNON.   I'll be back in no time.

(*Kisses her and rushes down the garden.*)

CECILY.   What an impetuous boy he is! I like his hair so much.
I must enter his proposal in my diary.

(*Enter* MERRIMAN.)

MERRIMAN.   A Miss Fairfax has just called to see Mr Worthing.
On very important business Miss Fairfax states.

CECILY.   Isn't Mr Worthing in his library?

MERRIMAN.   Mr Worthing went over in the direction of the
Rectory some time ago.

CECILY.   Pray ask the lady to come out here; Mr Worthing is
sure to be back soon. And you can bring tea.

MERRIMAN.   Yes, Miss.   (*Goes out.*)

CECILY.   Miss Fairfax! I suppose one of the many good elderly
women who are associated with Uncle Jack in some of his
philanthropic work in London. I don't quite like women
who are interested in philanthropic work. I think it is so
forward of them.

(*Enter* MERRIMAN.)

MERRIMAN.   Miss Fairfax.

(*Enter* GWENDOLEN.)   (*Exit* MERRIMAN.)

CECILY.   (*Advancing to meet her.*) Pray let me introduce myself
to you. My name is Cecily Cardew.

GWENDOLEN.   Cecily Cardew? (*Moving to her and shaking hands.*)
What a very sweet name! Something tells me that we are
going to be great friends. I like you already more than I can
say. My first impressions of people are never wrong.

CECILY.   How nice of you to like me so much after we have
known each other such a comparatively short time. Pray
sit down.

GWENDOLEN.   (*Still standing up.*) I may call you Cecily, may I
not?

CECILY.   With pleasure!

GWENDOLEN.   And you will always call me Gwendolen, won't
you?

CECILY.   If you wish.

GWENDOLEN.   Then that is all quite settled, is it not?

CECILY.   I hope so. (*A pause. They both sit down together.*)

GWENDOLEN.   Perhaps this might be a favourable opportunity
for my mentioning who I am. My father is Lord Bracknell.
You have never heard of Papa, I suppose?

CECILY.   I don't think so.

GWENDOLEN.   Outside the family circle, Papa, I am glad to say, is entirely unknown. I think that is quite as it should be. The home seems to me to be the proper sphere for the man. And certainly once a man begins to neglect his domestic duties he becomes painfully effeminate, does he not? And I don't like that. It makes men so very attractive. Cecily, Mamma, whose views on education are remarkably strict, has brought me up to be extremely short-sighted; it is part of her system; so do you mind my looking at you through my glasses?

CECILY.   Oh! not at all, Gwendolen. I am very fond of being looked at.

GWENDOLEN.   (*After examining* CECILY *carefully through a lorgnette.*) You are here on a short visit I suppose.

CECILY.   Oh no! I live here.

GWENDOLEN.   (*Severely.*) Really? Your mother, no doubt, or some female relative of advanced years, resides here also?

CECILY.   Oh no! I have no mother, nor, in fact, any relations.

GWENDOLEN.   Indeed?

CECILY.   My dear guardian, with the assistance of Miss Prism, has the arduous task of looking after me.

GWENDOLEN.   Your guardian?

CECILY.   Yes, I am Mr Worthing's ward.

GWENDOLEN.   Oh! It is strange he never mentioned to me that he had a ward. How secretive of him! He grows more interesting hourly. I am not sure, however, that the news inspires me with feelings of unmixed delight. (*Rising and going to her.*) I am very fond of you, Cecily; I have liked you ever since I met you! But I am bound to state that now that I know that you are Mr Worthing's ward, I cannot help expressing a wish you were – well just a little older than you seem to be – and not quite so very alluring in appearance. In fact, if I may speak candidly –

CECILY.   Pray do! I think that whenever one has anything unpleasant to say, one should always be quite candid.

GWENDOLEN.   Well, to speak with perfect candour, Cecily, I wish that you were fully forty-two, and more than usually plain for your age. Ernest has a strong upright nature. He is the very soul of truth and honour. Disloyalty would be as impossible to him as deception. But even men of the noblest possible moral character are extremely susceptible to the influence of the physical charms of others. Modern, no less than ancient history, supplies us with many most painful examples of what I refer to. If it were not so, indeed, history would be quite unreadable.

CECILY.   I beg your pardon, Gwendolen, did you say Ernest?

GWENDOLEN.   Yes.

CECILY.   Oh, but it is not Mr Ernest Worthing who is my guardian. It is his brother – his elder brother.

GWENDOLEN.   (*Sitting down again.*) Ernest never mentioned to me that he had a brother.

CECILY.   I am sorry to say they have not been on good terms for a long time.

GWENDOLEN.   Ah! that accounts for it. And now that I think of it I have never heard any man mention his brother. The subject seems distasteful to most men. Cecily, you have lifted a load from my mind. I was growing almost anxious. It would have been terrible if any cloud had come across a friendship like ours, would it not? Of course you are quite, quite sure that it is not Mr Ernest Worthing who is your guardian?

CECILY.   Quite sure. (*A pause.*) In fact, I am going to be his.

GWENDOLEN.   (*Enquiringly.*) I beg your pardon?

CECILY.   (*Rather shy and confidingly.*) Dearest Gwendolen, there is no reason why I should make a secret of it to you. Our little county newspaper is sure to chronicle the fact next week. Mr Ernest Worthing and I are engaged to be married.

GWENDOLEN.   (*Quite politely, rising.*) My darling Cecily, I think there must be some slight error. Mr Ernest Worthing is engaged to me. The announcement will appear in the *Morning Post* on Saturday at the latest.

CECILY.   (*Very politely, rising.*) I am afraid you must be under some misconception. Ernest proposed to me exactly ten minutes ago. (*Shows diary.*)

GWENDOLEN.   (*Examines diary through her lorgnette carefully.*) It is certainly very curious, for he asked me to be his wife yesterday afternoon at 5:30. If you would care to verify the incident, pray do so. (*Produces diary of her own.*) I never travel without my diary. One should have something sensational to read in the train. I am so sorry, dear Cecily, if it is any disappointment to you, but I am afraid *I* have the prior claim.

CECILY.   It would distress me more than I can tell you, dear Gwendolen, if it caused you any mental or physical anguish, but I feel bound to point out that since Ernest proposed to you he clearly has changed his mind.

GWENDOLEN.   (*Meditatively.*) If the poor fellow has been entrapped into any foolish promise I shall consider 'it my duty to rescue him at once, and with a firm hand.

CECILY.   (*Thoughtfully and sadly.*) Whatever unfortunate entanglement my dear boy may have got into, I will never reproach him with it after we are married.

GWENDOLEN.   Do you allude to me, Miss Cardew, as an entanglement? You are presumptuous. On an occasion of this kind it becomes more than a moral duty to speak one's mind. It becomes a pleasure.

CECILY.   Do you suggest, Miss Fairfax, that I entrapped Ernest into an engagement? How dare you? This is no time for wearing the shallow mask of manners. When I see a spade I call it a spade.

GWENDOLEN.   (*Satirically.*) I am glad to say that I have never seen a spade. It is obvious that our social spheres have been widely different.

(*Enter* MERRIMAN, *followed by the footman. He carries a salver, table cloth, and plate stand.* CECILY *is about to retort. The presence of the servants exercises a restraining influence, under which both girls chafe.*)

MERRIMAN.   Shall I lay tea here as usual, Miss?

CECILY.   (*Sternly, in a calm voice.*) Yes, as usual. (MERRIMAN *begins' to clear table and lay cloth. A long pause.* CECILY *and* GWENDOLEN *glare at each other.*)

GWENDOLEN.   Are there many interesting walks in the vicinity, Miss Cardew?

CECILY.   Oh! yes! a great many. From the top of one of the hills quite close one can see five counties.

GWENDOLEN.   Five counties! I don't think I should like that. I hate crowds.

CECILY.   (*Sweetly.*) I suppose that is why you live in town? (GWENDOLEN *bites her lip, and beats her foot nervously with her parasol.*)

GWENDOLEN.   (*Looking round.*) Quite a well-kept garden this is, Miss Cardew.

CECILY.   So glad you like it, Miss Fairfax.

GWENDOLEN.   I had no idea there were any flowers in the country.

CECILY.   Oh, flowers are as common here, Miss Fairfax, as people are in London.

GWENDOLEN.   Personally I cannot understand how anybody manages to exist in the country, if anybody who is anybody does. The country always bores me to death.

CECILY.   Ah! This is what the newspapers call agricultural depression, is it not? I believe the aristocracy are suffering very much from it just at present. It is almost an epidemic amongst them, I have been told. May I offer you some tea, Miss Fairfax?

GWENDOLEN.   (*With elaborate politeness.*) Thank you. (*Aside.*) Detestable girl! But I require tea!

CECILY.   (*Sweetly.*) Sugar?

GWENDOLEN.   (*Superciliously.*) No, thank you. Sugar is not fashionable any more. (CECILY *looks angrily at her, takes up the tongs and puts four lumps of sugar into the cup.*)

CECILY.   (*Severely.*) Cake or bread and butter?

GWENDOLEN.   (*In a bored manner.*) Bread and butter, please. Cake is rarely seen at the best houses nowadays.

CECILY.   (*Cuts a very large slice of cake, and puts it on the tray.*) Hand that to Miss Fairfax. (MERRIMAN *does so, and goes out with footman.* GWENDOLEN *drinks the tea and makes a grimace. Puts down cup at once, reaches out her hand to the bread and butter, looks at it, and finds it is cake. Rises in indignation.*)

GWENDOLEN.   You have filled my tea with lumps of sugar, and though I asked most distinctly for bread and butter, you have given me cake. I am known for the gentleness of my disposition, and the extraordinary sweetness of my nature, but I warn you, Miss Cardew, you may go too far.

CECILY.   (*Rising.*) To save my poor, innocent, trusting boy from the machinations of any other girl there are no lengths to which I would not go.

GWENDOLEN.   From the moment I saw you I distrusted you. I felt that you were false and deceitful. I am never deceived in such matters. My first impressions of people are invariably right.

CECILY.   It seems to me, Miss Fairfax, that I am trespassing on your valuable time. No doubt you have many other calls of a similar character to make in the neighbourhood.

(*Enter* JACK.)

GWENDOLEN.   (*Catching sight of him.*) Ernest! My own Ernest!

JACK.   Gwendolen! Darling! (*Offers to kiss her.*)

GWENDOLEN.   (*Drawing back.*) A moment! May I ask if you are engaged to be married to this young lady? (*Points to* CECILY.)

JACK.   (*Laughing.*) To dear little Cecily! Of course not! What could have put such an idea into your pretty little head?

GWENDOLEN.   Thank you. You may! (*Offers her cheek.*)

CECILY.   (*Very sweetly.*) I knew there must be some misunderstanding, Miss Fairfax. The gentleman whose arm is at present round your waist is my dear guardian, Mr John Worthing.

GWENDOLEN.   I beg your pardon?

CECILY.   This is Uncle Jack.

GWENDOLEN.   (*Receding.*) Jack! Oh!

(*Enter* ALGERNON.)

CECILY.   Here is Ernest.

ALGERNON.   (*Goes straight over to* CECILY *without noticing anyone else.*) My own love! (*Offers to kiss her.*)

CECILY.   (*Drawing back.*) A moment, Ernest! May I ask you – are you engaged to be married to this young lady?

ALGERNON.   (*Looking round.*) To what young lady? Good heavens! Gwendolen!

CECILY.   Yes! to good heavens, Gwendolen, I mean to Gwendolen.

ALGERNON.   (*Laughing.*) Of course not! What could have put such an idea into your pretty little head?

CECILY.   Thank you. (*Presenting her cheek to be kissed.*) You may. (ALGERNON *kisses her.*)

GWENDOLEN.   I felt there was some slight error, Miss Cardew. The gentleman who is how embracing you is my cousin, Mr Algernon Moncrieff.

CECILY.   (*Breaking away from* ALGERNON.) Algernon Moncrieff! Oh! (*The two girls move towards each other and put their arms round each other's waists as if for protection.*)

CECILY.   Are you called Algernon?

ALGERNON.   I cannot deny it.

CECILY.   Oh!

GWENDOLEN.   Is your name really John?

JACK.   (*Standing rather proudly.*) I could deny it if I liked. I could
deny anything if I liked. But my name certainly is John. It has
been John for years.

CECILY.   (*To* GWENDOLEN.) A gross deception has been
practised on both of us.

GWENDOLEN.   My poor wounded Cecily!

CECILY.   My sweet wronged Gwendolen!

GWENDOLEN.   (*Slowly and seriously.*) You will call me sister, will
you not? (*They embrace.* JACK *and* ALGERNON *groan and walk up
and down.*)

CECILY.   (*Rather brightly.*) There is just one question I would like
to be allowed to ask my guardian.

GWENDOLEN.   An admirable idea! Mr Worthing, there is just
one question I would like to be permitted to put to you.
Where is your brother Ernest? We are both engaged to be
married to your brother Ernest, so it is a matter of some
importance to us to know where your brother Ernest is at
present.

JACK.   (*Slowly and hesitatingly.*) Gwendolen – Cecily – it is very
painful for me to be forced to speak the truth. It is the first
time in my life that I have ever been reduced to such a
painful position, and I am really quite inexperienced in doing
anything of the kind. However I will tell you quite frankly
that I have no brother Ernest. I have no brother at all. I never
had a brother in my life, and I certainly have not the smallest
intention of ever having one in the future.

CECILY.   (*Surprised.*) No brother at all?

JACK.   (*Cheerily.*) None!

GWENDOLEN.   (*Severely.*) Had you never a brother of any kind?

JACK.   (*Pleasantly.*) Never. Not even of any kind.

GWENDOLEN.   I am afraid it is quite clear, Cecily, that neither
of us is engaged to be married to anyone.

CECILY.   It is not a very pleasant position for a young girl
suddenly to find herself in. Is it?

GWENDOLEN.   Let us go into the house. They will hardly
venture to come after us there.

CECILY.   No, men are so cowardly, aren't they?

(*They retire into the house with scornful looks.*)

JACK.   This ghastly state of things is what you call Bunburying,
I suppose?

ALGERNON.   Yes, and a perfectly wonderful Bunbury it is. The
most wonderful Bunbury I have ever had in my life.

JACK.   Well, you've no right whatsoever to Bunbury here.

ALGERNON.   That is absurd. One has a right to Bunbury
anywhere one chooses. Every serious Bunburyist knows
that.

JACK.   Serious Bunburyist! Good Heavens!

ALGERNON.   Well, one must be serious about something, if one
wants to have any amusement in life. I happen to be serious
about Bunburying. What on earth you are serious about I
haven't got the remotest idea. About everything, I should
fancy. You have such an absolutely trivial nature.

JACK.   Well, the only small satisfaction I have in the whole of
this wretched business is that your friend Bunbury is quite
exploded. You won't be able to run down to the country
quite so often as you used to do, dear Algy. And a very good
thing too.

ALGERNON.   Your brother is a little off colour, isn't he, dear
Jack? You won't be able to disappear to London quite so
frequently as your wicked custom was. And not a bad
thing either.

JACK.   As for your conduct towards Miss Cardew, I must say that
your taking in a sweet, simple, innocent girl like that is quite
inexcusable. To say nothing of the fact that she is my ward.

ALGERNON.   I can see no possible defence at all for your
deceiving a brilliant, clever, thoroughly experienced young
lady like Miss Fairfax. To say nothing of the fact that she is
my cousin.

JACK.   I wanted to be engaged to Gwendolen, that is all. I
love her.

ALGERNON.   Well, I simply wanted to be engaged to Cecily. I
adore her.

JACK.   There is certainly no chance of your marrying Miss
Cardew.

ALGERNON.   I don't think there is much likelihood, Jack, of you
and Miss Fairfax being united.

JACK.   Well, that is no business of yours.

ALGERNON.   If it was my business, I wouldn't talk about it. (*Begins to eat muffins.*) It is very vulgar to talk about one's business. Only people like stockbrokers do that, and then merely at dinner parties.

JACK.   How you can sit there, calmly eating muffins when we are in this horrible trouble, I can't make out. You seem to me to be perfectly heartless.

ALGERNON.   Well, I can't eat muffins in an agitated manner. The butter would probably get on my cuffs. One should always eat muffins quite calmly. It is the only way to eat them.

JACK.   I say it's perfectly heartless your eating muffins at all, under the circumstances.

ALGERNON.   When I am in trouble, eating is the only thing that consoles me. Indeed, when I am in really great trouble, as anyone who knows me intimately will tell you, I refuse everything except food and drink. At the present moment I am eating muffins because I am unhappy. Besides, I am particularly fond of muffins. (*Rising.*)

JACK.   (*Rising.*) Well, that is no reason why you should eat them all in that greedy way. (*Takes muffins from* ALGERNON.)

ALGERNON.   (*Offering tea-cake.*) I wish you would have tea-cake instead. I don't like tea-cake.

JACK.   Good Heavens! I suppose a man may eat his own muffins in his own garden.

ALGERNON.   But you have just said it was perfectly heartless to eat muffins.

JACK.   I said it was perfectly heartless of you, under the circumstances. That is a very different thing.

ALGERNON.   That may be. But the muffins are the same. (*He seizes the muffin-dish from* JACK.)

JACK.   Algy, I wish to goodness you would go.

ALGERNON.   You can't possibly ask me to go without having some dinner. It's absurd. I never go without my dinner. No one ever does, except vegetarians and people like that. Besides I have just made arrangements with Dr Chasuble to be christened at a quarter to six under the name of Ernest.

JACK.   My dear fellow, the sooner you give up that nonsense the better. I made arrangements this morning with Dr Chasuble to be christened myself at 5:30, and I naturally will take the name of Ernest. Gwendolen would wish it. We can't both be

christened Ernest. It's absurd. Besides, I have a perfect right
to be christened if I like. There is no evidence at all that I ever
have been christened by anybody. I should think it extremely
probable I never was, and so does Dr Chasuble. It is entirely
different in your case. You have been christened already.

ALGERNON.   Yes, but I have not been christened for years.

JACK.   Yes, but you have been christened. That is the important
thing.

ALGERNON.   Quite so. So I know my constitution can stand
it. If you are not quite sure about your ever having been
christened, I must say I think it rather dangerous your
venturing on it now. It might make you very unwell.
You can hardly have forgotten that someone very closely
connected with you was very nearly carried off this week
in Paris by a severe chill.

JACK.   Yes, but you said yourself that a severe chill was not
hereditary.

ALGERNON.   It usen't to be, I know – but I daresay it is
now. Science is always making wonderful improvements
in things.

JACK.   (*Picking up the muffin-dish.*) Oh, that is nonsense; you are
always talking nonsense.

ALGERNON.   Jack, you are at the muffins again! I wish you
wouldn't. There are only two left. (*Takes them.*) I told you
I was particularly fond of muffins.

JACK.   But I hate tea-cake.

ALGERNON.   Why on earth then do you allow tea-cake to be
served up for your guests? What ideas you have of hospitality!

JACK.   Algernon! I have already told you to go. I don't want you
here. Why don't you go!

ALGERNON.   I haven't quite finished my tea yet! and there is still
one muffin left. (JACK *groans, and sinks into a chair*, ALGERNON
still continues eating.)

ACT-DROP.

THIRD ACT

Scene. Morning-room at the Manor House.

(GWENDOLEN and CECILY are at the window, looking out into
the garden.)

GWENDOLEN.   The fact that they did not follow us at once into
the house, as anyone else would have done, seems to me to
show that they have some sense of shame left.

CECILY.   They have been eating muffins. That looks like
repentance.

GWENDOLEN.   (*After a pause.*) They don't seem to notice us at
all. Couldn't you cough?

CECILY.   But I haven't got a cough.

GWENDOLEN.   They're looking at us. What effrontery!

CECILY.   They're approaching. That's very forward of them.

GWENDOLEN.   Let us preserve a dignified silence.

CECILY.   Certainly. It's the only thing to do now.

(*Enter* JACK *followed by* ALGERNON. *They whistle some dreadful
popular air from a British opera.*)

GWENDOLEN.   This dignified silence seems to produce an
unpleasant effect.

CECILY.   A most distasteful one.

GWENDOLEN.   But we will not be the first to speak.

CECILY.   Certainly not.

GWENDOLEN.   Mr Worthing, I have something very particular
to ask you. Much depends on your reply.

CECILY.   Gwendolen, your common sense is invaluable. Mr
Moncrieff, kindly answer me the following question. Why
did you pretend to be my guardian's brother?

ALGERNON.   In order that I might have an opportunity of
meeting you.

CECILY.   (*To* GWENDOLEN.) That certainly seems a satisfactory
explanation, does it not?

GWENDOLEN.   Yes, dear, if you can believe him.

CECILY.   I don't. But that does not affect the wonderful beauty
of his answer.

GWENDOLEN.   True. In matters of grave importance, style, not
sincerity is the vital thing. Mr Worthing, what explanation
can you offer to me for pretending to have a brother? Was
it in order that you might have an opportunity of coming up
to town to see me as often as possible?

JACK.   Can you doubt it, Miss Fairfax?

GWENDOLEN.   I have the gravest doubts upon the subject. But
I intend to crush them. This is not the moment for German
scepticism. (*Moving to* CECILY.) Their explanations appear to

be quite satisfactory, especially Mr Worthing's. That seems to me to have the stamp of truth upon it.

CECILY.   I am more than content with what Mr Moncrieff said. His voice alone inspires one with absolute credulity.

GWENDOLEN.   Then you think we should forgive them?

CECILY.   Yes. I mean no.

GWENDOLEN.   True! I had forgotten. There are principles at stake that one cannot surrender. Which of us should tell them? The task is not a pleasant one.

CECILY.   Could we not both speak at the same time?

GWENDOLEN.   An excellent idea! I nearly always speak at the same time as other people. Will you take the time from me?

CECILY.   Certainly. (GWENDOLEN *beats time with uplifted finger*.)

GWENDOLEN AND CECILY.   (*Speaking together*.) Your Christian names are still an insuperable barrier. That is all!

JACK AND ALGERNON.   (*Speaking together*.) Our Christian names! Is that all? But we are going to be christened this afternoon.

GWENDOLEN.   (*To* JACK.) For my sake you are prepared to do this terrible thing?

JACK.   I am.

CECILY.   (*To* ALGERNON.) To please me you are ready to face this fearful ordeal?

ALGERNON.   I am!

GWENDOLEN.   How absurd to talk of the equality of the sexes! Where questions of self-sacrifice are concerned, men are infinitely beyond us.

JACK.   We are. (*Clasps hands with* ALGERNON.)

CECILY.   They have moments of physical courage of which we women know absolutely nothing.

GWENDOLEN.   (*To* JACK.) Darling!

ALGERNON.   (*To* CECILY.) Darling. (*They fall into each other's arms*.)

(*Enter* MERRIMAN. *When he enters he coughs loudly, seeing the situation*.)

MERRIMAN.   Ahem! Ahem! Lady Bracknell!

JACK.   Good Heavens!

(*Enter* LADY BRACKNELL. *The couples separate in alarm. Exit* MERRIMAN.)

LADY BRACKNELL.   Gwendolen! What does this mean?

GWENDOLEN.   Merely that I am engaged to be married to Mr Worthing, Mamma.

LADY BRACKNELL.   Come here. Sit down. Sit down immediately. Hesitation of any kind is a sign of mental decay in the young, of physical weakness in the old. (*Turns to* JACK.) Apprised, sir, of my daughter's sudden flight by her trusty maid, whose confidence I purchased by means of a small coin, I followed her at once by a luggage train. Her unhappy father is, I am glad to say, under the impression that she is attending a more than usually lengthy lecture by the University Extension Scheme on the influence of a permanent income on thought. I do not propose to undeceive him. Indeed I have never undeceived him on any question. I would consider it wrong. But of course, you will clearly understand that all communication between yourself and my daughter must cease immediately from this moment. On this point, as indeed on all points, I am firm.

JACK.   I am engaged to be married to Gwendolen, Lady Bracknell!

LADY BRACKNELL.   You are nothing of the kind, sir. And now, as regards Algernon! . . . Algernon!

ALGERNON.   Yes, Aunt Augusta.

LADY BRACKNELL.   May I ask if it is in this house that your invalid friend Mr Bunbury resides?

ALGERNON.   (*Stammering.*) Oh! No! Bunbury doesn't live here. Bunbury is somewhere else at present. In fact, Bunbury is dead.

LADY BRACKNELL.   Dead! When did Mr Bunbury die? His death must have been extremely sudden.

ALGERNON.   (*Airily.*) Oh! I killed Bunbury this afternoon. I mean poor Bunbury died this afternoon.

LADY BRACKNELL.   What did he die of?

ALGERNON.   Bunbury? Oh, he was quite exploded.

LADY BRACKNELL.   Exploded! Was he the victim of a revolutionary outrage? I was not aware that Mr Bunbury was interested in social legislation. If so, he is well punished for his morbidity.

ALGERNON.   My dear Aunt Augusta, I mean he was found out! The doctors found out that Bunbury could not live, that is what I mean – so Bunbury died.

LADY BRACKNELL. He seems to have had great confidence in the opinion of his physicians. I am glad, however, that he made up his mind at the last to some definite course of action, and acted under proper medical advice. And now that we have finally got rid of this Mr Bunbury, may I ask, Mr Worthing, who is that young person whose hand my nephew Algernon is now holding in what seems to me a peculiarly unnecessary manner?

JACK. That lady is Miss Cecily Cardew, my ward. (LADY BRACKNELL *bows coldly to* CECILY.)

ALGERNON. I am engaged to be married to Cecily. Aunt Augusta.

LADY BRACKNELL. I beg your pardon?

CECILY. Mr Moncrieff and I are engaged to be married, Lady Bracknell.

LADY BRACKNELL. (*With a shiver, crossing to the sofa and sitting down.*) I do not know whether there is anything peculiarly exciting in the air of this particular part of Hertfordshire, but the number of engagements that go on seems to me considerably above the proper average that statistics have laid down for our guidance. I think some preliminary enquiry on my part would not be out of place. Mr Worthing, is Miss Cardew at all connected with any of the larger railway stations in London? I merely desire information. Until yesterday I had no idea that there were any families or persons whose origin was a Terminus. (JACK *looks perfectly furious, but restrains himself.*)

JACK. (*In a clear, cold voice.*) Miss Cardew is the granddaughter of the late Mr Thomas Cardew of 149, Belgrave Square, SW; Gervase Park, Dorking, Surrey; and the Sporran, Fifeshire, NB.

LADY BRACKNELL. That sounds not unsatisfactory. Three addresses always inspire confidence, even in tradesmen. But what proof have I of their authenticity?

JACK. I have carefully preserved the Court Guides of the period. They are open to your inspection, Lady Bracknell.

LADY BRACKNELL. (*Grimly.*) I have known strange errors in that publication.

JACK. Miss Cardew's family solicitors are Messrs Markby, Markby, and Markby.

LADY BRACKNELL.   Markby, Markby, and Markby? A firm of
the very highest position in their profession. Indeed I am told
that one of the Mr Markbys is occasionally to be seen at dinner
parties. So far I am satisfied.

JACK.   (*Very irritably.*) How extremely kind of you, Lady
Bracknell! I have also in my possession, you will be
pleased to hear, certificates of Miss Cardew's birth, baptism,
whooping cough, registration, vaccination, confirmation,
and the measles; both the German and the English variety.

LADY BRACKNELL.   Ah! A life crowded with incident, I see;
though perhaps somewhat too exciting for a young girl. I
am not myself in favour of premature experiences. (*Rises,
looks at her watch.*) Gwendolen! the time approaches for our
departure. We have not a moment to lose. As a matter of
form, Mr Worthing, I had better ask you if Miss Cardew has
any little fortune?

JACK.   Oh! about a hundred and thirty thousand pounds in the
Funds. That is all. Good-bye, Lady Bracknell. So pleased to
have seen you.

LADY BRACKNELL.   (*Sitting down again.*) A moment, Mr
Worthing. A hundred and thirty thousand pounds! And
in the Funds! Miss Cardew seems to me a most attractive
young lady, now that I look at her. Few girls of the present
day have any really solid qualities, any of the qualities that
last, and improve with time. We live, I regret to say, in an
age of surfaces. (*To* CECILY.) Come over here, dear. (CECILY
goes across.) Pretty child! your dress is sadly simple, and your
hair seems almost as nature might have left it. But we can
soon alter all that. A thoroughly experienced French maid
produces a really marvellous result in a very brief space
of time. I remember recommending one to young Lady
Lancing, and after three months her own husband did not
know her.

JACK.   (*Aside.*) And after six months nobody knew her.

LADY BRACKNELL.   (*Glares at* JACK *for a few moments. Then bends,
with a practised smile, to* CECILY.) Kindly turn round, sweet
child. (CECILY *turns completely round.*) No, the side view is what
I want. (CECILY *presents her profile.*) Yes, quite as I expected.
There are distinct social possibilities in your profile. The two
weak points in our age are its want of principle and its want

of profile. The chin a little higher, dear. Style largely depends on the way the chin is worn. They are worn very high, just at present. Algernon!

ALGERNON.   Yes, Aunt Augusta!

LADY BRACKNELL.   There are distinct social possibilities in Miss Cardew's profile.

ALGERNON.   Cecily is the sweetest, dearest, prettiest girl in the whole world. And I don't care twopence about social possibilities.

LADY BRACKNELL.   Never speak disrespectfully of Society, Algernon. Only people who can't get into it do that. (*To* CECILY.) Dear child, of course you know that Algernon has nothing but his debts to depend upon. But I do not approve of mercenary marriages. When I married Lord Bracknell I had no fortune of any kind. But I never dreamed for a moment of allowing that to stand in my way. Well, I suppose I must give my consent.

ALGERNON.   Thank you, Aunt Augusta.

LADY BRACKNELL.   Cecily, you may kiss me!

CECILY.   (*Kisses her.*) Thank you, Lady Bracknell.

LADY BRACKNELL.   You may also address me as Aunt Augusta for the future.

CECILY.   Thank you, Aunt Augusta.

LADY BRACKNELL.   The marriage, I think, had better take place quite soon.

ALGERNON.   Thank you, Aunt Augusta.

CECILY.   Thank you, Aunt Augusta.

LADY BRACKNELL.   To speak frankly, I am not in favour of long engagements. They give people the opportunity of finding out each other's character before marriage, which I think is never advisable.

JACK.   I beg your pardon for interrupting you, Lady Bracknell, but this engagement is quite out of the question. I am Miss Cardew's guardian, and she cannot marry without my consent until she comes of age. That consent I absolutely decline to give.

LADY BRACKNELL.   Upon what grounds may I ask? Algernon is an extremely, I may almost say an ostentatiously, eligible young man. He has nothing, but he looks everything. What more can one desire?

JACK.   It pains me very much to have to speak frankly to you, Lady Bracknell, about your nephew, but the fact is that I do not approve at all of his moral character. I suspect him of being untruthful. (ALGERNON *and* CECILY *look at him in indignant amazement.*)

LADY BRACKNELL.   Untruthful! My nephew Algernon? Impossible! He is an Oxonian.

JACK.   I fear there can be no possible doubt about the matter. This afternoon, during my temporary absence in London on an important question of romance, he obtained admission to my house by means of the false pretence of being my brother. Under an assumed name he drank, I've just been informed by my butler, an entire pint bottle of my Perrier-Jouet, Brut, '89; a wine I was specially reserving for myself. Continuing his disgraceful deception, he succeeded in the course of the afternoon in alienating the affections of my only ward. He subsequently stayed to tea, and devoured every single muffin. And what makes his conduct all the more heartless is, that he was perfectly well aware from the first that I have no brother, that I never had a brother, and that I don't intend to have a brother, not even of any kind. I distinctly told him so myself yesterday afternoon.

LADY BRACKNELL.   Ahem! Mr Worthing, after careful consideration I have decided entirely to overlook my nephew's conduct to you.

JACK.   That is very generous of you, Lady Bracknell. My own decision, however, is unalterable. I decline to give my consent.

LADY BRACKNELL.   (*To* CECILY.) Come here, sweet child. (CECILY *goes over.*) How old are you, dear?

CECILY.   Well, I am really only eighteen, but I always admit to twenty when I go to evening parties.

LADY BRACKNELL.   You are perfectly right in making some slight alteration. Indeed, no woman should ever be quite accurate about her age. It looks so calculating. . . . (*In a meditative manner.*) Eighteen, but admitting to twenty at evening parties. Well, it will not be very long before you are of age and free from the restraints of tutelage. So I don't think your guardian's consent is, after all, a matter of any importance.

JACK.   Pray excuse me, Lady Bracknell, for interrupting you again, but it is only fair to tell you that according to the terms of her grandfather's will Miss Cardew does not come legally of age till she is thirty-five.

LADY BRACKNELL.   That does not seem to me to be a grave objection. Thirty-five is a very attractive age. London society is full of women of the very highest birth who have, of their own free choice, remained thirty-five for years. Lady Dumbleton is an instance in point. To my own knowledge she has been thirty-five ever since she arrived at the age of forty, which was many years ago now. I see no reason why our dear Cecily should not be even still more attractive at the age you mention than she is at present. There will be a large accumulation of property.

CECILY.   Algy, could you wait for me till I was thirty-five?

ALGERNON.   Of course I could, Cecily. You know I could.

CECILY.   Yes, I felt it instinctively, but I couldn't wait all that time. I hate waiting even five minutes for anybody. It always makes me rather cross. I am not punctual myself, I know, but I do like punctuality in others, and waiting, even to be married, is quite out of the question.

ALGERNON.   Then what is to be done, Cecily?

CECILY.   I don't know, Mr Moncrieff.

LADY BRACKNELL.   My dear Mr Worthing, as Miss Cardew states positively that she cannot wait till she is thirty-five – a remark which I am bound to say seems to me to show a somewhat impatient nature – I would beg of you to reconsider your decision.

JACK.   But my dear Lady Bracknell, the matter is entirely in your own hands. The moment you consent to my marriage with Gwendolen, I will most gladly allow your nephew to form an alliance with my ward.

LADY BRACKNELL.   (*Rising and drawing herself up.*) You must be quite aware that what you propose is out of the question.

JACK.   Then a passionate celibacy is all that any of us can look forward to.

LADY BRACKNELL.   That is not the destiny I propose for Gwendolen. Algernon, of course, can choose for himself. (*Pulls out her watch.*) Come, dear; (GWENDOLEN *rises*) we have already missed five, if not six, trains. To miss any more might expose us to comment on the platform.

(*Enter* DR CHASUBLE.)

CHASUBLE.   Everything is quite ready for the christenings.

LADY BRACKNELL.   The christenings, sir! Is not that somewhat premature?

CHASUBLE.   (*Looking rather puzzled, and pointing to* JACK *and* ALGERNON.) Both these gentlemen have expressed a desire for immediate baptism.

LADY BRACKNELL.   At their age? The idea is grotesque and irreligious! Algernon, I forbid you to be baptized. I will not hear of such excesses. Lord Bracknell would be highly displeased if he learned that that was the way in which you wasted your time and money.

CHASUBLE.   Am I to understand then that there are to be no christenings at all this afternoon?

JACK.   I don't think that, as things are now, it would be of much practical value to either of us, Dr Chasuble.

CHASUBLE.   I am grieved to hear such sentiments from you, Mr Worthing. They savour of the heretical views of the Anabaptists, views that I have completely refuted in four of my unpublished sermons. However, as your present mood seems to be one peculiarly secular, I will return to the church at once. Indeed, I have just been informed by the pew-opener that for the last hour and a half Miss Prism has been waiting for me in the vestry.

LADY BRACKNELL.   (*Starting.*) Miss Prism! Did I hear you mention a Miss Prism?

CHASUBLE.   Yes, Lady Bracknell. I am on my way to join her.

LADY BRACKNELL.   Pray allow me to detain you for a moment. This matter may prove to be one of vital importance to Lord Bracknell and myself. Is this Miss Prism a female of repellent aspect, remotely connected with education?

CHASUBLE.   (*Somewhat indignantly.*) She is the most cultivated of ladies, and the very picture of respectability.

LADY BRACKNELL.   It is obviously the same person. May I ask what position she holds in your household?

CHASUBLE.   (*Severely.*) I am a celibate, madam.

JACK.   (*Interposing.*) Miss Prism, Lady Bracknell, has been for the last three years Miss Cardew's esteemed governess and valued companion.

LADY BRACKNELL.   In spite of what I hear of her, I must see her at once. Let her be sent for.

CHASUBLE.   (*Looking off.*) She approaches; she is nigh.

(*Enter* MISS PRISM *hurriedly.*)

MISS PRISM.   I was told you expected me in the vestry, dear Canon. I have been waiting for you there for an hour and three quarters. (*Catches sight of* LADY BRACKNELL *who has fixed her with a stony glare.* MISS PRISM *grows pale and quails. She looks anxiously round as if desirous to escape.*)

LADY BRACKNELL.   (*In a severe, judicial voice.*) Prism! (MISS PRISM *bows her head in shame.*) Come here, Prism! (MISS PRISM *approaches in a humble manner.*) Prism! Where is that baby? (*General consternation. The* CANON *starts back in horror.* ALGERNON *and* JACK *pretend to be anxious to shield* CECILY *and* GWENDOLEN *from hearing the details of a terrible public scandal.*) Twenty-eight years ago, Prism, you left Lord Bracknell's house, Number 104, Upper Grosvenor Street, in charge of a perambulator that contained a baby, of the male sex. You never returned. A few weeks later, through the elaborate investigations of the Metropolitan police, the perambulator was discovered at midnight, standing by itself in a remote corner of Bayswater. It contained the manuscript of a three-volume novel of more than usually revolting sentimentality. (MISS PRISM *starts in involuntary indignation.*) But the baby was not there! (*Everyone looks at* MISS PRISM.) Prism! Where is that baby? (*A pause.*)

MISS PRISM.   Lady Bracknell, I admit with shame that I do not know. I only wish I did. The plain facts of the case are these. On the morning of the day you mention, a day that is for ever branded on my memory, I prepared as usual to take the baby out in its perambulator. I had also with me a somewhat old, but capacious handbag, in which I had intended to place the manuscript of a work of fiction that I had written during my few unoccupied hours. In a moment of mental abstraction, for which I never can forgive myself, I deposited the manuscript in the bassinette, and placed the baby in the handbag.

JACK. (*Who has been listening attentively.*) But where did you deposit the handbag?

MISS PRISM.   Do not ask me, Mr Worthing.

JACK.   Miss Prism, this is a matter of no small importance to me. I insist on knowing where you deposited the handbag that contained that infant.

MISS PRISM.   I left it in the cloakroom of one of the larger railway stations in London.

JACK.   What railway station?

MISS PRISM.   (*Quite crushed.*) Victoria. The Brighton line. (*Sinks into a chair.*)

JACK.   I must retire to my room for a moment. Gwendolen, wait here for me.

GWENDOLEN.   If you are not too long, I will wait here for you all my life. (*Exit* JACK *in great excitement.*)

CHASUBLE.   What do you think this means, Lady Bracknell?

LADY BRACKNELL.   I dare not even suspect, Dr Chausuble. I need hardly tell you that in families of high position strange coincidences are not supposed to occur. They are hardly considered the thing. (*Noises heard overhead as if someone was throwing trunks about. Everyone looks up.*)

CECILY.   Uncle Jack seems strangely agitated.

CHASUBLE.   Your guardian has a very emotional nature.

LADY BRACKNELL.   This noise is extremely unpleasant. It sounds as if he was having an argument. I dislike arguments of any kind. They are always vulgar, and often convincing.

CHASUBLE.   (*Looking up.*) It has stopped now. (*The noise is redoubled.*)

LADY BRACKNELL.   I wish he would arrive at some conclusion.

GWENDOLEN.   This suspense is terrible. I hope it will last.

(*Enter* JACK *with a handbag of black leather in his hand.*)

JACK.   (*Rushing over to* MISS PRISM.) Is this the handbag, Miss Prism? Examine it carefully before you speak. The happiness of more than one life depends on your answer.

MISS PRISM.   (*Calmly.*) It seems to be mine. Yes, here is the injury it received through the upsetting of a Gower Street omnibus in younger and happier days. Here is the stain on the lining caused by the explosion of a temperance beverage, an incident that occurred at Leamington. And here, on the lock, are my initials. I had forgotten that in an extravagant mood I had had them placed there. The bag is undoubtedly mine. I am delighted to have it so unexpectedly restored to me. It has been a great inconvenience being without it all these years.

JACK.   (*In a pathetic voice.*) Miss Prism, more is restored to you than this handbag. I was the baby you placed in it.

MISS PRISM.   (*Amazed.*) You?

JACK.   (*Embracing her.*) Yes . . . mother!

MISS PRISM.   (*Recoiling in indignant astonishment.*) Mr Worthing! I am unmarried!

JACK.   Unmarried! I do not deny that is a serious blow. But after all, who has the right to cast a stone against one who has suffered? Cannot repentance wipe out an act of folly? Why should there be one law for men, and another for women? Mother, I forgive you. (*Tries to embrace her again.*)

MISS PRISM.   (*Still more indignant.*) Mr Worthing, there is some error. (*Pointing to* LADY BRACKNELL.) There is the lady who can tell you who you really are.

JACK.   (*After a pause.*) Lady Bracknell, I hate to seem inquisitive, but would you kindly inform me who I am?

LADY BRACKNELL.   I am afraid that the news I have to give you will not altogether please you. You are the son of my poor sister, Mrs Moncrieff, and consequently Algernon's elder brother.

JACK.   Algy's elder brother! Then I have a brother after all. I knew I had a brother! I always said I had a brother! Cecily, – how could you have ever doubted that I had a brother? (*Seizes hold of* ALGERNON.) Dr Chasuble, my unfortunate brother. Miss Prism, my unfortunate brother. Gwendolen, my unfortunate brother. Algy, you young scoundrel, you will have to treat me with more respect in the future. You have never behaved to me like a brother in all your life.

ALGERNON.   Well, not till today, old boy, I admit. I did my best, however, though I was out of practice. (*Shakes hands.*)

GWENDOLEN.   (*To* JACK.) My own! But what own are you? What is your Christian name, now that you have become someone else?

JACK.   Good Heavens! . . . I had quite forgotten that point. Your decision on the subject of my name is irrevocable, I suppose?

GWENDOLEN.   I never change, except in my affections.

CECILY.   What a noble nature you have, Gwendolen!

JACK.   Then the question had better be cleared up at once. Aunt Augusta, a moment. At the time when Miss Prism left me in the handbag, had I been christened already?

LADY BRACKNELL.   Every luxury that money could buy, including christening, had been lavished on you by your fond and doting parents.

JACK.   Then I was christened! That is settled. Now, what name was I given? Let me know the worst.

LADY BRACKNELL.   Being the eldest son you were naturally christened after your father.

JACK.   (*Irritably.*) Yes, but what was my father's Christian name?

LADY BRACKNELL.   (*Meditatively.*) I cannot at the present moment recall what the General's Christian name was. But I have no doubt he had one. He was eccentric, I admit. But only in later years. And that was the result of the Indian climate, and marriage, and indigestion, and other things of that kind.

JACK.   Algy! Can't you recollect what our father's Christian name was?

ALGERNON.   My dear boy, we were never even on speaking terms. He died before I was a year old.

JACK.   His name would appear in the Army Lists of the period, I suppose, Aunt Augusta?

LADY BRACKNELL.   The General was essentially a man of peace, except in his domestic life. But I have no doubt his name would appear in any military directory.

JACK.   The Army Lists of the last forty years are here. These delightful records should have been my constant study. (*Rushes to bookcase and tears the books out.*) M. Generals . . . Mallam, Maxbohm, Magley, what ghastly names they have – Markby, Migsby, Mobbs, Moncrieff! Lieutenant 1840, Captain, Lieutenant-Colonel, Colonel, General 1869, Christian names, Ernest John. (*Puts book very quietly down and speaks quite calmly.*) I always told you, Gwendolen, my name was Ernest, didn't I? Well, it is Ernest after all. I mean it naturally is Ernest.

LADY BRACKNELL.   Yes, I remember now that the General was called Ernest. I knew I had some particular reason for disliking the name.

GWENDOLEN.   Ernest! My own Ernest! I felt from the first that you could have no other name!

JACK.   Gwendolen, it is a terrible thing for a man to find out suddenly that all his life he has been speaking nothing but the truth. Can you forgive me?

GWENDOLEN.   I can. For I feel that you are sure to change.

JACK.   My own one!

CHASUBLE.   (*To* MISS PRISM.) Lætitia! (*Embraces her.*)

MISS PRISM.   (*Enthusiastically.*) Frederick! At last!

ALGERNON.   Cecily! (*Embraces her.*) At last!

JACK.   Gwendolen! (*Embraces her.*) At last!

LADY BRACKNELL.   My nephew, you seem to be displaying signs of triviality.

JACK.   On the contrary, Aunt Augusta, I've now realized for the first time in my life the vital Importance of Being Earnest.

CURTAIN.

The Gribsby Episode

This episode appears in the four-act version of *Earnest* published in *The Complete Works of Oscar Wilde* edited by J.B. Foreman (London: Collins, 1966). It belongs to the draft of the play that Wilde completed in late 1894. This scene was not part of the text submitted to the Lord Chamberlain's office, which controlled the licensing of theatrical productions. The Gribsby episode was removed, and so the original second and third acts of *Earnest* in manuscript were merged into one. In other words, four acts were condensed into three. Gribsby makes his appearance at the point where Miss Prism has just remarked 'We must not be premature in our judgements' (p. 58). The four- and three-act versions more or less reconverge where Cecily informs Algernon: 'It is always painful to part from people whom one has known for a very brief space of time' (p. 60).

The three-act version is the one which has usually been performed on stage; and it is said that it was Wilde's preferred text. What happens in the Gribsby episode bears upon events in Wilde's life. He himself was often in debt. As he wrote from the Savoy Hotel to Alfred Douglas in March 1893: 'My bill here is £49 per week. I have also got a new sitting-room over the Thames. Why are you not here, my dear, my wonderful boy? I fear I must leave; no money, no credit, and a heart of lead' (*Letters*, ed. Rupert Hart-Davis, London: Rupert Hart-Davis, 1962, p. 337).

MERRIMAN.   Mr Ernest's luggage, sir. I have unpacked it and put it in the room next to your own.

ALGERNON.   I am afraid I can't stay more than a week, Jack, this time.

CECILY.   A week? Will you really be able to stay over Monday?

ALGERNON.   I think I can manage to stop over Monday, now.

CECILY.   I am so glad.

MERRIMAN.   (*To* ERNEST.) I beg your pardon, sir. There is an elderly gentleman wishes to see you. He has just come in a cab from the station.

(Holds card on salver.)

ALGERNON.   To see me?

MERRIMAN.   Yes, sir.

ALGERNON.   (*Reads card.*) Parker and Gribsby, Solicitors. I don't know anything about them. Who are they?

JACK.   (*Takes card.*) Parker and Gribsby: I wonder who they can be? I expect Ernest they have come about some business for your friend Bunbury. Perhaps Bunbury wants to make his will, and wishes you to be executor. (*To* MERRIMAN.) Show Messrs Parker and Gribsby in at once.

MERRIMAN.   There is only one gentleman in the hall, sir.

JACK.   Show either Mr Parker or Mr Gribsby in.

MERRIMAN.   Yes, sir.

(Exit.)

JACK.   I hope, Ernest, that I may rely on the statement you made to me last week when I finally settled all your bills for you. I hope you have no outstanding accounts of any kind.

ALGERNON.   I haven't any debts at all, dear Jack. Thanks to your generosity, I don't owe a penny, except for a few neckties I believe.

JACK.   I am sincerely glad to hear it.

(*Enter* MERRIMAN.)

MERRIMAN.   Mr Gribsby.

(*Enter* GRIBSBY.) (*Exit* MERRIMAN.)

GRIBSBY.   (*To* CANON CHASUBLE.) Mr Ernest Worthing?

MISS PRISM.   (*Indicating* ALGERNON.) This is Mr Ernest Worthing.

GRIBSBY.   Mr Ernest Worthing?

ALGERNON.   Yes.

GRIBSBY.   Of B.4, The Albany—?

ALGERNON.   Yes, that is my address—

GRIBSBY.   I am very sorry, Mr Worthing, but we have a writ of attachment for 20 days against you at the suit of the Savoy Hotel Co. Limited for £762. 14. 2.

ALGERNON.   What perfect nonsense! I never dine at the Savoy at my own expense. I always dine at Willis's. It is far more expensive. I don't owe a penny to the Savoy.

GRIBSBY.   The writ is marked as having been served on you personally at the Albany on May the 27th. Judgement was given in default against you on the fifth of June – Since then we have written to you no less than thirteen times, without receiving any reply. In the interest of our clients we had no option but to obtain an order for committal of your person. But, no doubt, Mr Worthing, you will be able to settle the account, without any further unpleasantness. Seven and six should be added to the bill of costs for the expense of the cab which was hired for your convenience in case of any necessity of removal, but that I am sure is a contingency that is not likely to occur.

ALGERNON.   Removal! What on earth do you mean by removal? I haven't the smallest intention of going away. I am staying here for a week. I am staying with my brother. (*Points to* JACK.)

GRIBSBY.   (*To* JACK.) Pleased to meet you, sir.

ALGERNON.   (*To* GRIBSBY.) If you imagine I am going up to town the moment I arrive you are extremely mistaken.

GRIBSBY.   I am merely a Solicitor myself. I do not employ personal violence of any kind. The officer of the Court whose function it is to seize the person of the debtor is waiting in the fly outside. He has considerable experience in these matters. In the point of fact he has arrested in the course of his duties nearly all the younger sons of the aristocracy, as well as several eldest sons, besides of course a good many members of the House of Lords. His style and manner are considered extremely good. Indeed, he looks more like a betting man than a court-official. That is why we always employ him. But no doubt you will prefer to pay the bill.

ALGERNON.   Pay it? How on earth am I going to do that? You don't suppose I have got any money? How perfectly silly you are. No gentleman ever has any money.

GRIBSBY.   My experience is that it is usually relations who pay.

JACK.   Kindly allow me to see this bill, Mr Gribsby – (*Turns over immense folio*.) – £762. 14. 2 since last October. I am bound to say I never saw such reckless extravagance in all my life. (*Hands it to* DR CHASUBLE.)

MISS PRISM.   £762 for eating! How grossly materialistic! There can be little good in any young man who eats so much, and so often.

CHASUBLE.   It certainly is a painful proof of the disgraceful luxury of the age. We are far away from Wordsworth's plain living and high thinking.

JACK.   Now, Dr Chasuble, do you consider that I am in any way called upon to pay this monstrous account for my brother?

CHASUBLE.   I am bound to say that I do not think so. It would be encouraging his profligacy.

MISS PRISM.   As a man sows, so let him reap. The proposed incarceration might be most salutary. It is to be regretted that it is only for 20 days.

JACK.   I am quite of your opinion.

ALGERNON.   My dear fellow, how ridiculous you are! You know perfectly well that the bill is really yours.

JACK.   Mine?

ALGERNON.   Yes: you know it is.

CHASUBLE.   Mr Worthing, if this is a jest, it is out of place.

MISS PRISM.   It is gross effrontery. Just what I expected from him.

CECILY.   It is ingratitude. I didn't expect that.

JACK.   Never mind what he says. This is the way he always goes on. (*To* ALGERNON.) You mean to say that you are not Ernest Worthing, residing at B.4, The Albany? I wonder, as you are at it, that you don't deny being my brother at all. Why don't you?

ALGERNON.   Oh! I am not going to do that, my dear fellow, it would be absurd. Of course, I'm your brother. And that is why you should pay this bill for me. What is the use of having a brother, if he doesn't pay one's bills for one?

JACK.   Personally, if you ask me, I don't see *any* use in having a brother. As for paying your bill I have not the smallest intention of doing anything of the kind. Dr Chasuble, the worthy Rector of this parish, and Miss Prism, in whose admirable and sound judgement I place great reliance, are both of opinion that incarceration would do you a great deal of good. And I think so too.

GRIBSBY.   (*Pulls out watch.*) I am sorry to disturb this pleasant family meeting, but time presses. We have to be at Holloway not later than four o'clock; otherwise it is difficult to obtain admission. The rules are very strict.

ALGERNON.   Holloway!

GRIBSBY.   It is at Holloway that detentions of this character take place always.

ALGERNON.   Well, I really am not going to be imprisoned in the suburbs for having dined in the West End. It is perfectly ridiculous.

GRIBSBY.   The bill is for suppers, not for dinners.

ALGERNON.   I really don't care. All I say is that I am not going to be imprisoned in the suburbs.

GRIBSBY.   The surroundings I admit are middle class: but the gaol itself is fashionable and well-aired: and there are ample opportunities of taking exercise at certain stated hours of the day. In the case of a medical certificate, which is always easy to obtain, the hours can be extended.

ALGERNON.   Exercise! Good God! no gentleman ever takes exercise. You don't seem to understand what a gentleman is.

GRIBSBY.   I have met so many of them, sir, that I am afraid I don't. There are the most curious varieties of them. The result of cultivation, no doubt. Will you kindly come now, sir, if it will not be inconvenient to you.

ALGERNON.   (*Appealingly.*) Jack!

MISS PRISM.   Pray be firm, Mr Worthing.

CHASUBLE.   This is an occasion on which any weakness would be out of place. It would be a form of self-deception.

JACK.   I am quite firm: and I don't know what weakness or deception of any kind is.

CECILY.   Uncle Jack! I think you have a little money of mine haven't you? Let me pay this bill. I wouldn't like your own brother to be in prison.

JACK.   Oh! you can't pay it, Cecily, that is nonsense.

CECILY.   Then you will, won't you? I think you would be sorry if you thought your own brother was shut up. Of course, I am quite disappointed with him.

JACK.   You won't speak to him again, Cecily, will you?

CECILY.   Certainly not. Unless, of course, he speaks to me first; it would be very rude not to answer him.

JACK.   Well, I'll take care he doesn't speak to you. I'll take care he doesn't speak to any body in this house. The man should be cut. Mr Gribsby—

GRIBSBY.   Yes, sir.

JACK.   I'll pay this bill for my brother. It is the last bill I shall ever pay for him too. How much is it?

GRIBSBY.   £762. 14. 2. May I ask your full name, sir?

JACK.   Mr John Worthing, JP, the Manor House, Woolton. Does that satisfy you?

GRIBSBY.   Oh! certainly, sir, certainly. It was a mere formality. (*To* MISS PRISM.) Handsome place. Ah! the cab will be 5/9 extra: hired for the convenience of the client.

JACK.   All right.

MISS PRISM.   I must say that I think such generosity quite foolish. Especially paying the cab.

CHASUBLE.   (*With a wave of the hand.*) The heart has its wisdom as well as the head, Miss Prism.

JACK.   Payable to Gribsby and Parker I suppose?

GRIBSBY.   Yes, sir. Kindly don't cross the cheque. Thank you.

JACK.   You are Gribsby aren't you? What is Parker like?

GRIBSBY.   I am both, sir. Gribsby when I am on unpleasant business, Parker on occasions of a less severe kind.

JACK.   The next time I see you I hope you will be Parker.

GRIBSBY.   I hope so, sir. (*To* DR CHASUBLE.) Good day. (DR CHASUBLE *bows coldly.*) Good day. (MISS PRISM *bows coldly.*) Hope I shall have the pleasure of meeting you again. (*To* ALGERNON.)

ALGERNON.   I sincerely hope not. What ideas you have of the sort of society a gentleman wants to mix in. No gentleman ever wants to know a Solicitor, who wants to imprison one in the suburbs.

GRIBSBY.   Quite so, quite so.

ALGERNON.   By the way, Gribsby. Gribsby, you are not to go back to the station in that cab. That is my cab. It was taken for my convenience. You and the gentleman who looks like the betting man have got to walk to the station, and a very good thing too. Solicitors don't walk nearly enough. They bolt. But they don't walk. I don't know any solicitor who takes sufficient exercise. As a rule they sit in stuffy offices all day long neglecting their business.

JACK.   You can take the cab, Mr Gribsby.

GRIBSBY.   Thank you, sir.

Exit.

The Critic as Artist

A DIALOGUE. Persons: Gilbert and Ernest. Scene: the library of a house in Piccadilly, overlooking the Green Park.

GILBERT.   (*At the piano.*) My dear Ernest, what are you laughing at?

ERNEST.   (*Looking up.*) At a capital story that I have just come across in this volume of Reminiscences that I have found on your table.

GILBERT.   What is the book? Ah! I see. I have not read it yet. Is it good?

ERNEST.   Well, while you have been playing, I have been turning over the pages with some amusement, though, as a rule, I dislike modern memoirs. They are generally written by people who have either entirely lost their memories, or have never done anything worth remembering; which, however, is, no doubt, the true explanation of their popularity, as the English public always feels perfectly at its ease when a mediocrity is talking to it.

GILBERT.   Yes: the public is wonderfully tolerant. It forgives everything except genius. But I must confess that I like all memoirs. I like them for their form, just as much as for their matter. In literature mere egotism is delightful. It is what fascinates us in the letters of personalities so different as Cicero and Balzac, Flaubert and Berlioz, Byron and Madame de Sévigné. Whenever we come across it, and, strangely enough, it is rather rare, we cannot but welcome it, and do not easily forget it. Humanity will always love Rousseau for having confessed his sins, not to a priest, but to the world, and the couchant nymphs that Cellini wrought in bronze for the castle of King Francis, the green and gold Perseus, even, that in the open Loggia at Florence shows the moon the dead terror that once turned life to stone, have not given it more pleasure than has that autobiography in which the supreme scoundrel of the Renaissance relates the story of his splendour and his shame. The opinions, the character, the achievements of the man, matter very little. He may be a sceptic like the gentle Sieur de Montaigne, or a saint like the bitter son of Monica, but when he tells us his own secrets he can always charm our ears to listening and our lips to silence. The mode of thought that Cardinal Newman represented – if that can be called a mode of thought which seeks to solve intellectual problems by a denial of the supremacy of the intellect – may not, cannot, I think, survive. But the world will never weary of watching that troubled soul in its progress from darkness to darkness. The lonely church at Littlemore, where 'the breath of the morning is damp, and worshippers are few', will always be dear to it, and whenever men see the yellow snapdragon blossoming on the wall of Trinity they will think of that gracious undergraduate who saw in the flower's sure recurrence a prophecy that he would abide for ever with the Benign Mother of his days – a prophecy that Faith, in her wisdom or her folly, suffered not to be fulfilled. Yes; autobiography is irresistible. Poor, silly, conceited Mr Secretary Pepys has chattered his way into the circle of the Immortals, and, conscious that indiscretion is the better part of valour, bustles about among them in that 'shaggy purple gown with gold buttons and looped lace' which he is so fond of describing to us, perfectly at his ease, and prattling, to his own and our infinite pleasure, of the Indian blue petticoat that he bought for his wife, of the 'good hog's harslet', and the 'pleasant French fricassee of veal' that he loved to eat, of his game of bowls with Will Joyce, and his 'gadding after beauties', and his reciting of *Hamlet* on a Sunday, and his playing of the viol on week days, and other wicked or trivial things. Even in actual life egotism is not

without its attractions. When people talk to us about others
they are usually dull. When they talk to us about themselves
they are nearly always interesting, and if one could shut them
up, when they become wearisome, as easily as one can shut
up a book of which one has grown wearied, they would be
perfect absolutely.

ERNEST.   There is much virtue in that If, as Touchstone would
say. But do you seriously propose that every man should
become his own Boswell? What would become of our industrious compilers of Lives and Recollections in that case?

GILBERT.   What has become of them? They are the pest of
the age, nothing more and nothing less. Every great man
nowadays has his disciples, and it is always Judas who writes
the biography.

ERNEST.   My dear fellow!

GILBERT.   I am afraid it is true. Formerly we used to canonize
our heroes. The modern method is to vulgarize them. Cheap
editions of great books may be delightful, but cheap editions
of great men are absolutely detestable.

ERNEST.   May I ask, Gilbert, to whom you allude?

GILBERT.   Oh! to all our second-rate *littérateurs*. We are overrun
by a set of people who, when poet or painter passes away,
arrive at the house along with the undertaker, and forget that
their one duty is to behave as mutes. But we won't talk about
them. They are the mere body-snatchers of literature. The
dust is given to one, and the ashes to another, and the soul
is out of their reach. And now, let me play Chopin to you,
or Dvořák? Shall I play you a fantasy by Dvořák? He writes
passionate, curiously-coloured things.

ERNEST.   No; I don't want music just at present. It is far too
indefinite. Besides, I took the Baroness Bernstein down to
dinner last night, and, though absolutely charming in every
other respect, she insisted on discussing music as if it were
actually written in the German language. Now, whatever
music sounds like, I am glad to say that it does not sound
in the smallest degree like German. There are forms of
patriotism that are really quite degrading. No; Gilbert, don't
play any more. Turn round and talk to me. Talk to me till the
white-horned day comes into the room. There is something
in your voice that is wonderful.

GILBERT.   (*Rising from the piano.*) I am not in a mood for talking
to-night. I really am not. How horrid of you to smile!
Where are the cigarettes? Thanks. How exquisite these single
daffodils are! They seem to be made of amber and cool ivory.
They are like Greek things of the best period. What was the
story in the confessions of the remorseful Academician that
made you laugh? Tell it to me. After playing Chopin, I feel
as if I had been weeping over sins that I had never committed,
and mourning over tragedies that were not my own. Music
always seems to me to produce that effect. It creates for one
a past of which one has been ignorant, and fills one with
a sense of sorrows that have been hidden from one's tears.
I can fancy a man who had led a perfectly commonplace
life, hearing by chance some curious piece of music, and
suddenly discovering that his soul, without his being
conscious of it, had passed through terrible experiences,
and known fearful joys, or wild romantic loves, or great
renunciations. And so tell me this story, Ernest. I want to
be amused.

ERNEST.   Oh! I don't know that it is of any importance. But I
thought it a really admirable illustration of the true value of
ordinary art-criticism. It seems that a lady once gravely asked
the remorseful Academician, as you call him, if his celebrated
picture of 'A Spring-Day at Whiteley's', or 'Waiting for the
Last Omnibus', or some subject of that kind, was all painted
by hand?

GILBERT.   And was it?

ERNEST.   You are quite incorrigible. But, seriously speaking,
what is the use of art-criticism? Why cannot the artist be
left alone, to create a new world if he wishes it, or, if not,
to shadow forth the world which we already know, and
of which, I fancy, we would each one of us be wearied
if Art, with her fine spirit of choice and delicate instinct
of selection, did not, as it were, purify it for us, and give
to it a momentary perfection. It seems to me that the
imagination spreads, or should spread, a solitude around it,
and works best in silence and in isolation. Why should the
artist be troubled by the shrill clamour of criticism? Why
should those who cannot create take upon themselves to
estimate the value of creative work? What can they know

about it? If a man's work is easy to understand, an explanation is unnecessary . . .

GILBERT.   And if his work is incomprehensible, an explanation is wicked.

ERNEST.   I did not say that.

GILBERT.   Ah! but you should have. Nowadays, we have so few mysteries left to us that we cannot afford to part with one of them. The members of the Browning Society, like the theologians of the Broad Church Party, or the authors of Mr Walter Scott's Great Writers Series, seem to me to spend their time in trying to explain their divinity away. Where one had hoped that Browning was a mystic they have sought to show that he was simply inarticulate. Where one had fancied that he had something to conceal, they have proved that he had but little to reveal. But I speak merely of his incoherent work. Taken as a whole the man was great. He did not belong to the Olympians, and had all the incompleteness of the Titan. He did not survey, and it was but rarely that he could sing. His work is marred by struggle, violence and effort, and he passed not from emotion to form, but from thought to chaos. Still, he was great. He has been called a thinker, and was certainly a man who was always thinking, and always thinking aloud; but it was not thought that fascinated him, but rather the processes by which thought moves. It was the machine he loved, not what the machine makes. The method by which the fool arrives at his folly was as dear to him as the ultimate wisdom of the wise. So much, indeed, did the subtle mechanism of mind fascinate him that he despised language, or looked upon it as an incomplete instrument of expression. Rhyme, that exquisite echo which in the Muse's hollow hill creates and answers its own voice; rhyme, which in the hands of the real artist becomes not merely a material element of metrical beauty, but a spiritual element of thought and passion also, waking a new mood, it may be, or stirring a fresh train of ideas, or opening by mere sweetness and suggestion of sound some golden door at which the Imagination itself had knocked in vain; rhyme, which can turn man's utterance to the speech of gods; rhyme, the one chord we have added to the Greek lyre, became in Robert Browning's hands a grotesque, misshapen thing, which at times made him masquerade in poetry as a low comedian, and ride Pegasus too often with his tongue in his cheek. There are moments when he wounds us by monstrous music. Nay, if he can only get his music by breaking the strings of his lute, he breaks them, and they snap in discord, and no Athenian tettix, making melody from tremulous wings, lights on the ivory horn to make the movement perfect, or the interval less harsh. Yet, he was great: and though he turned language into ignoble clay, he made from it men and women that live. He is the most Shakespearian creature since Shakespeare. If Shakespeare could sing with myriad lips, Browning could stammer through a thousand mouths. Even now, as I am speaking, and speaking not against him but for him, there glides through the room the pageant of his persons. There, creeps Fra Lippo Lippi with his cheeks still burning from some girl's hot kiss. There, stands dread Saul with the lordly male-sapphires gleaming in his turban. Mildred Tresham is there, and the Spanish monk, yellow with hatred, and Blougram, and Ben Ezra, and the Bishop of St Praxed's. The spawn of Setebos gibbers in the corner, and Sebald, hearing Pippa pass by, looks on Ottima's haggard face, and loathes her and his own sin, and himself. Pale as the white satin of his doublet, the melancholy king watches with dreamy treacherous eyes too loyal Strafford pass forth to his doom, and Andrea shudders as he hears the cousins whistle in the garden, and bids his perfect wife go down. Yes, Browning was great. And as what will he be remembered? As a poet? Ah, not as a poet! He will be remembered as a writer of fiction, as the most supreme writer of fiction, it may be, that we have ever had. His sense of dramatic situation was unrivalled, and, if he could not answer his own problems, he could at least put problems forth, and what more should an artist do? Considered from the point of view of a creator of character he ranks next to him who made Hamlet. Had he been articulate, he might have sat beside him. The only man who can touch the hem of his garment is George Meredith. Meredith is a prose Browning, and so is Browning. He used poetry as a medium for writing in prose.

ERNEST.   There is something in what you say, but there is not everything in what you say. In many points you are unjust.

GILBERT.   It is difficult not to be unjust to what one loves. But
let us return to the particular point at issue. What was it that
you said?

ERNEST.   Simply this: that in the best days of art there were no
art-critics.

GILBERT.   I seem to have heard that observation before, Ernest.
It has all the vitality of error and all the tediousness of an
old friend.

ERNEST.   It is true. Yes: there is no use your tossing your
head in that petulant manner. It is quite true. In the best
days of art there were no art-critics. The sculptor hewed
from the marble block the great white-limbed Hermes that
slept within it. The waxers and gilders of images gave tone
and texture to the statue, and the world, when it saw it,
worshipped and was dumb. He poured the glowing bronze
into the mould of sand, and the river of red metal cooled
into noble curves and took the impress of the body of a
god. With enamel or polished jewels he gave sight to the
sightless eyes. The hyacinth-like curls grew crisp beneath his
graver. And when, in some dim frescoed fane, or pillared
sunlit portico, the child of Leto stood upon his pedestal,
those who passed by, διὰ λαμπροτάτου βαίνοντες ἁβρῶς
αἰθέρος, became conscious of a new influence that had
come across their lives, and dreamily, or with a sense of
strange and quickening joy, went to their homes or daily
labour, or wandered, it may be, through the city gates to
that nymph-haunted meadow where young Phædrus bathed
his feet, and, lying there on the soft grass, beneath the tall
wind-whispering planes and flowering *agnus castus*, began
to think of the wonder of beauty, and grew silent with
unaccustomed awe. In those days the artist was free. From
the river valley he took the fine clay in his fingers, and
with a little tool of wood or bone, fashioned it into forms
so exquisite that the people gave them to the dead as their
playthings, and we find them still in the dusty tombs on
the yellow hillside by Tanagra, with the faint gold and the
fading crimson still lingering about hair and lips and raiment.
On a wall of fresh plaster, stained with bright sandyx or
mixed with milk and saffron, he pictured one who trod
with tired feet the purple white-starred fields of asphodel,

101

one 'in whose eyelids lay the whole of the Trojan War', Polyxena, the daughter of Priam; or figured Odysseus, the wise and cunning, bound by tight cords to the mast-step, that he might listen without hurt to the singing of the Sirens, or wandering by the clear river of Acheron, where the ghosts of fishes flitted over the pebbly bed; or showed the Persian in trews and mitre flying before the Greek at Marathon, or the galleys clashing their beaks of brass in the little Salaminian bay. He drew with silverpoint and charcoal upon parchment and prepared cedar. Upon ivory and rose-coloured terracotta he painted with wax, making the wax fluid with juice of olives, and with heated irons making it firm. Panel and marble and linen canvas became wonderful as his brush swept across them; and life seeing her own image, was still, and dared not speak. All life, indeed, was his, from the merchants seated in the market-place to the cloaked shepherd lying on the hill; from the nymph hidden in the laurels and the faun that pipes at noon, to the king whom, in long green-curtained litter, slaves bore upon oil-bright shoulders, and fanned with peacock fans. Men and women, with pleasure or sorrow in their faces, passed before him. He watched them, and their secret became his. Through form and colour he re-created a world.

All subtle arts belonged to him also. He held the gem against the revolving disk, and the amethyst became the purple couch for Adonis, and across the veined sardonyx sped Artemis with her hounds. He beat out the gold into roses, and strung them together for necklace or armlet. He beat out the gold into wreaths for the conqueror's helmet, or into palmates for the Tyrian robe, or into masks for the royal dead. On the back of the silver mirror he graved Thetis borne by her Nereids, or love-sick Phædra with her nurse, or Persephone, weary of memory, putting poppies in her hair. The potter sat in his shed, and, flower-like from the silent wheel, the vase rose up beneath his hands. He decorated the base and stem and ears with pattern of dainty olive-leaf, or foliated acanthus, or curved and crested wave. Then in black or red he painted lads wrestling, or in the race: knights in full armour, with strange heraldic shields and curious visors, leaning from shell-shaped chariot over rearing steeds: the gods seated at the feast or working their miracles: the heroes in their victory or in their pain. Sometimes he would etch in thin vermilion lines upon a ground of white the languid bridegroom and his bride, with Eros hovering round them – an Eros like one of Donatello's angels, a little laughing thing with gilded or with azure wings. On the curved side he would write the name of his friend. ΚΑΛΟΣ ΑΛΚΙΒΙΑΔΗΣ or ΚΑΛΟΣ ΧΑΡΜΙΔΗΣ or tells us the story of his days. Again, on the rim of the wide flat cup he would draw the stag browsing, or the lion at rest, as his fancy willed it. From the tiny perfume-bottle laughed Aphrodite at her toilet, and, with bare-limbed Mænads in his train, Dionysus danced round the wine-jar on naked must-stained feet, while, satyr-like, the old Silenus sprawled upon the bloated skins, or shook that magic spear which was tipped with a fretted fir-cone, and wreathed with dark ivy. And no one came to trouble the artist at his work. No irresponsible chatter disturbed him. He was not worried by opinions. By the Ilyssus, says Arnold somewhere, there was no Higginbotham. By the Ilyssus, my dear Gilbert, there were no silly art congresses bringing provincialism to the provinces and teaching the mediocrity how to mouth. By the Ilyssus there were no tedious magazines about art, in which the industrious prattle of what they do not understand. On the reed-grown banks of that little stream strutted no ridiculous journalism monopolizing the seat of judgement when it should be apologising in the dock. The Greeks had no art-critics.

GILBERT.   Ernest, you are quite delightful, but your views are terribly unsound. I am afraid that you have been listening to the conversation of some one older than yourself. That is always a dangerous thing to do, and if you allow it to degenerate into a habit you will find it absolutely fatal to any intellectual development. As for modern journalism, it is not my business to defend it. It justifies its own existence by the great Darwinian principle of the survival of the vulgarest. I have merely to do with literature.

ERNEST.   But what is the difference between literature and journalism?

GILBERT.   Oh! journalism is unreadable, and literature is not read. That is all. But with regard to your statement that the

Greeks had no art-critics, I assure you that is quite absurd. It would be more just to say that the Greeks were a nation of art-critics.

ERNEST.   Really?

GILBERT.   Yes, a nation of art-critics. But I don't wish to destroy the delightfully unreal picture that you have drawn of the relation of the Hellenic artist to the intellectual spirit of his age. To give an accurate description of what has never occurred is not merely the proper occupation of the historian, but the inalienable privilege of any man of parts and culture. Still less do I desire to talk learnedly. Learned conversation is either the affectation of the ignorant or the profession of the mentally unemployed. And, as for what is called improving conversation, that is merely the foolish method by which the still more foolish philanthropist feebly tries to disarm the just rancour of the criminal classes. No: let me play to you some mad scarlet thing by Dvořák. The pallid figures on the tapestry are smiling at us, and the heavy eyelids of my bronze Narcissus are folded in sleep. Don't let us discuss anything solemnly. I am but too conscious of the fact that we are born in an age when only the dull are treated seriously, and I live in terror of not being misunderstood. Don't degrade me into the position of giving you useful information. Education is an admirable thing, but it is well to remember from time to time that nothing that is worth knowing can be taught. Through the parted curtains of the window I see the moon like a clipped piece of silver. Like gilded bees the stars cluster round her. The sky is a hard hollow sapphire. Let us go out into the night. Thought is wonderful, but adventure is more wonderful still. Who knows but we may meet Prince Florizel of Bohemia, and hear the fair Cuban tell us that she is not what she seems?

ERNEST.   You are horribly wilful. I insist on your discussing this matter with me. You have said that the Greeks were a nation of art-critics. What art-criticism have they left us?

GILBERT.   My dear Ernest, even if not a single fragment of art-criticism had come down to us from Hellenic or Hellenistic days, it would be none the less true that the Greeks were a nation of art-critics, and that they invented the criticism of art just as they invented the criticism of everything else.

For, after all, what is our primary debt to the Greeks? Simply the critical spirit. And, this spirit, which they exercised on questions of religion and science, of ethics and metaphysics, of politics and education, they exercised on questions of art also, and, indeed, of the two supreme and highest arts, they have left us the most flawless system of criticism that the world has ever seen.

ERNEST.   But what are the two supreme and highest arts?

GILBERT.   Life and Literature, life and the perfect expression of life. The principles of the former, as laid down by the Greeks, we may not realize in an age so marred by false ideals as our own. The principles of the latter, as they laid them down, are, in many cases, so subtle that we can hardly understand them. Recognizing that the most perfect art is that which most fully mirrors man in all his infinite variety, they elaborated the criticism of language, considered in the light of the mere material of that art, to a point to which we, with our accentual system of reasonable or emotional emphasis, can barely if at all attain; studying, for instance, the metrical movements of a prose as scientifically as a modern musician studies harmony and counterpoint, and, I need hardly say, with much keener æsthetic instinct. In this they were right, as they were right in all things. Since the introduction of printing, and the fatal development of the habit of reading amongst the middle and lower classes of this country, there has been a tendency in literature to appeal more and more to the eye, and less and less to the ear which is really the sense which, from the standpoint of pure art, it should seek to please, and by whose canons of pleasure it should abide always. Even the work of Mr Pater, who is, on the whole, the most perfect master of English prose now creating amongst us, is often far more like a piece of mosaic than a passage in music, and seems, here and there, to lack the true rhythmical life of words and the fine freedom and richness of effect that such rhythmical life produces. We, in fact, have made writing a definite mode of composition, and have treated it as a form of elaborate design. The Greeks, upon the other hand, regarded writing simply as a method of chronicling. Their test was always the spoken word in its musical and metrical relations. The voice was the medium, and the ear the critic. I have sometimes thought that the story of Homer's blindness might be really an artistic myth, created in critical days, and serving to remind us, not merely that the great poet is always a seer, seeing less with the eyes of the body than he does with the eyes of the soul, but that he is a true singer also, building his song out of music, repeating each line over and over again to himself till he has caught the secret of its melody, chaunting in darkness the words that are winged with light. Certainly, whether this be so or not, it was to his blindness, as an occasion, if not as a cause, that England's great poet owed much of the majestic movement and sonorous splendour of his later verse. When Milton could no longer write he began to sing. Who would match the measures of *Comus* with the measures of *Samson Agonistes*, or of *Paradise Lost* or *Regained*? When Milton became blind he composed, as every one should compose, with the voice purely, and so the pipe or reed of earlier days became that mighty many-stopped organ whose rich reverberant music has all the stateliness of Homeric verse, if it seeks not to have its swiftness, and is the one imperishable inheritance of English literature sweeping through all the ages, because above them, and abiding with us ever, being immortal in its form. Yes: writing has done much harm to writers. We must return to the voice. That must be our test, and perhaps then we shall be able to appreciate some of the subtleties of Greek art-criticism.

As it now is, we cannot do so. Sometimes, when I have written a piece of prose that I have been modest enough to consider absolutely free from fault, a dreadful thought comes over me that I may have been guilty of the immoral effeminacy of using trochaic and tribrachic movements, a crime for which a learned critic of the Augustan age censures with most just severity the brilliant if somewhat paradoxical Hegesias. I grow cold when I think of it, and wonder to myself if the admirable ethical effect of the prose of that charming writer, who once in a spirit of reckless generosity towards the uncultivated portion of our community proclaimed the monstrous doctrine that conduct is three-fourths of life, will not some day be entirely annihilated by the discovery that the pæons have been wrongly placed.

ERNEST.   Ah! now you are flippant.

GILBERT.   Who would not be flippant when he is gravely told
that the Greeks had no art-critics? I can understand it being
said that the constructive genius of the Greeks lost itself in
criticism, but not that the race to whom we owe the critical
spirit did not criticize. You will not ask me to give you a
survey of Greek art criticism from Plato to Plotinus. The
night is too lovely for that, and the moon, if she heard us,
would put more ashes on her face than are there already. But
think merely of one perfect little work of æsthetic criticism,
Aristotle's *Treatise on Poetry*. It is not perfect in form, for it is
badly written, consisting perhaps of notes dotted down for an
art lecture, or of isolated fragments destined for some larger
book, but in temper and treatment it is perfect, absolutely.
The ethical effect of art, its importance to culture, and its
place in the formation of character, had been done once
for all by Plato; but here we have art treated, not from the
moral, but from the purely æsthetic point of view. Plato had,
of course, dealt with many definitely artistic subjects, such as
the importance of unity in a work of art, the necessity for tone
and harmony, the æsthetic value of appearances, the relation
of the visible arts to the external world, and the relation of
fiction to fact. He first perhaps stirred in the soul of man
that desire that we have not yet satisfied, the desire to know
the connection between Beauty and Truth, and the place of
Beauty in the moral and intellectual order of the Kosmos.
The problems of idealism and realism, as he sets them forth,
may seem to many to be somewhat barren of result in the
metaphysical sphere of abstract being in which he places
them, but transfer them to the sphere of art, and you will
find that they are still vital and full of meaning. It may be that
it is as a critic of Beauty that Plato is destined to live, and that
by altering the name of the sphere of his speculation we shall
find a new philosophy. But Aristotle, like Goethe, deals with
art primarily in its concrete manifestations, taking Tragedy,
for instance, and investigating the material it uses, which is
language, its subject-matter, which is life, the method by
which it works, which is action, the conditions under which
it reveals itself, which are those of theatric presentation, its
logical structure, which is plot, and its final æsthetic appeal,

which is to the sense of beauty realized through the passions
of pity and awe. That purification and spiritualizing of the
nature which he calls κάθαρσις is, as Goethe saw, essentially
aesthetic, and is not moral, as Lessing fancied. Concerning
himself primarily with the impression that the work of art
produces, Aristotle sets himself to analyse that impression,
to investigate its source, to see how it is engendered. As
a physiologist and psychologist, he knows that the health
of a function resides in energy. To have a capacity for a
passion and not to realize it, is to make oneself incomplete
and limited. The mimic spectacle of life that Tragedy affords
cleanses the bosom of much 'perilous stuff', and by presenting
high and worthy objects for the exercise of the emotions
purifies and spiritualizes the man; nay, not merely does it
spiritualize him, but it initiates him also into noble feelings
of which he might else have known nothing, the word
κάθαρσις having, it has sometimes seemed to me, a definite
allusion to the rite of initiation, if indeed that be not, as I
am occasionally tempted to fancy, its true and only meaning
here. This is of course a mere outline of the book. But you
see what a perfect piece of æsthetic criticism it is. Who
indeed but a Greek could have analysed art so well? After
reading it, one does not wonder any longer that Alexandria
devoted itself so largely to art-criticism, and that we find the
artistic temperaments of the day investigating every question
of style and manner, discussing the great Academic schools
of painting, for instance, such as the school of Sicyon, that
sought to preserve the dignified traditions of the antique
mode, or the realistic and impressionist schools, that aimed
at reproducing actual life, or the elements of ideality in
portraiture, or the artistic value of the epic form in an age
so modern as theirs, or the proper subject-matter for the
artist. Indeed, I fear that the inartistic temperaments of the day
busied themselves also in matters of literature and art, for the
accusations of plagiarism were endless, and such accusations
proceed either from the thin colourless lips of impotence, or
from the grotesque mouths of those who, possessing nothing
of their own, fancy that they can gain a reputation for wealth
by crying out that they have been robbed. And I assure you,
my dear Ernest, that the Greeks chattered about painters

quite as much as people do nowadays, and had their private views, and shilling exhibitions, and Arts and Crafts guilds, and Pre-Raphaelite movements, and movements towards realism, and lectured about art, and wrote essays on art, and produced their art-historians, and their archæologists, and all the rest of it. Why, even the theatrical managers of travelling companies brought their dramatic critics with them when they went on tour, and paid them very handsome salaries for writing laudatory notices. Whatever, in fact, is modern in our life we owe to the Greeks. Whatever is an anachronism is due to mediævalism. It is the Greeks who have given us the whole system of art-criticism, and how fine their critical instinct was, may be seen from the fact that the material they criticized with most care was, as I have already said, language. For the material that painter or sculptor uses is meagre in comparison with, that of words. Words have not merely music as sweet as that of viol and lute, colour as rich and vivid as any that makes lovely for us the canvas of the Venetian or the Spaniard, and plastic form no less sure and certain than that which reveals itself in marble or in bronze, but thought and passion and spirituality are theirs also, are theirs indeed alone. If the Greeks had criticized nothing but language, they would still have been the great art-critics of the world. To know the principles of the highest art is to know the principles of all the arts.

But I see that the moon is hiding behind a sulphur-coloured cloud. Out of a tawny mane of drift she gleams like a lion's eye. She is afraid that I will talk to you of Lucian and Longinus, of Quinctilian and Dionysius, of Pliny and Fronto and Pausanias, of all those who in the antique world wrote or lectured upon art matters. She need not be afraid. I am tired of my expedition into the dim, dull abyss of facts. There is nothing left for me now but the divine μονόχρονος ἡδονή of another cigarette. Cigarettes have at least the charm of leaving one unsatisfied.

ERNEST.   Try one of mine. They are rather good. I get them direct from Cairo. The only use of our *attachés* is that they supply their friends with excellent tobacco. And as the moon has hidden herself, let us talk a little longer. I am quite ready to admit that I was wrong in what I said about the Greeks.

They were, as you have pointed out, a nation of art-critics. I acknowledge it, and I feel a little sorry for them. For the creative faculty is higher than the critical. There is really no comparison between them.

GILBERT.   The antithesis between them is entirely arbitrary. Without the critical faculty, there is no artistic creation at all, worthy of the name. You spoke a little while ago of that fine spirit of choice and delicate instinct of selection by which the artist realizes life for us, and gives to it a momentary perfection. Well, that spirit of choice, that subtle tact of omission, is really the critical faculty in one of its most characteristic moods, and no one who does not possess this critical faculty can create anything at all in art. Arnold's definition of literature as a criticism of life was not very felicitous in form, but it showed how keenly he recognized the importance of the critical element in all creative work.

ERNEST.   I should have said that great artists worked unconsciously, that they were 'wiser than they knew', as, I think, Emerson remarks somewhere.

GILBERT.   It is really not so, Ernest. All fine imaginative work is self-conscious and deliberate. No poet sings because he must sing. At least, no great poet does. A great poet sings because he chooses to sing. It is so now, and it has always been so. We are sometimes apt to think that the voices that sounded at the dawn of poetry were simpler, fresher and more natural than ours, and that the world which the early poets looked at, and through which they walked, had a kind of poetical quality of its own, and almost without changing could pass into song. The snow lies thick now upon Olympus, and its steep scarped sides are bleak and barren, but once, we fancy, the white feet of the Muses brushed the dew from the anemones in the morning, and at evening came Apollo to sing to the shepherds in the vale. But in this we are merely lending to other ages what we desire, or think we desire, for our own. Our historical sense is at fault. Every century that produces poetry is, so far, an artificial century, and the work that seems to us to be the most natural and simple product of its time is always the result of the most self-conscious effort. Believe me, Ernest, there is no fine art without self-consciousness, and self-consciousness and the critical spirit are one.

ERNEST.   I see what you mean, and there is much in it. But
    surely you would admit that the great poems of the early
    world, the primitive, anonymous collective poems, were
    the result of the imagination of races, rather than of the
    imagination of individuals?

GILBERT.   Not when they became poetry. Not when they
    received a beautiful form. For there is no art where there
    is no style, and no style where there is no unity, and unity
    is of the individual. No doubt Homer had old ballads and
    stories to deal with, as Shakespeare had chronicles and plays
    and novels from which to work, but they were merely his
    rough material. He took them, and shaped them into song.
    They become his, because he made them lovely. They were
    built out of music,

> 'And so not built at all,
> And therefore built for ever.'

The longer one studies life and literature, the more strongly
one feels that behind everything that is wonderful stands
the individual, and that it is not the moment that makes
the man, but the man who creates the age. Indeed, I am
inclined to think that each myth and legend that seems to
us to spring out of the wonder, or terror, or fancy of tribe
and nation, was in its origin the invention of one single
mind. The curiously limited number of the myths seems
to me to point to this conclusion. But we must not go off
into questions of comparative mythology. We must keep to
criticism. And what I want to point out is this. An age that has
no criticism is either an age in which art is immobile, hieratic,
and confined to the reproduction of formal types, or an age
that possesses no art at all. There have been critical ages that
have not been creative, in the ordinary sense of the word,
ages in which the spirit of man has sought to set in order the
treasures of his treasure-house, to separate the gold from the
silver, and the silver from the lead, to count over the jewels,
and to give names to the pearls. But there has never been a
creative age that has not been critical also. For it is the critical
faculty that invents fresh forms. The tendency of creation is to
repeat itself. It is to the critical instinct that we owe each new
school that springs up, each new mould that art finds ready to

111

its hand. There is really not a single form that art now uses
that does not come to us from the critical spirit of Alexandria,
where these forms were either stereotyped or invented or
made perfect. I say Alexandria, not merely because it was
there that the Greek spirit became most self-conscious, and
indeed ultimately expired in scepticism and theology, but
because it was to that city, and not to Athens, that Rome
turned for her models, and it was through the survival, such
as it was, of the Latin language that culture lived at all. When,
at the Renaissance, Greek literature dawned upon Europe,
the soil had been in some measure prepared for it. But, to
get rid of the details of history, which are always wearisome
and usually inaccurate, let us say generally, that the forms
of art have been due to the Greek critical spirit. To it we
owe the epic, the lyric, the entire drama in every one of its
developments, including burlesque, the idyll, the romantic
novel, the novel of adventure, the essay, the dialogue, the
oration, the lecture, for which perhaps we should not forgive
them, and the epigram, in all the wide meaning of that word.
In fact, we owe it everything, except the sonnet, to which,
however, some curious parallels of thought-movement may
be traced in the Anthology, American journalism, to which
no parallel can be found anywhere, and the ballad in sham
Scotch dialect, which one of our most industrious writers
has recently proposed should be made the basis for a final
and unanimous effort on the part of our second-rate poets
to make themselves really romantic. Each new school, as it
appears, cries out against criticism, but it is to the critical
faculty in man that it owes its origin. The mere creative
instinct does not innovate, but reproduces.

ERNEST.   You have been talking of criticism as an essential part
of the creative spirit, and I now fully accept your theory. But
what of criticism outside creation? I have a foolish habit of
reading periodicals, and it seems to me that most modern
criticism is perfectly valueless.

GILBERT.   So is most modern creative work also. Mediocrity
weighing mediocrity in the balance, and incompetence
applauding its brother – that is the spectacle which the
artistic activity of England affords us from time to time.
And yet, I feel I am a little unfair in this matter. As a rule,

the critics – I speak, of course, of the higher class, of those in fact who write for the sixpenny papers – are far more cultured than the people whose work they are called upon to review. This is, indeed, only what one would expect, for criticism demands infinitely more cultivation than creation does.

ERNEST.   Really?

GILBERT.   Certainly. Anybody can write a three-volumed novel. It merely requires a complete ignorance of both life and literature. The difficulty that I should fancy the reviewer feels is the difficulty of sustaining any standard. Where there is no style a standard must be impossible. The poor reviewers are apparently reduced to be the reporters of the police-court of literature, the chroniclers of the doings of the habitual criminals of art. It is sometimes said of them that they do not read all through the works they are called upon to criticize. They do not. Or at least they should not. If they did so, they would become confirmed misanthropes, or if I may borrow a phrase from one of the pretty Newnham graduates, confirmed womanthropes for the rest of their lives. Nor is it necessary. To know the vintage and quality of a wine one need not drink the whole cask. It must be perfectly easy in half an hour to say whether a book is worth anything or worth nothing. Ten minutes are really sufficient, if one has the instinct for form. Who wants to wade through a dull volume? One tastes it, and that is quite enough – more than enough, I should imagine. I am aware that there are many honest workers in painting as well as in literature who object to criticism entirely. They are quite right. Their work stands in no intellectual relation to their age. It brings us no new element of pleasure. It suggests no fresh departure of thought, or passion, or beauty. It should not be spoken of. It should be left to the oblivion that it deserves.

ERNEST.   But, my dear fellow – excuse me for interrupting you – you seem to me to be allowing your passion for criticism to lead you a great deal too far. For, after all, even you must admit that it is much more difficult to do a thing than to talk about it.

GILBERT.   More difficult to do a thing than to talk about it? Not at all. That is a gross popular error. It is very much more difficult to talk about a thing than to do it. In the sphere of actual life that is of course obvious. Anybody can make history. Only a great man can write it. There is no mode of action, no form of emotion, that we do not share with the lower animals. It is only by language that we rise above them, or above each other – by language, which is the parent, and not the child, of thought. Action, indeed, is always easy, and when presented to us in its most aggravated, because most continuous form, which I take to be that of real industry, becomes simply the refuge of people who have nothing whatsoever to do. No, Ernest, don't talk about action. It is a blind thing dependent on external influences, and moved by an impulse of whose nature it is unconscious. It is a thing incomplete in its essence, because limited by accident, and ignorant of its direction, being always at variance with its aim. Its basis is the lack of imagination. It is the last resource of those who know not how to dream.

ERNEST.   Gilbert, you treat the world as if it were a crystal ball. You hold it in your hand, and reverse it to please a wilful fancy. You do nothing but re-write history.

GILBERT.   The one duty we owe to history is to re-write it. That is not the least of the tasks in store for the critical spirit. When we have fully discovered the scientific laws that govern life, we shall realize that the one person who has more illusions than the dreamer is the man of action. He, indeed, knows neither the origin of his deeds nor their results. From the field in which he thought that he had sown thorns, we have gathered for our vintage, and the fig-tree that he planted for our pleasure is as barren as the thistle, and more bitter. It is because Humanity has never known where it was going that it has been able to find its way.

ERNEST.   You think, then, that in the sphere of action a conscious aim is a delusion?

GILBERT.   It is worse than a delusion. If we lived long enough to see the results of our actions it may be that those who call themselves good would be sickened with a dull remorse, and those whom the world calls evil stirred by a noble joy. Each little thing that we do passes into the great machine of life which may grind our virtues to powder and make them worthless, or transform our sins into elements of a new civilization, more marvellous and more splendid than any that has gone before. But men are the slaves of words. They rage against Materialism, as they call it, forgetting that there has been no material improvement that has not spiritualized the world, and that there have been few, if any, spiritual awakenings that have not wasted the world's faculties in barren hopes, and fruitless aspirations, and empty or trammelling creeds. What is termed Sin is an essential element of progress. Without it the world would stagnate, or grow old, or become colourless. By its curiosity Sin increases the experience of the race. Through its intensified assertion of individualism, it saves us from monotony of type. In its rejection of the current notions about morality, it is one with the higher ethics. And as for the virtues! What are the virtues? Nature, M. Renan tells us, cares little about chastity, and it may be that it is to the shame of the Magdalen, and not to their own purity, that the Lucretias of modern life owe their freedom from stain. Charity, as even those of whose religion it makes a formal part have been compelled to acknowledge, creates a multitude of evils. The mere existence of conscience, that faculty of which people prate so much nowadays, and are so ignorantly proud, is a sign of our imperfect development. It must be merged in instinct before we become fine. Self-denial is simply a method by which man arrests his progress, and self-sacrifice a survival of the mutilation of the savage, part of that old worship of pain which is so terrible a factor in the history of the world, and which even now makes its victims day by day, and has its altars in the land. Virtues! Who knows what the virtues are? Not you. Not I. Not any one. It is well for our vanity that we slay the criminal, for if we suffered him to live he might show us what we had gained by his crime. It is well for his peace that the saint goes to his martyrdom. He is spared the sight of the horror of his harvest.

ERNEST.   Gilbert, you sound too harsh a note. Let us go back to the more gracious fields of literature. What was it you said? That it was more difficult to talk about a thing than to do it?

GILBERT.   (*After a pause.*) I believe I ventured upon that simple truth. Surely you see now that I am right? When man acts he is a puppet. When he describes he is a poet. The whole secret lies in that. It was easy enough on the sandy plains

by windy Ilion to send the notched arrow from the painted
bow, or to hurl against the shield of hide and flamelike brass
the long ash-handled spear. It was easy for the adulterous
queen to spread the Tyrian carpets for her lord, and then,
as he lay couched in the marble bath, to throw over his
head the purple net, and call to her smooth-faced lover to
stab through the meshes at the heart that should have broken
at Aulis. For Antigone even, with Death waiting for her as
her bridegroom, it was easy to pass through the tainted air
at noon, and climb the hill, and strew with kindly earth the
wretched naked corse that had no tomb. But what of those
who wrote about these things? What of those who gave them
reality, and made them live for ever? Are they not greater than
the men and women they sing of? 'Hector that sweet knight
is dead', and Lucian tells us how in the dim under-world
Menippus saw the bleaching skull of Helen, and marvelled
that it was for so grim a favour that all those horned ships
were launched, those beautiful mailed men laid low, those
towered cities brought to dust. Yet, every day the swanlike
daughter of Leda comes out on the battlements, and looks
down at the tide of war. The greybeards wonder at her
loveliness, and she stands by the side of the king. In his
chamber of stained ivory lies her leman. He is polishing his
dainty armour, and combing the scarlet plume. With squire
and page, her husband passes from tent to tent. She can see his
bright hair, and hears, or fancies that she hears, that clear cold
voice. In the courtyard below, the son of Priam is buckling
on his brazen cuirass. The white arms of Andromache are
around his neck. He sets his helmet on the ground, lest their
babe should be frightened. Behind the embroidered curtains
of his pavilion sits Achilles, in perfumed raiment, while in
harness of gilt and silver the friend of his soul arrays himself
to go forth to the fight. From a curiously carven chest that
his mother Thetis had brought to his ship-side, the Lord of
the Myrmidons takes out that mystic chalice that the lip of
man had never touched, and cleanses it with brimstone, and
with fresh water cools it, and, having washed his hands, fills
with black wine its burnished hollow, and spills the thick
grape-blood upon the ground in honour of Him whom
at Dodona barefooted prophets worshipped, and prays to

Him, and knows not that he prays in vain, and that by the
hands of two knights from Troy, Panthous' son, Euphorbus,
whose lovelocks were looped with gold, and the Priamid, the
lion-hearted, Patroklus, the comrade of comrades, must meet
his doom. Phantoms, are they? Heroes of mist and mountain?
Shadows in a song? No: they are real. Action! What is action?
It dies at the moment of its energy. It is a base concession to
fact. The world is made by the singer for the dreamer.

ERNEST.   While you talk it seems to me to be so.

GILBERT.   It is so in truth. On the mouldering citadel of Troy
lies the lizard like a thing of green bronze. The owl has
built her nest in the palace of Priam. Over the empty plain
wander shepherd and goatherd with their flocks, and where,
on the wine-surfaced, oily sea, οἶνοψ πόντος as Homer calls
it, copper-prowed and streaked with vermilion, the great galleys
of the Danaoi came in their gleaming crescent, the lonely
tunny-fisher sits in his little boat and watches the bobbing
corks of his net. Yet, every morning the doors of the city
are thrown open, and on foot, or in horse-drawn chariot,
the warriors go forth to battle, and mock their enemies from
behind their iron masks. All day long the fight rages, and
when night comes the torches gleam by the tents, and the
cresset burns in the hall. Those who live in marble or on
painted panel, know of life but a single exquisite instant,
eternal indeed in its beauty, but limited to one note of passion or one mood of calm. Those whom the poet makes live
have their myriad emotions of joy and terror, of courage and
despair, of pleasure and of suffering. The seasons come and
go in glad or saddening pageant, and with winged or leaden
feet the years pass by before them. They have their youth
and their manhood, they are children, and they grow old.
It is always dawn for St Helena, as Veronese saw her at the
window. Through the still morning air the angels bring her
the symbol of God's pain. The cool breezes of the morning
lift the gilt threads from her brow. On that little hill by the
city of Florence, where the lovers of Giorgione are lying, it
is always the solstice of noon, of noon made so languorous
by summer suns that hardly can the slim naked girl dip into
the marble tank the round bubble of clear glass, and the long
fingers of the lute-player rest idly upon the chords. It is

twilight always for the dancing nymphs whom Corot set
free among the silver poplars of France. In eternal twilight
they move, those frail diaphanous figures, whose tremulous
white feet seem not to touch the dew-drenched grass they
tread on. But those who walk in epos, drama, or romance,
see through the labouring months the young moons wax and
wane, and watch the night from evening unto morning star,
and from sunrise unto sunsetting, can note the shifting day
with all its gold and shadow. For them, as for us, the flowers
bloom and wither, and the Earth, that Green-tressed Goddess
as Coleridge calls her, alters her raiment for their pleasure.
The statue is concentrated to one moment of perfection. The
image stained upon the canvas possesses no spiritual element
of growth or change. If they know nothing of death, it is
because they know little of life, for the secrets of life and
death belong to those, and those only, whom the sequence
of time affects, and who possess not merely the present but
the future, and can rise or fall from a past of glory or of
shame. Movement, that problem of the visible arts, can be
truly realized by Literature alone. It is Literature that shows
us the body in its swiftness and the soul in its unrest.

ERNEST.   Yes; I see now what you mean. But, surely, the higher
you place the creative artist, the lower must the critic rank.

GILBERT.   Why so?

ERNEST.   Because the best that he can give us will be but an
echo of rich music, a dim shadow of clear-outlined form. It
may, indeed, be that life is chaos, as you tell me that it is;
that its martyrdoms are mean and its heroisms ignoble; and
that it is the function of Literature to create, from the rough
material of actual existence, a new world that will be more
marvellous, more enduring, and more true than the world
that common eyes look upon, and through which common
natures seek to realize their perfection. But surely, if this new
world has been made by the spirit and touch of a great artist,
it will be a thing so complete and perfect that there will be
nothing left for the critic to do. I quite understand now, and
indeed admit most readily, that it is far more difficult to talk
about a thing than to do it. But it seems to me that this sound
and sensible maxim, which is really extremely soothing to

one's feelings, and should be adopted as its motto by every
Academy of Literature all over the world, applies only to
the relations that exist between Art and Life, and not to any
relations that there may be between Art and Criticism.

GILBERT.   But, surely, Criticism is itself an art. And just as
artistic creation implies the working of the critical faculty,
and, indeed, without it cannot be said to exist at all, so
Criticism is really creative in the highest sense of the word.
Criticism is, in fact, both creative and independent.

ERNEST.   Independent?

GILBERT.   Yes; independent. Criticism is no more to be judged
by any low standard of imitation or resemblance than is the
work of poet or sculptor. The critic occupies the same
relation to the work of art that he criticizes as the artist does
to the visible world of form and colour, or the unseen world
of passion and of thought. He does not even require for the
perfection of his art the finest materials. Anything will serve
his purpose. And just as out of the sordid and sentimental
amours of the silly wife of a small country doctor in the
squalid village of Yonville-l'Abbaye, near Rouen, Gustave
Flaubert was able to create a classic, and make a masterpiece
of style, so, from subjects of little or of no importance, such
as the pictures in this year's Royal Academy, or in any year's
Royal Academy for that matter, Mr Lewis Morris's poems,
M. Ohnet's novels, or the plays of Mr Henry Arthur Jones,
the true critic can, if it be his pleasure so to direct or waste his
faculty of contemplation, produce work that will be flawless
in beauty and instinct with intellectual subtlety. Why not?
Dulness is always an irresistible temptation for brilliancy, and
stupidity is the permanent *Bestia Trionfans* that calls wisdom
from its cave. To an artist so creative as the critic, what does
subject-matter signify? No more and no less than it does to the
novelist and the painter. Like them, he can find his motives
everywhere. Treatment is the test. There is nothing that has
not in it suggestion or challenge.

ERNEST.   But is Criticism really a creative art?

GILBERT.   Why should it not be? It works with materials, and
puts them into a form that is at once new and delightful.
What more can one say of poetry? Indeed, I would call
criticism a creation within a creation. For just as the great

artists, from Homer and Æschylus, down to Shakespeare and Keats, did not go directly to life for their subject-matter, but sought for it in myth, and legend, and ancient tale, so the critic deals with materials that others have, as it were, purified for him, and to which imaginative form and colour have been already added. Nay, more, I would say that the highest Criticism, being the purest form of personal impression, is in its way more creative than creation, as it has least reference to any standard external to itself, and is, in fact, its own reason for existing, and, as the Greeks would put it, in itself, and to itself, an end. Certainly, it is never trammelled by any shackles of verisimilitude. No ignoble considerations of probability, that cowardly concession to the tedious repetitions of domestic or public life, affect it ever. One may appeal from fiction unto fact. But from the soul there is no appeal.

ERNEST.   From the soul?

GILBERT.   Yes, from the soul. That is what the highest criticism really is, the record of one's own soul. It is more fascinating than history, as it is concerned simply with oneself. It is more delightful than philosophy, as its subject is concrete and not abstract, real and not vague. It is the only civilized form of autobiography, as it deals not with the events, but with the thoughts of one's life; not with life's physical accidents of deed or circumstance, but with the spiritual moods and imaginative passions of the mind. I am always amused by the silly vanity of those writers and artists of our day who seem to imagine that the primary function of the critic is to chatter about their second-rate work. The best that one can say of most modern creative art is that it is just a little less vulgar than reality, and so the critic, with his fine sense of distinction and sure instinct of delicate refinement, will prefer to look into the silver mirror or through the woven veil, and will turn his eyes away from the chaos and clamour of actual existence, though the mirror be tarnished and the veil be torn. His sole aim is to chronicle his own impressions. It is for him that pictures are painted, books written, and marble hewn into form.

ERNEST.   I seem to have heard another theory of Criticism.

GILBERT.   Yes: it has been said by one whose gracious memory
we all revere, and the music of whose pipe once lured
Proserpina from her Sicilian fields, and made those white
feet stir, and not in vain, the Cumnor cowslips, that the
proper aim of Criticism is to see the object as in itself it really
is. But this is a very serious error, and takes no cognizance of
Criticism's most perfect form, which is in its essence purely
subjective, and seeks to reveal its own secret and not the
secret of another. For the highest Criticism deals with art
not as expressive but as impressive purely.

ERNEST.   But is that really so?

GILBERT.   Of course it is. Who cares whether Mr Ruskin's
views on Turner are sound or not? What does it matter?
That mighty and majestic prose of his, so fervid and so
fiery-coloured in its noble eloquence, so rich in its elaborate
symphonic music, so sure and certain, at its best, in subtle
choice of word and epithet, is at least as great a work of art
as any of those wonderful sunsets that bleach or rot on their
corrupted canvases in England's Gallery; greater indeed, one
is apt to think at times, not merely because its equal beauty
is more enduring, but on account of the fuller variety of its
appeal, soul speaking to soul in those long-cadenced lines,
not through form and colour alone, though through these,
indeed, completely and without loss, but with intellectual
and emotional utterance, with lofty passion and with loftier
thought, with imaginative insight, and with poetic aim;
greater, I always think, even as Literature is the greater art.
Who, again, cares whether Mr Pater has put into the portrait
of Monna Lisa something that Lionardo never dreamed of?
The painter may have been merely the slave of an archaic
smile, as some have fancied, but whenever I pass into the
cool galleries of the Palace of the Louvre, and stand before
that strange figure 'set in its marble chair in that cirque of
fantastic rocks, as in some faint light under sea', I murmur
to myself, 'She is older than the rocks among which she sits;
like the vampire, she has been dead many times, and learned
the secrets of the grave; and has been a diver in deep seas,
and keeps their fallen day about her; and trafficked for strange
webs with Eastern merchants; and, as Leda, was the mother
of Helen of Troy, and, as St Anne, the mother of Mary; and

all this has been to her but as the sound of lyres and flutes,
and lives only in the delicacy with which it has moulded the
changing lineaments, and tinged the eyelids and the hands.'
And I say to my friend, 'The presence that thus so strangely
rose beside the waters is expressive of what in the ways of a
thousand years man had come to desire'; and he answers me,
'Hers is the head upon which all "the ends of the world are
come", and the eyelids are a little weary.'

And so the picture becomes more wonderful to us than it
really is, and reveals to us a secret of which, in truth, it knows
nothing, and the music of the mystical prose is as sweet in
our ears as was that flute-player's music that lent to the lips
of La Gioconda those subtle and poisonous curves. Do you
ask me what Lionardo would have said had any one told him
of this picture that 'all the thoughts and experience of the
world had etched and moulded there in that which they had
of power to refine and make expressive the outward form,
the animalism of Greece, the lust of Rome, the reverie of
the Middle Age with its spiritual ambition and imaginative
loves, the return of the Pagan world, the sins of the Borgias?'
He would probably have answered that he had contemplated
none of these things, but had concerned himself simply with
certain arrangements of lines and masses, and with new and
curious colour-harmonies of blue and green. And it is for
this very reason that the criticism which I have quoted
is criticism of the highest kind. It treats the work of art
simply as a starting-point for a new creation. It does not
confine itself – let us at least suppose so for the moment –
to discovering the real intention of the artist and accepting that
as final. And in this it is right, for the meaning of any
beautiful created thing is, at least, as much in the soul of
him who looks at it, as it was in his soul who wrought it.
Nay, it is rather the beholder who lends to the beautiful
thing its myriad meanings, and makes it marvellous for us,
and sets it in some new relation to the age, so that it becomes
a vital portion of our lives, and a symbol of what we pray
for, or perhaps of what, having prayed for, we fear that we
may receive. The longer I study, Ernest, the more clearly
I see that the beauty of the visible arts is, as the beauty of
music, impressive primarily, and that it may be marred, and

indeed often is so, by any excess of intellectual intention on the part of the artist. For when the work is finished it has, as it were, an independent life of its own, and may deliver a message far other than that which was put into its lips to say. Sometimes, when I listen to the overture to *Tannhäuser*, I seem indeed to see that comely knight treading delicately on the flower-strewn grass, and to hear the voice of Venus calling to him from the caverned hill. But at other times it speaks to me of a thousand different things, of myself, it may be, and my own life, or of the lives of others whom one has loved and grown weary of loving, or of the passions that man has known, or of the passions that man has not known, and so has sought for. To-night it may fill one with that ΕΡΩΣ ΤΩΝ ΑΔΥΝΑΤΩΝ, that *Amour de l'Impossible*, which falls like a madness on many who think they live securely and out of reach of harm, so that they sicken suddenly with the poison of unlimited desire, and, in the infinite pursuit of what they may not obtain, grow faint and swoon or stumble. To-morrow, like the music of which Aristotle and Plato tell us, the noble Dorian music of the Greek, it may perform the office of a physician, and give us an anodyne against pain, and heal the spirit that is wounded, and 'bring the soul into harmony with all right things'. And what is true about music is true about all the arts. Beauty has as many meanings as man has moods. Beauty is the symbol of symbols. Beauty reveals everything, because it expresses nothing. When it shows us itself, it shows us the whole fiery-coloured world.

ERNEST.   But is such work as you have talked about really criticism?

GILBERT.   It is the highest Criticism, for it criticizes not merely the individual work of art, but Beauty itself, and fills with wonder a form which the artist may have left void, or not understood, or understood incompletely.

ERNEST.   The highest Criticism, then, is more creative than creation, and the primary aim of the critic is to see the object as in itself it really is not; that is your theory, I believe?

GILBERT.   Yes, that is my theory. To the critic the work of art is simply a suggestion for a new work of his own, that need not necessarily bear any obvious resemblance to the thing it criticizes. The one characteristic of a beautiful form is that one can put into it whatever one wishes, and see in it whatever one chooses to see; and the Beauty, that gives to creation its universal and æsthetic element, makes the critic a creator in his turn, and whispers of a thousand different things which were not present in the mind of him who carved the statue or painted the panel or graved the gem.

It is sometimes said by those who understand neither the nature of the highest Criticism nor the charm of the highest Art, that the pictures that the critic loves most to write about are those that belong to the anecdotage of painting, and that deal with scenes taken out of literature or history. But this is not so. Indeed, pictures of this kind are far too intelligible. As a class, they rank with illustrations, and even considered from this point of view are failures, as they do not stir the imagination, but set definite bounds to it. For the domain of the painter is, as I suggested before, widely different from that of the poet. To the latter belongs life in its full and absolute entirety; not merely the beauty that men look at, but the beauty that men listen to also; not merely the momentary grace of form or the transient gladness of colour, but the whole sphere of feeling, the perfect cycle of thought. The painter is so far limited that it is only through the mask of the body that he can show us the mystery of the soul; only through conventional images that he can handle ideas; only through its physical equivalents that he can deal with psychology. And how inadequately does he do it then, asking us to accept the torn turban of the Moor for the noble rage of Othello, or a dotard in a storm for the wild madness of Lear! Yet it seems as if nothing could stop him. Most of our elderly English painters spend their wicked and wasted lives in poaching upon the domain of the poets, marring their motives by clumsy treatment, and striving to render, by visible form or colour, the marvel of what is invisible, the splendour of what is not seen. Their pictures are, as a natural consequence, insufferably tedious. They have degraded the invisible arts into the obvious arts, and the one thing not worth looking at is the obvious. I do not say that poet and painter may not treat of the same subject. They have always done so, and will always do so. But while the poet can be pictorial or not, as he chooses, the painter must be pictorial always. For a painter is limited, not to what he sees in nature, but to what upon canvas may be seen.

And so, my dear Ernest, pictures of this kind will not really fascinate the critic. He will turn from them to such works as make him brood and dream and fancy, to works that possess the subtle quality of suggestion, and seem to tell one that even from them there is an escape into a wider world. It is sometimes said that the tragedy of an artist's life is that he cannot realize his ideal. But the true tragedy that dogs the steps of most artists is that they realize their ideal too absolutely. For, when the ideal is realized, it is robbed of its wonder and its mystery, and becomes simply a new starting-point for an ideal that is other than itself. This is the reason why music is the perfect type of art. Music can never reveal its ultimate secret. This, also, is the explanation of the value of limitations in art. The sculptor gladly surrenders imitative colour, and the painter the actual dimensions of form, because by such renunciations they are able to avoid too definite a presentation of the Real, which would be mere imitation, and too definite a realization of the Ideal, which would be too purely intellectual. It is through its very incompleteness that Art becomes complete in beauty, and so addresses itself, not to the faculty of recognition nor to the faculty of reason, but to the æsthetic sense alone, which, while accepting both reason and recognition as stages of apprehension, subordinates them both to a pure synthetic impression of the work of art as a whole, and, taking whatever alien emotional elements the work may possess, uses their very complexity as a means by which a richer unity may be added to the ultimate impression itself. You see, then, how it is that the æsthetic critic rejects those obvious modes of art that have but one message to deliver, and having delivered it become dumb and sterile, and seeks rather for such modes as suggest reverie and mood, and by their imaginative beauty make all interpretations true, and no interpretation final. Some resemblance, no doubt, the creative work of the critic will have to the work that has stirred him to creation, but it will be such resemblance as exists, not between Nature and the mirror that the painter of landscape or figure may be supposed to hold up to her,

125

but between Nature and the work of the decorative artist. Just as on the flowerless carpets of Persia, tulip and rose blossom indeed and are lovely to look on, though they are not reproduced in visible shape or line; just as the pearl and purple of the sea-shell is echoed in the church of St Mark at Venice; just as the vaulted ceiling of the wondrous chapel at Ravenna is made gorgeous by the gold and green and sapphire of the peacock's tail, though the birds of Juno fly not across it; so the critic reproduces the work that he criticizes in a mode that is never imitative, and part of whose charm may really consist in the rejection of resemblance, and shows us in this way not merely the meaning but also the mystery of Beauty, and, by transforming each art into literature, solves once for all the problem of Art's unity.

But I see it is time for supper. After we have discussed some Chambertin and a few ortolans, we will pass on to the question of the critic considered in the light of the interpreter.

ERNEST.   Ah! you admit, then, that the critic may occasionally be allowed to see the object as in itself it really is.

GILBERT.   I am not quite sure. Perhaps I may admit it after supper. There is a subtle influence in supper.

PART II

A DIALOGUE: Persons: the same. Scene: the same.

ERNEST.   The ortolans were delightful, and the Chambertin perfect, and now let us return to the point at issue.

GILBERT.   Ah! don't let us do that. Conversation should touch everything, but should concentrate itself on nothing. Let us talk about *Moral Indignation, its Cause and Cure*, a subject on which I think of writing: or about *The Survival of Thersites*, as shown by the English comic papers; or about any topic that may turn up.

ERNEST.   No; I want to discuss the critic and criticism. You have told me that the highest criticism deals with art, not as expressive, but as impressive purely, and is consequently both creative and independent, is in fact an art by itself, occupying the same relation to creative work that creative work does to the visible world of form and colour, or the unseen world of passion and of thought. Well, now, tell me, will not the critic be sometimes a real interpreter?

GILBERT.   Yes; the critic will be an interpreter, if he chooses. He can pass from his synthetic impression of the work of art as a whole, to an analysis or exposition of the work itself, and in this lower sphere, as I hold it to be, there are many delightful things to be said and done. Yet his object will not always be to explain the work of art. He may seek rather to deepen its mystery, to raise round it, and round its maker, that mist of wonder which is dear to both gods and worshippers alike. Ordinary people are 'terribly at ease in Zion'. They propose to walk arm in arm with the poets, and have a glib ignorant way of saying 'Why should we read what is written about Shakespeare and Milton? We can read the plays and the poems. That is enough.' But an appreciation of Milton is, as the late Rector of Lincoln remarked once, the reward of consummate scholarship. And he who desires to understand Shakespeare truly must understand the relations in which Shakespeare stood to the Renaissance and the Reformation, to the age of Elizabeth and the age of James; he must be familiar with the history of the struggle for supremacy between the old classical forms and the new spirit of romance, between the school of Sidney, and Daniel, and Jonson, and the school of Marlowe and Marlowe's greater son; he must know the materials that were at Shakespeare's disposal, and the method in which he used them, and the conditions of theatric presentation in the sixteenth and seventeenth century, their limitations and their opportunities for freedom, and the literary criticism of Shakespeare's day, its aims and modes and canons; he must study the English language in its progress, and blank or rhymed verse in its various developments; he must study the Greek drama, and the connection between the art of the creator of the Agamemnon and the art of the creator of Macbeth; in a word, he must be able to bind Elizabethan London to the Athens of Pericles, and to learn Shakespeare's true position in the history of European drama and the drama of the world. The critic will certainly be an interpreter, but he will not treat Art as a riddling Sphinx, whose shallow secret may be guessed and revealed by one whose feet are

wounded and who knows not his name. Rather, he will
look upon Art as a goddess whose mystery it is his province
to intensify, and whose majesty his privilege to make more
marvellous in the eyes of men.

And here, Ernest, this strange thing happens. The critic will
indeed be an interpreter, but he will not be an interpreter
in the sense of one who simply repeats in another form a
message that has been put into his lips to say. For, just as
it is only by contact with the art of foreign nations that the
art of a country gains that individual and separate life that
we call nationality, so, by curious inversion, it is only by
intensifying his own personality that the critic can interpret
the personality and work of others, and the more strongly
this personality enters into the interpretation the more
real the interpretation becomes, the more satisfying, the
more convincing, and the more true.

ERNEST.   I would have said that personality would have been a
disturbing element.

GILBERT.   No; it is an element of revelation. If you wish to
understand others you must intensify your own individualism.

ERNEST.   What, then, is the result?

GILBERT.   I will tell you, and perhaps I can tell you best by
definite example. It seems to me that, while the literary
critic stands of course first, as having the wider range, and
larger vision, and nobler material, each of the arts has a critic,
as it were, assigned to it. The actor is a critic of the drama.
He shows the poet's work under new conditions, and by a
method special to himself. He takes the written word, and
action, gesture and voice become the media of revelation.
The singer or the player on lute and viol, is the critic of
music. The etcher of a picture robs the painting of its fair
colours, but shows us by the use of a new material its true
colour-quality, its tones and values, and the relations of its
masses, and so is, in his way, a critic of it, for the critic is he
who exhibits to us a work of art in a form different from that
of the work itself, and the employment of a new material is
a critical as well as a creative element. Sculpture, too, has
its critic, who may be either the carver of a gem, as he
was in Greek days, or some painter like Mantegna, who
sought to reproduce on canvas the beauty of plastic line

and the symphonic dignity of processional bas-relief. And in the case of all these creative critics of art it is evident that personality is an absolute essential for any real interpretation. When Rubinstein plays to us the *Sonata Appassionata* of Beethoven, he gives us not merely Beethoven, but also himself, and so gives us Beethoven absolutely – Beethoven re-interpreted through a rich artistic nature, and made vivid and wonderful to us by a new and intense personality. When a great actor plays Shakespeare we have the same experience. His own individuality becomes a vital part of the interpretation. People sometimes say that actors give us their own Hamlets, and not Shakespeare's; and this fallacy – for it is a fallacy – is, I regret to say, repeated by that charming and graceful writer who has lately deserted the turmoil of literature for the peace of the House of Commons, I mean the author of *Obiter Dicta*. In point of fact, there is no such thing as Shakespeare's Hamlet. If Hamlet has something of the definiteness of a work of art, he has also all the obscurity that belongs to life. There are as many Hamlets as there are melancholies.

ERNEST.   As many Hamlets as there are melancholies?

GILBERT.   Yes: and as art springs from personality, so it is only to personality that it can be revealed, and from the meeting of the two comes right interpretative criticism.

ERNEST.   The critic, then, considered as the interpreter, will give no less than he receives, and lend as much as he borrows?

GILBERT.   He will be always showing us the work of art in some new relation to our age. He will always be reminding us that great works of art are living things – are, in fact, the only things that live. So much, indeed, will he feel this, that I am certain that, as civilization progresses and we become more highly organized, the elect spirits of each age, the critical and cultured spirits, will grow less and less interested in actual life, and *will seek to gain their impressions almost entirely from what Art has touched*. For Life is terribly deficient in form. Its catastrophes happen in the wrong way and to the wrong people. There is a grotesque horror about its comedies, and its tragedies seem to culminate in farce. One is always wounded when one approaches it. Things last either too long, or not long enough.

129

ERNEST.   Poor life! Poor human life! Are you not even touched
   by the tears that the Roman poet tells us are part of its
   essence.

GILBERT.   Too quickly touched by them, I fear. For when one
   looks back upon the life that was so vivid in its emotional
   intensity, and filled with such fervent moments of ecstasy or
   of joy, it all seems to be a dream and an illusion. What are
   the unreal things, but the passions that once burned one like
   fire? What are the incredible things, but the things that one
   has faithfully believed? What are the improbable things? The
   things that one has done oneself. No, Ernest; life cheats us
   with shadows, like a puppet-master. We ask it for pleasure.
   It gives it to us, with bitterness and disappointment in its
   train. We come across some noble grief that we think will
   lend the purple dignity of tragedy to our days, but it passes
   away from us, and things less noble take its place, and on some
   grey windy dawn, or odorous eve of silence and of silver, we
   find ourselves looking with callous wonder, or dull heart of
   stone, at the tress of gold-flecked hair that we had once so
   wildly worshipped and so madly kissed.

ERNEST.   Life then is a failure?

GILBERT.   From the artistic point of view, certainly. And the
   chief thing that makes life a failure from this artistic point of
   view is the thing that lends to life its sordid security, the fact
   that one can never repeat exactly the same emotion. How
   different it is in the world of Art! On a shelf of the bookcase
   behind you stands the *Divine Comedy*, and I know that, if
   I open it at a certain place, I shall be filled with a fierce
   hatred of some one who has never wronged me, or stirred
   by a great love for some one whom I shall never see. There
   is no mood or passion that Art cannot give us, and those
   of us who have discovered her secret can settle beforehand
   what our experiences are going to be. We can choose our day
   and select our hour. We can say to ourselves, 'To-morrow,
   at dawn, we shall walk with grave Virgil through the valley of
   the shadow of death', and lo! the dawn finds us in the obscure
   wood, and the Mantuan stands by our side. We pass through
   the gate of the legend fatal to hope, and with pity or with joy
   behold the horror of another world. The hypocrites go by,
   with their painted faces and their cowls of gilded lead. Out of

the ceaseless winds that drive them, the carnal look at us, and
we watch the heretic rending his flesh, and the glutton lashed
by the rain. We break the withered branches from the tree
in the grove of the Harpies, and each dull-hued poisonous
twig bleeds with red blood before us, and cries aloud with
bitter cries. Out of a horn of fire Odysseus speaks to us,
and when from his sepulchre of flame the great Ghibelline
rises, the pride that triumphs over the torture of that bed
becomes ours for a moment. Through the dim purple air fly
those who have stained the world with the beauty of their
sin, and in the pit of loathsome disease, dropsy-stricken and
swollen of body into the semblance of a monstrous lute, lies
Adamo di Brescia, the coiner of false coin. He bids us listen
to his misery; we stop, and with dry and gaping lips he tells
us how he dreams day and night of the brooks of clear water
that in cool dewy channels gush down the green Casentine
hills. Sinon, the false Greek of Troy, mocks at him. He smites
him in the face, and they wrangle. We are fascinated by their
shame, and loiter, till Virgil chides us and leads us away to that
city turreted by giants where great Nimrod blows his horn.
Terrible things are in store for us, and we go to meet them
in Dante's raiment and with Dante's heart. We traverse the
marshes of the Styx, and Argenti swims to the boat through
the slimy waves. He calls to us, and we reject him. When we
hear the voice of his agony we are glad, and Virgil praises
us for the bitterness of our scorn. We tread upon the cold
crystal of Cocytus, in which traitors stick like straws in glass.
Our foot strikes against the head of Bocca. He will not tell us
his name, and we tear the hair in handfuls from the screaming
skull. Alberigo prays us to break the ice upon his face that he
may weep a little. We pledge our word to him, and when
he has uttered his dolorous tale we deny the word that we
have spoken, and pass from him; such cruelty being courtesy
indeed, for who more base than he who has mercy for the
condemned of God? In the jaws of Lucifer we see the man
who sold Christ, and in the jaws of Lucifer the men who slew
Cæsar. We tremble, and come forth to re-behold the stars.

In the land of Purgation the air is freer, and the holy
mountain rises into the pure light of day. There is peace
for us, and for those who for a season abide in it there

is some peace also, though, pale from the poison of the
Maremma, Madonna Pia passes before us, and Ismene, with the
sorrow of earth still lingering about her, is there. Soul after
soul makes us share in some repentance or some joy. He
whom the mourning of his widow taught to drink the sweet
wormwood of pain, tells us of Nella praying in her lonely
bed, and we learn from the mouth of Buonconte how a
single tear may save a dying sinner from the fiend. Sordello,
that noble and disdainful Lombard, eyes us from afar like a
couchant lion. When he learns that Virgil is one of Mantua's
citizens, he falls upon his neck, and when he learns that he
is the singer of Rome he falls before his feet. In that valley
whose grass and flowers are fairer than cleft emerald and
Indian wood, and brighter than scarlet and silver, they are
singing who in the world were kings; but the lips of Rudolph
of Hapsburg do not move to the music of the others, and
Philip of France beats his breast and Henry of England sits
alone. On and on we go, climbing the marvellous stair, and
the stars become larger than their wont, and the song of
the kings grows faint, and at length we reach the seven
trees of gold and the garden of the Earthly Paradise. In a
griffin-drawn chariot appears one whose brows are bound
with olive, who is veiled in white, and mantled in green,
and robed in a vesture that is coloured like live fire. The
ancient flame wakes within us. Our blood quickens through
terrible pulses. We recognize her. It is Beatrice, the woman
we have worshipped. The ice congealed about our heart
melts. Wild tears of anguish break from us, and we bow our
forehead to the ground, for we know that we have sinned.
When we have done penance, and are purified, and have
drunk of the fountain of Lethe and bathed in the fountain
of Eunoe, the mistress of our soul raises us to the Paradise
of Heaven. Out of that eternal pearl, the moon, the face of
Piccarda Donati leans to us. Her beauty troubles us for a
moment, and when, like a thing that falls through water, she
passes away, we gaze after her with wistful eyes. The sweet
planet of Venus is full of lovers. Cunizza, the sister of Ezzelin,
the lady of Sordello's heart, is there, and Folco, the passionate
singer of Provence, who in sorrow for Azalais forsook the
world, and the Canaanitish harlot whose soul was the first

that Christ redeemed. Joachim of Flora stands in the sun, and, in the sun, Aquinas recounts the story of St Francis and Bonaventure the story of St Dominic. Through the burning rubies of Mars, Cacciaguida approaches. He tells us of the arrow that is shot from the bow of exile, and how salt tastes the bread of another, and how steep are the stairs in the house of a stranger. In Saturn the soul sings not, and even she who guides us dare not smile. On a ladder of gold the flames rise and fall. At last, we see the pageant of the Mystical Rose. Beatrice fixes her eyes upon the face of God to turn them not again. The beatific vision is granted to us; we know the Love that moves the sun and all the stars.

Yes, we can put the earth back six hundred courses and make ourselves one with the great Florentine, kneel at the same altar with him, and share his rapture and his scorn. And if we grow tired of an antique time, and desire to realize our own age in all its weariness and sin, are there not books that can make us live more in one single hour than life can make us live in a score of shameful years? Close to your hand lies a little volume, bound in some Nile-green skin that has been powdered with gilded nenuphars and smoothed with hard ivory. It is the book that Gautier loved, it is Baudelaire's masterpiece. Open it at that sad madrigal that begins

'Que m'importe que tu sois sage?
Sois belle! et sois triste!'

and you will find yourself worshipping sorrow as you have never worshipped joy. Pass on to the poem on the man who tortures himself, let its subtle music steal into your brain and colour your thoughts, and you will become for a moment what he was who wrote it; nay, not for a moment only, but for many barren moonlit nights and sunless sterile days will a despair that is not your own make its dwelling within you, and the misery of another gnaw your heart away. Read the whole book, suffer it to tell even one of its secrets to your soul, and your soul will grow eager to know more, and will feed upon poisonous honey, and seek to repent of strange crimes of which it is guiltless, and to make atonement for terrible pleasures that it has never known. And then, when you are tired of these flowers of evil, turn to the flowers that grow in the garden of Perdita, and in their dew-drenched chalices cool your fevered brow, and let their loveliness heal and restore your soul; or wake from his forgotten tomb the sweet Syrian, Meleager, and bid the lover of Heliodore make you music, for he too has flowers in his song, red pomegranate blossoms, and irises that smell of myrrh, ringed daffodils and dark blue hyacinths, and marjoram and crinkled ox-eyes. Dear to him was the perfume of the bean-field at evening, and dear to him the odorous eared-spikenard that grew on the Syrian hills, and the fresh green thyme, the wine-cup's charm. The feet of his love as she walked in the garden were like lilies set upon lilies. Softer than sleep-laden poppy petals were her lips, softer than violets and as scented. The flame-like crocus sprang from the grass to look at her. For her the slim narcissus stored the cool rain; and for her the anemones forgot the Sicilian winds that wooed them. And neither crocus, nor anemone, nor narcissus was as fair as she was.

It is a strange thing, this transference of emotion. We sicken with the same maladies as the poets, and the singer lends us his pain. Dead lips have their message for us, and hearts that have fallen to dust can communicate their joy. We run to kiss the bleeding mouth of Fantine, and we follow Manon Lescaut over the whole world. Ours is the love-madness of the Tyrian, and the terror of Orestes is ours also. There is no passion that we cannot feel, no pleasure that we may not gratify, and we can choose the time of our initiation and the time of our freedom also. Life! Life! Don't let us go to life for our fulfilment or our experience. It is a thing narrowed by circumstances, incoherent in its utterance, and without that fine correspondence of form and spirit which is the only thing that can satisfy the artistic and critical temperament. It makes us pay too high a price for its wares, and we purchase the meanest of its secrets at a cost that is monstrous and infinite.

ERNEST.   Must we go, then, to Art for everything?

GILBERT.   For everything. Because Art does not hurt us. The tears that we shed at a play are a type of the exquisite sterile emotions that it is the function of Art to awaken. We weep, but we are not wounded. We grieve, but our grief is not bitter. In the actual life of man, sorrow, as Spinoza says somewhere, is a passage to a lesser perfection. But the sorrow with which Art fills us both purifies and initiates, if I may quote once more from the great art-critic of the Greeks. It is through Art, and through Art only, that we can realize our perfection; through Art, and through Art only, that we can shield ourselves from the sordid perils of actual existence. This results not merely from the fact that nothing that one can imagine is worth doing, and that one can imagine everything, but from the subtle law that emotional forces, like the forces of the physical sphere, are limited in extent and energy. One can feel so much, and no more. And how can it matter with what pleasure life tries to tempt one, or with what pain it seeks to maim and mar one's soul, if in the spectacle of the lives of those who have never existed one has found the true secret of joy, and wept away one's tears over their deaths who, like Cordelia and the daughter of Brabantio, can never die?

ERNEST.   Stop a moment. It seems to me that in everything that you have said there is something radically immoral.

GILBERT.   All art is immoral.

ERNEST.   All art?

GILBERT.   Yes. For emotion for the sake of emotion is the aim of art, and emotion for the sake of action is the aim of life, and of that practical organization of life that we call society. Society, which is the beginning and basis of morals, exists simply for the concentration of human energy, and in order to ensure its own continuance and healthy stability it demands, and no doubt rightly demands, of each of its citizens that he should contribute some form of productive labour to the common weal, and toil and travail that the day's work may be done. Society often forgives the criminal; it never forgives the dreamer. The beautiful sterile emotions that art excites in us are hateful in its eyes, and so completely are people dominated by the tyranny of this dreadful social ideal that they are always coming shamelessly up to one at Private Views and other places that are open to the general public, and saying in a loud stentorian voice, 'What are you doing?' whereas 'What are you thinking?' is the only question that any single civilized being should ever be allowed to whisper to another. They mean well, no doubt, these honest beaming folk. Perhaps that is the reason why they are so excessively tedious. But some one should teach them that while, in the opinion of society, Contemplation is the gravest sin of which any citizen can be guilty, in the opinion of the highest culture it is the proper occupation of man.

ERNEST.   Contemplation?

GILBERT.   Contemplation. I said to you some time ago that it was far more difficult to talk about a thing than to do it. Let me say to you now that to do nothing at all is the most difficult thing in the world, the most difficult and the most intellectual. To Plato, with his passion for wisdom, this was the noblest form of energy. To Aristotle, with his passion for knowledge, this was the noblest form of energy also. It was to this that the passion for holiness led the saint and the mystic of mediaeval days.

ERNEST.   We exist, then, to do nothing?

GILBERT.   It is to do nothing that the elect exist. Action is limited and relative. Unlimited and absolute is the vision of him who sits at ease and watches, who walks in loneliness and dreams. But we who are born at the close of this wonderful age are at once too cultured and too critical, too intellectually subtle and too curious of exquisite pleasures, to accept any speculations about life in exchange for life itself. To us the *città divina* is colourless, and the *fruitio Dei* without meaning. Metaphysics do not satisfy our temperaments, and religious ecstasy is out of date. The world through which the Academic philosopher becomes 'the spectator of all time and of all existence' is not really an ideal world, but simply a world of abstract ideas. When we enter it, we starve amidst the chill mathematics of thought. The courts of the city of God are not open to us now. Its gates are guarded by Ignorance, and to pass them we have to surrender all that in our nature is most divine. It is enough that our fathers believed. They have exhausted the faith-faculty of the species. Their legacy to us is the scepticism of which they were afraid. Had they put it into words, it might not live within us as thought. No, Ernest, no. We cannot go back to the saint. There is far more to be learned from the sinner. We cannot go back to the philosopher, and the mystic leads us astray. Who, as Mr Pater suggests somewhere, would exchange the curve of a single rose-leaf for that formless intangible Being which Plato rates so high? What to us is the Illumination of Philo, the Abyss of Eckhart, the Vision of Böhme, the monstrous Heaven itself that was revealed to Swedenborg's blinded eyes? Such things are less than the yellow trumpet of one daffodil of the field, far less than the meanest of the visible arts; for, just as Nature is matter struggling into mind, so Art is mind expressing itself under the conditions of matter, and thus, even in the lowliest of her manifestations, she speaks to both sense and soul alike. To the aesthetic temperament the vague is always repellent. The Greeks were a nation of artists, because they were spared the sense of the infinite. Like Aristotle, like Goethe after he had read Kant, we desire the concrete, and nothing but the concrete can satisfy us.

ERNEST.   What then do you propose?

GILBERT.   It seems to me that with the development of the critical spirit we shall be able to realize, not merely our own lives, but the collective life of the race, and so to make ourselves absolutely modern, in the true meaning of the word modernity. For he to whom the present is the only thing that is present, knows nothing of the age in which he lives. To realize the nineteenth century, one must realize every century that has preceded it and that has contributed to its making. To know anything about oneself one must know all about others. There must be no mood with which one cannot sympathize, no dead mode of life that one cannot make alive. Is this impossible? I think not. By revealing to us the absolute mechanism of all action, and so freeing us from the self-imposed and trammelling burden of moral responsibility, the scientific principle of Heredity has become, as it were, the warrant for the contemplative life. It has shown us that we are never less free than when we try to act. It has hemmed us round with the nets of the hunter, and written upon the wall the prophecy of our doom. We may not watch it, for it is within us. We may not see it, save in a mirror that mirrors the soul. It is Nemesis without her mask. It is the last of the Fates, and the most terrible. It is the only one of the Gods whose real name we know.

And yet, while in the sphere of practical and external life it has robbed energy of its freedom and activity of its choice, in the subjective sphere, where the soul is at work, it comes to us, this terrible shadow, with many gifts in its hands, gifts of strange temperaments and subtle susceptibilities, gifts of wild ardours and chill moods of indifference, complex multiform gifts of thoughts that are at variance with each other, and passions that war against themselves. And so, it is not our own life that we live, but the lives of the dead, and the soul that dwells within us is no single spiritual entity, making us personal and individual, created for our service, and entering into us for our joy. It is something that has dwelt in fearful places, and in ancient sepulchres has made its abode. It is sick with many maladies, and has memories of curious sins. It is wiser than we are, and its wisdom is bitter. It fills us with impossible desires, and makes us follow what we know we cannot gain. One thing, however, Ernest, it can do for us. It can lead us away from surroundings whose beauty is dimmed to us by the mist of familiarity, or whose ignoble ugliness and sordid claims are marring the perfection of our development. It can help us to leave the age in which we were born, and to pass into other ages, and find ourselves not exiled from their air. It can teach us how to escape from our experience, and to realize the experiences of those who are greater than we are. The pain of Leopardi crying out against life becomes our pain. Theocritus blows on his pipe, and we laugh with the lips of nymph and shepherd. In the wolfskin of Pierre Vidal we flee before the hounds, and in the armour of Lancelot we ride from the bower of the Queen. We have whispered the secret of our love beneath the cowl of Abelard, and in the stained raiment of Villon have put our shame into song. We can see the dawn through Shelley's eyes, and when we wander with Endymion the Moon grows amorous of our youth. Ours is the anguish of Atys, and ours the weak rage and noble sorrows of the Dane. Do you think that it is the imagination that enables us to live these countless lives? Yes: it is the imagination; and the imagination is the result of heredity. It is simply concentrated race-experience.

ERNEST.   But where in this is the function of the critical spirit?

GILBERT.   The culture that this transmission of racial experiences makes possible can be made perfect by the critical spirit alone, and indeed may be said to be one with it. For who is the true critic but he who bears within himself the dreams, and ideas, and feelings of myriad generations, and to whom no form of thought is alien, no emotional impulse obscure? And who the true man of culture, if not he who by fine scholarship and fastidious rejection has made instinct self-conscious and intelligent, and can separate the work that has distinction from the work that has it not, and so by contact and comparison makes himself master of the secrets of style and school, and understands their meanings, and listens to their voices, and develops that spirit of disinterested curiosity which is the real root, as it is the real flower, of the intellectual life, and thus attains to intellectual clarity, and, having learned 'the best that is known and thought in the world', lives – it is not fanciful to say so – with those who are the Immortals.

Yes, Ernest: the contemplative life, the life that has for its aim not *doing* but *being*, and not *being* merely, but *becoming* – that is what the critical spirit can give us. The gods live thus: either brooding over their own perfection, as Aristotle tells us, or, as Epicurus fancied, watching with the calm eyes of the spectator the tragi-comedy of the world that they have made. We, too, might live like them, and set ourselves to witness with appropriate emotions the varied scenes that man and nature afford. We might make ourselves spiritual by detaching ourselves from action, and become perfect by the rejection of energy. It has often seemed to me that Browning felt something of this. Shakespeare hurls Hamlet into active life, and makes him realize his mission by effort. Browning might have given us a Hamlet who would have realized his mission by thought. Incident and event were to him unreal or unmeaning. He made the soul the protagonist of life's tragedy, and looked on action as the one undramatic element of a play. To us, at any rate, the ΒΙΟΣ ΘΕΩΡΗΤΙΚΟΣ is the true ideal. From the high tower of Thought we can look out at the world. Calm, and self-centred, and complete, the aesthetic critic contemplates life, and no arrow drawn at a venture can pierce between the joints of his harness. He at least is safe. He has discovered how to live.

Is such a mode of life immoral? Yes: all the arts are immoral, except those baser forms of sensual or didactic art that seek to excite to action of evil or of good. For action of every kind belongs to the sphere of ethics. The aim of art is simply to create a mood. Is such a mode of life unpractical? Ah! it is not so easy to be unpractical as the ignorant Philistine imagines. It were well for England if it were so. There is no country in the world so much in need of unpractical people as this country of ours. With us, Thought is degraded by its constant association with practice. Who that moves in the stress and turmoil of actual existence, noisy politician, or brawling social reformer, or poor narrow-minded priest blinded by the sufferings of that unimportant section of the community among whom he has cast his lot, can seriously claim to be able to form a disinterested intellectual judgement about any one thing? Each of the professions means a prejudice. The necessity for a career forces every one to take sides. We live in the age of the overworked, and the under-educated; the age in which people are so industrious that they become absolutely stupid. And, harsh though it may sound, I cannot help saying that such people deserve their doom. The sure way of knowing nothing about life is to try to make oneself useful.

ERNEST.   A charming doctrine, Gilbert.

GILBERT.   I am not sure about that, but it has at least the minor merit of being true. That the desire to do good to others produces a plentiful crop of prigs is the least of the evils of which it is the cause. The prig is a very interesting psychological study, and though of all poses a moral pose is the most offensive, still to have a pose at all is something. It is a formal recognition of the importance of treating life from a definite and reasoned standpoint. That Humanitarian Sympathy wars against Nature, by securing the survival of the failure, may make the man of science loathe its facile virtues. The political economist may cry out against it for putting the improvident on the same level as the provident, and so robbing life of the strongest, because most sordid, incentive to industry. But, in the eyes of the thinker, the real harm that emotional sympathy does is that it limits knowledge, and so prevents us from solving any single social problem. We are trying at present to stave off the coming crisis, the coming revolution as my friends the Fabianists call it, by means of doles and alms. Well, when the revolution or crisis arrives, we shall be powerless, because we shall know nothing. And so, Ernest, let us not be deceived. England will never be civilized till she has added Utopia to her dominions. There is more than one of her colonies that she might with advantage surrender for so fair a land. What we want are unpractical people who see beyond the moment, and think beyond the day. Those who try to lead the people can only do so by following the mob. It is through the voice of one crying in the wilderness that the ways of the gods must be prepared.

But perhaps you think that in beholding for the mere joy of beholding, and contemplating for the sake of contemplation, there is something that is egotistic. If you think so, do not say so. It takes a thoroughly selfish age, like our own, to deify self-sacrifice. It takes a thoroughly grasping age, such as that in which we live, to set above the fine intellectual virtues, those shallow and emotional virtues that are an immediate practical benefit to itself. They miss their aim, too, these philanthropists and sentimentalists of our day, who are always chattering to one about one's duty to one's neighbour. For the development of the race depends on the development of the individual, and where self-culture has ceased to be the ideal, the intellectual standard is instantly lowered, and, often, ultimately lost. If you meet at dinner a man who has spent his life in educating himself – a rare type in our time, I admit, but still one occasionally to be met with – you rise from table richer, and conscious that a high ideal has for a moment touched and sanctified your days. But oh! my dear Ernest, to sit next a man who has spent his life in trying to educate others! What a dreadful experience that is! How appalling is that ignorance which is the inevitable result of the fatal habit of imparting opinions! How limited in range the creature's mind proves to be! How it wearies us, and must weary himself, with its endless repetitions and sickly reiteration! How lacking it is in any element of intellectual growth! In what a vicious circle it always moves!

141

ERNEST.   You speak with strange feeling, Gilbert. Have you
    had this dreadful experience, as you call it, lately?

GILBERT.   Few of us escape it. People say that the schoolmaster
    is abroad. I wish to goodness he were. But the type of which,
    after all, he is only one, and certainly the least important,
    of the representatives, seems to me to be really dominating
    our lives; and just as the philanthropist is the nuisance of the
    ethical sphere, so the nuisance of the intellectual sphere is
    the man who is so occupied in trying to educate others, that
    he has never had any time to educate himself. No, Ernest,
    self–culture is the true ideal of man. Goethe saw it, and the
    immediate debt that we owe to Goethe is greater than the
    debt we owe to any man since Greek days. The Greeks saw
    it, and have left us, as their legacy to modern thought, the
    conception of the contemplative life as well as the critical
    method by which alone can that life be truly realized. It was
    the one thing that made the Renaissance great, and gave us
    Humanism. It is the one thing that could make our own
    age great also; for the real weakness of England lies, not
    in incomplete armaments or unfortified coasts, not in the
    poverty that creeps through sunless lanes, or the drunkenness
    that brawls in loathsome courts, but simply in the fact that
    her ideals are emotional and not intellectual.

        I do not deny that the intellectual ideal is difficult of
    attainment, still less that it is, and perhaps will be for years
    to come, unpopular with the crowd. It is so easy for people
    to have sympathy with suffering. It is so difficult for them to
    have sympathy with thought. Indeed, so little do ordinary
    people understand what thought really is, that they seem to
    imagine that, when they have said that a theory is dangerous,
    they have pronounced its condemnation, whereas it is only
    such theories that have any true intellectual value. An
    idea that is not dangerous is unworthy of being called an
    idea at all.

ERNEST.   Gilbert, you bewilder me. You have told me that all
    art is, in its essence, immoral. Are you going to tell me now
    that all thought is, in its essence, dangerous?

GILBERT.   Yes, in the practical sphere it is so. The security
    of society lies in custom and unconscious instinct, and the
    basis of the stability of society, as a healthy organism, is the

complete absence of any intelligence amongst its members. The great majority of people being fully aware of this, rank themselves naturally on the side of that splendid system that elevates them to the dignity of machines, and rage so wildly against the intrusion of the intellectual faculty into any question that concerns life, that one is tempted to define man as a rational animal who always loses his temper when he is called upon to act in accordance with the dictates of reason. But let us turn from the practical sphere, and say no more about the wicked philanthropists, who, indeed, may well be left to the mercy of the almond-eyed sage of the Yellow River, Chuang Tsŭ the wise, who has proved that such well-meaning and offensive busybodies have destroyed the simple and spontaneous virtue that there is in man. They are a wearisome topic, and I am anxious to get back to the sphere in which criticism is free.

ERNEST.   The sphere of the intellect?

GILBERT.   Yes. You remember that I spoke of the critic as being in his own way as creative as the artist, whose work, indeed, may be merely of value in so far as it gives to the critic a suggestion for some new mood of thought and feeling which he can realize with equal, or perhaps greater, distinction of form, and, through the use of a fresh medium of expression, make differently beautiful and more perfect. Well, you seemed to be a little sceptical about the theory. But perhaps I wronged you?

ERNEST.   I am not really sceptical about it, but I must admit that I feel very strongly that such work as you describe the critic producing – and creative such work must undoubtedly be admitted to be – is, of necessity, purely subjective, whereas the greatest work is objective always, objective and impersonal.

GILBERT.   The difference between objective and subjective work is one of external form merely. It is accidental, not essential. All artistic creation is absolutely subjective. The very landscape that Corot looked at was, as he said himself, but a mood of his own mind; and those great figures of Greek or English drama that seem to us to possess an actual existence of their own, apart from the poets who shaped and fashioned them, are, in their ultimate analysis, simply the

143

poets themselves, not as they thought they were, but as they thought they were not; and by such thinking came in strange manner, though but for a moment, really so to be. For out of ourselves we can never pass, nor can there be in creation what in the creator was not. Nay, I would say that the more objective a creation appears to be, the more subjective it really is. Shakespeare might have met Rosencrantz and Guildenstern in the white streets of London, or seen the serving-men of rival houses bite their thumbs at each other in the open square; but Hamlet came out of his soul, and Romeo out of his passion. They were elements of his nature to which he gave visible form, impulses that stirred so strongly within him that he had, as it were perforce, to suffer them to realize their energy, not on the lower plane of actual life, where they would have been trammelled and constrained and so made imperfect, but on that imaginative plane of art where Love can indeed find in Death its rich fulfilment, where one can stab the eavesdropper behind the arras, and wrestle in a new-made grave, and make a guilty king drink his own hurt, and see one's father's spirit, beneath the glimpses of the moon, stalking in complete steel from misty wall to wall. Action being limited would have left Shakespeare unsatisfied and unexpressed; and, just as it is because he did nothing that he has been able to achieve everything, so it is because he never speaks to us of himself in his plays that his plays reveal him to us absolutely, and show us his true nature and temperament far more completely than do those strange and exquisite sonnets, even, in which he bares to crystal eyes the secret closet of his heart. Yes, the objective form is the most subjective in matter. Man is least himself when he talks in his own person. Give him a mask, and he will tell you the truth.

ERNEST. The critic, then, being limited to the subjective form, will necessarily be less able fully to express himself than the artist, who has always at his disposal the forms that are impersonal and objective.

GILBERT. Not necessarily, and certainly not at all if he recognizes that each mode of criticism is, in its highest development, simply a mood, and that we are never more true to ourselves than when we are inconsistent. The æsthetic critic, constant only to the principle of beauty in all things, will ever be looking for fresh impressions, winning from the various schools the secret of their charm, bowing, it may be, before foreign altars, or smiling, if it be his fancy, at strange new gods. What other people call one's past has, no doubt, everything to do with them, but has absolutely nothing to do with oneself. The man who regards his past is a man who deserves to have no future to look forward to. When one has found expression for a mood, one has done with it. You laugh; but believe me it is so. Yesterday it was Realism that charmed one. One gained from it that *nouveau frisson* which it was its aim to produce. One analysed it, explained it, and wearied of it. At sunset came the *Luministe* in painting, and the *Symboliste* in poetry, and the spirit of mediaevalism, that spirit which belongs not to time but to temperament, woke suddenly in wounded Russia, and stirred us for a moment by the terrible fascination of pain. To-day the cry is for Romance, and already the leaves are tremulous in the valley, and on the purple hill-tops walks Beauty with slim gilded feet. The old modes of creation linger, of course. The artists reproduce either themselves or each other, with wearisome iteration. But Criticism is always moving on, and the critic is always developing.

Nor, again, is the critic really limited to the subjective form of expression. The method of the drama is his, as well as the method of the epos. He may use dialogue, as he did who set Milton talking to Marvel on the nature of comedy and tragedy, and made Sidney and Lord Brooke discourse on letters beneath the Penshurst oaks; or adopt narration, as Mr Pater is fond of doing, each of whose Imaginary Portraits – is not that the title of the book? – presents to us, under the fanciful guise of fiction, some fine and exquisite piece of criticism, one on the painter Watteau, another on the philosophy of Spinoza, a third on the Pagan elements of the early Renaissance, and the last, and in some respects the most suggestive, on the source of that Aufklärung, that enlightening which dawned on Germany in the last century, and to which our own culture owes so great a debt. Dialogue, certainly, that wonderful literary form which, from Plato to Lucian, and from Lucian to Giordano

Bruno, and from Bruno to that grand old Pagan in whom Carlyle took such delight, the creative critics of the world have always employed, can never lose for the thinker its attraction as a mode of expression. By its means he can both reveal and conceal himself, and give form to every fancy, and reality to every mood. By its means he can exhibit the object from each point of view, and show it to us in the round, as a sculptor shows us things gaining in this manner all the richness and reality of effect that comes from those side issues that are suddenly suggested by the central idea in its progress, and really illumine the idea more completely, or from those felicitous after-thoughts that give a fuller completeness to the central scheme, and yet convey something of the delicate charm of chance.

ERNEST. By its means, too, he can invent an imaginary antagonist, and convert him when he chooses by some absurdly sophistical argument.

GILBERT. Ah! it is so easy to convert others. It is so difficult to convert oneself. To arrive at what one really believes, one must speak through lips different from one's own. To know the truth one must imagine myriads of falsehoods. For what is Truth? In matters of religion, it is simply the opinion that has survived. In matters of science, it is the ultimate sensation. In matters of art, it is one's last mood. And you see now, Ernest, that the critic has at his disposal as many objective forms of expression as the artist has. Ruskin put his criticism into imaginative prose, and is superb in his changes and contradictions; and Browning put his into blank verse, and made painter and poet yield us their secret; and M. Renan uses dialogue, and Mr Pater fiction, and Rossetti translated into sonnet-music the colour of Giorgione and the design of Ingres, and his own design and colour also, feeling, with the instinct of one who had many modes of utterance, that the ultimate art is literature, and the finest and fullest medium that of words.

ERNEST. Well, now that you have settled that the critic has at his disposal all objective forms, I wish you would tell me what are the qualities that should characterize the true critic.

GILBERT. What would you say they were?

ERNEST.   Well, I should say that a critic should above all
things be fair.

GILBERT.   Ah! not fair. A critic cannot be fair in the ordinary
sense of the word. It is only about things that do not interest
one that one can give a really unbiassed opinion, which is
no doubt the reason why an unbiassed opinion is always
absolutely valueless. The man who sees both sides of a
question is a man who sees absolutely nothing at all. Art
is a passion, and, in matters of art, Thought is inevitably
coloured by emotion, and so is fluid rather than fixed,
and, depending upon fine moods and exquisite moments,
cannot be narrowed into the rigidity of a scientific formula
or a theological dogma. It is to the soul that Art speaks, and
the soul may be made the prisoner of the mind as well as of
the body. One should, of course, have no prejudices; but, as
a great Frenchman remarked a hundred years ago, it is one's
business in such matters to have preferences, and when one
has preferences one ceases to be fair. It is only an auctioneer
who can equally and impartially admire all schools of Art.
No: fairness is not one of the qualities of the true critic. It
is not even a condition of criticism. Each form of Art with
which we come in contact dominates us for the moment
to the exclusion of every other form. We must surrender
ourselves absolutely to the work in question, whatever it
may be, if we wish to gain its secret. For the time, we must
think of nothing else, can think of nothing else, indeed.

ERNEST.   The true critic will be rational, at any rate, will he
not?

GILBERT.   Rational? There are two ways of disliking art,
Ernest. One is to dislike it. The other, to like it rationally.
For Art, as Plato saw, and not without regret, creates in
listener and spectator a form of divine madness. It does not
spring from inspiration, but it makes others inspired. Reason
is not the faculty to which it appeals. If one loves Art at all,
one must love it beyond all other things in the world, and
against such love, the reason, if one listened to it, would cry
out. There is nothing sane about the worship of beauty. It
is too splendid to be sane. Those of whose lives it forms the
dominant note will always seem to the world to be pure
visionaries.

ERNEST.   Well, at least, the critic will be sincere.

GILBERT.   A little sincerity is a dangerous thing, and a great deal
of it is absolutely fatal. The true critic will, indeed, always be
sincere in his devotion to the principle of beauty, but he will
seek for beauty in every age and in each school, and will
never suffer himself to be limited to any settled custom of
thought, or stereotyped mode of looking at things. He will
realize himself in many forms, and by a thousand different
ways, and will ever be curious of new sensations and fresh
points of view. Through constant change, and through
constant change alone, he will find his true unity. He
will not consent to be the slave of his own opinions. For
what is mind but motion in the intellectual sphere? The
essence of thought, as the essence of life, is growth. You
must not be frightened by words, Ernest. What people call
insincerity is simply a method by which we can multiply our
personalities.

ERNEST.   I am afraid I have not been fortunate in my
suggestions.

GILBERT.   Of the three qualifications you mentioned, two,
sincerity and fairness, were, if not actually moral, at least
on the borderland of morals, and the first condition of
criticism is that the critic should be able to recognize that
the sphere of Art and the sphere of Ethics are absolutely
distinct and separate. When they are confused, Chaos has
come again. They are too often confused in England now,
and though our modern Puritans cannot destroy a beautiful
thing, yet, by means of their extraordinary prurience, they
can almost taint beauty for a moment. It is chiefly, I regret
to say, through journalism that such people find expression. I
regret it because there is much to be said in favour of modern
journalism. By giving us the opinions of the uneducated, it
keeps us in touch with the ignorance of the community.
By carefully chronicling the current events of contemporary
life, it shows us of what very little importance such events
really are. By invariably discussing the unnecessary, it makes
us understand what things are requisite for culture, and what
are not. But it should not allow poor Tartuffe to write articles
upon modern art. When it does this it stultifies itself. And
yet Tartuffe's articles and Chadband's notes do this good, at

least. They serve to show how extremely limited is the area over which ethics, and ethical considerations, can claim to exercise influence. Science is out of the reach of morals, for her eyes are fixed upon eternal truths. Art is out of the reach of morals, for her eyes are fixed upon things beautiful and immortal and ever-changing. To morals belong the lower and less intellectual spheres. However, let these mouthing Puritans pass; they have their comic side. Who can help laughing when an ordinary journalist seriously proposes to limit the subject-matter at the disposal of the artist? Some limitation might well, and will soon, I hope, be placed upon some of our newspapers and newspaper writers. For they give us the bald, sordid, disgusting facts of life. They chronicle, with degrading avidity, the sins of the second-rate, and with the conscientiousness of the illiterate give us accurate and prosaic details of the doings of people of absolutely no interest whatsoever. But the artist, who accepts the facts of life, and yet transforms them into shapes of beauty, and makes them vehicles of pity or of awe, and shows their colour-element, and their wonder, and their true ethical import also, and builds out of them a world more real than reality itself, and of loftier and more noble import – who shall set limits to him? Not the apostles of that new Journalism which is but the old vulgarity 'writ large'. Not the apostles of that new Puritanism, which is but the whine of the hypocrite, and is both writ and spoken badly. The mere suggestion is ridiculous. Let us leave these wicked people, and proceed to the discussion of the artistic qualifications necessary for the true critic.

ERNEST.   And what are they? Tell me yourself.

GILBERT.   Temperament is the primary requisite for the critic – a temperament exquisitely susceptible to beauty, and to the various impressions that beauty gives us. Under what conditions, and by what means, this temperament is engendered in race or individual, we will not discuss at present. It is sufficient to note that it exists, and that there is in us a beauty-sense, separate from the other senses and above them, separate from the reason and of nobler import, separate from the soul and of equal value – a sense that leads some to create, and others, the finer spirits as I think, to contemplate merely. But to be purified and made perfect, this sense requires some form of exquisite environment. Without this it starves, or is dulled. You remember that lovely passage in which Plato describes how a young Greek should be educated, and with what insistence he dwells upon the importance of surroundings, telling us how the lad is to be brought up in the midst of fair sights and sounds, so that the beauty of material things may prepare his soul for the reception of the beauty that is spiritual. Insensibly, and without knowing the reason why, he is to develop that real love of beauty which, as Plato is never weary of reminding us, is the true aim of education. By slow degrees there is to be engendered in him such a temperament as will lead him naturally and simply to choose the good in preference to the bad, and, rejecting what is vulgar and discordant, to follow by fine instinctive taste all that possesses grace and charm and loveliness. Ultimately, in its due course, this taste is to become critical and self-conscious, but at first it is to exist purely as a cultivated instinct, and 'he who has received this true culture of the inner man will with clear and certain vision perceive the omissions and faults in art or nature, and with a taste that cannot err, while he praises, and finds his pleasure in what is good, and receives it into his soul, and so becomes good and noble, he will rightly blame and hate the bad, now in the days of his youth, even before he is able to know the reason why': and so, when, later on, the critical and self-conscious spirit develops in him, he 'will recognize and salute it as a friend with whom his education has made him long familiar'. I need hardly say, Ernest, how far we in England have fallen short of this ideal, and I can imagine the smile that would illuminate the glossy face of the Philistine if one ventured to suggest to him that the true aim of education was the love of beauty, and that the methods by which education should work were the development of temperament, the cultivation of taste, and the creation of the critical spirit.

Yet, even for us, there is left some loveliness of environment, and the dulness of tutors and professors matters very little when one can loiter in the grey cloisters at Magdalen, and listen to some flute-like voice singing in Waynfleete's chapel, or lie in the green meadow, among the strange snake-spotted

fritillaries, and watch the sunburnt noon smite to a finer gold
the tower's gilded vanes, or wander up the Christ Church
staircase beneath the vaulted ceiling's shadowy fans, or pass
through the sculptured gateway of Laud's building in the
College of St John. Nor is it merely at Oxford, or Cambridge,
that the sense of beauty can be formed and trained and
perfected. All over England there is a Renaissance of the
decorative Arts. Ugliness has had its day. Even in the houses
of the rich there is taste, and the houses of those who are
not rich have been made gracious and comely and sweet to
live in. Caliban, poor noisy Caliban, thinks that when he has
ceased to make mows at a thing, the thing ceases to exist.
But if he mocks no longer, it is because he has been met
with mockery, swifter and keener than his own, and for a
moment has been bitterly schooled into that silence which
should seal for ever his uncouth distorted lips. What has
been done up to now, has been chiefly in the clearing of
the way. It is always more difficult to destroy than it is to
create, and when what one has to destroy is vulgarity and
stupidity, the task of destruction needs not merely courage
but also contempt. Yet it seems to me to have been, in a
measure, done. We have got rid of what was bad. We have
now to make what is beautiful. And though the mission of
the Aesthetic Movement is to lure people to contemplate,
not to lead them to create, yet, as the creative instinct is
strong in the Celt, and it is the Celt who leads in art, there
is no reason why in future years this strange Renaissance
should not become almost as mighty in its way as was that
new birth of Art that woke many centuries ago in the cities
of Italy.

Certainly, for the cultivation of temperament, we must
turn to the decorative arts: to the arts that touch us, not
to the arts that teach us. Modern pictures are, no doubt,
delightful to look at. At least, some of them are. But they
are quite impossible to live with; they are too clever, too
assertive, too intellectual. Their meaning is too obvious, and
their method too clearly defined. One exhausts what they
have to say in a very short time, and then they become as
tedious as one's relations. I am very fond of the work of
many of the Impressionist painters of Paris and London.

Subtlety and distinction have not yet left the school. Some
of their arrangements and harmonies serve to remind one of
the unapproachable beauty of Gautier's immortal *Symphonie
en Blanc Majeur*, that flawless masterpiece of colour and music
which may have suggested the type as well as the titles of
many of their best pictures. For a class that welcomes the
incompetent with sympathetic eagerness, and that confuses
the bizarre with the beautiful, and vulgarity with truth,
they are extremely accomplished. They can do etchings
that have the brilliancy of epigrams, pastels that are as
fascinating as paradoxes, and as for their portraits, whatever
the commonplace may say against them, no one can deny
that they possess that unique and wonderful charm which
belongs to works of pure fiction. But even the Impressionists,
earnest and industrious as they are, will not do. I like them.
Their white keynote, with its variations in lilac, was an era
in colour. Though the moment does not make the man,
the moment certainly makes the Impressionist, and for the
moment in art, and the 'moment's monument' as Rossetti
phrased it, what may not be said? They are suggestive also.
If they have not opened the eyes of the blind, they have
at least given great encouragement to the short-sighted,
and while their leaders may have all the inexperience of
old age, their young men are far too wise to be ever
sensible. Yet they will insist on treating painting as if it
were a mode of autobiography invented for the use of the
illiterate, and are always prating to us on their coarse gritty
canvases of their unnecessary selves and their unnecessary
opinions, and spoiling by a vulgar over-emphasis that fine
contempt of nature which is the best and only modest
thing about them. One tires, at the end, of the work of
individuals whose individuality is always noisy, and generally
uninteresting. There is far more to be said in favour of that
newer school at Paris, the *Archaïcistes*, as they call themselves,
who, refusing to leave the artist entirely at the mercy of the
weather, do not find the ideal of art in mere atmospheric
effect, but seek rather for the imaginative beauty of design
and the loveliness of fair colour, and rejecting the tedious
realism of those who merely paint what they see, try to
see something worth seeing, and to see it not merely with

actual and physical vision, but with that nobler vision of the soul which is as far wider in spiritual scope as it is far more splendid in artistic purpose. They, at any rate, work under those decorative conditions that each art requires for its perfection, and have sufficient aesthetic instinct to regret those sordid and stupid limitations of absolute modernity of form which have proved the ruin of so many of the Impressionists. Still, the art that is frankly decorative is the art to live with. It is, of all our visible arts, the one art that creates in us both mood and temperament. Mere colour, unspoiled by meaning, and unallied with definite form, can speak to the soul in a thousand different ways. The harmony that resides in the delicate proportions of lines and masses becomes mirrored in the mind. The repetitions of pattern give us rest. The marvels of design stir the imagination. In the mere loveliness of the materials employed there are latent elements of culture. Nor is this all. By its deliberate rejection of Nature as the ideal of beauty, as well as of the imitative method of the ordinary painter, decorative art not merely prepares the soul for the reception of true imaginative work, but develops in it that sense of form which is the basis of creative no less than of critical achievement. For the real artist is he who proceeds, not from feeling to form, but from form to thought and passion. He does not first conceive an idea, and then say to himself, 'I will put my idea into a complex metre of fourteen lines', but, realizing the beauty of the sonnet-scheme, he conceives certain modes of music and methods of rhyme, and the mere form suggests what is to fill it and make it intellectually and emotionally complete. From time to time the world cries out against some charming artistic poet, because, to use its hackneyed and silly phrase, he has 'nothing to say'. But if he had something to say, he would probably say it, and the result would be tedious. It is just because he has no new message, that he can do beautiful work. He gains his inspiration from form, and from form purely, as an artist should. A real passion would ruin him. Whatever actually occurs is spoiled for art. All bad poetry springs from genuine feeling. To be natural is to be obvious, and to be obvious is to be inartistic.

ERNEST.   I wonder do you really believe what you say?

GILBERT.   Why should you wonder? It is not merely in art
    that the body is the soul. In every sphere of life Form is
    the beginning of things. The rhythmic harmonious gestures
    of dancing convey, Plato tells us, both rhythm and harmony
    into the mind. Forms are the food of faith, cried Newman
    in one of those great moments of sincerity that make us
    admire and know the man. He was right, though he may
    not have known how terribly right he was. The Creeds are
    believed, not because they are rational, but because they are
    repeated. Yes: Form is everything. It is the secret of life.
    Find expression for a sorrow, and it will become dear to
    you. Find expression for a joy, and you intensify its ecstasy.
    Do you wish to love? Use Love's Litany, and the words will
    create the yearning from which the world fancies that they
    spring. Have you a grief that corrodes your heart? Steep
    yourself in the language of grief, learn its utterance from
    Prince Hamlet and Queen Constance, and you will find
    that mere expression is a mode of consolation, and that
    Form, which is the birth of passion, is also the death of
    pain. And so, to return to the sphere of Art, it is Form
    that creates not merely the critical temperament, but also
    the aesthetic instinct, that unerring instinct that reveals to
    one all things under their conditions of beauty. Start with
    the worship of form, and there is no secret in art that will
    not be revealed to you, and remember that in criticism, as in
    creation, temperament is everything, and that it is, not by the
    time of their production, but by the temperaments to which
    they appeal, that the schools of art should be historically
    grouped.
ERNEST.   Your theory of education is delightful. But what
    influence will your critic, brought up in these exquisite
    surroundings, possess? Do you really think that any artist is
    ever affected by criticism?
GILBERT.   The influence of the critic will be the mere fact of
    his own existence. He will represent the flawless type. In him
    the culture of the century will see itself realized. You must
    not ask of him to have any aim other than the perfecting of
    himself. The demand of the intellect, as has been well said,
    is simply to feel itself alive. The critic may, indeed, desire
    to exercise influence; but, if so, he will concern himself

not with the individual, but with the age, which he will seek to wake into consciousness, and to make responsive, creating in it new desires and appetites, and lending it his larger vision and his nobler moods. The actual art of to-day will occupy him less than the art of to-morrow, far less than the art of yesterday, and as for this or that person at present toiling away, what do the industrious matter? They do their best, no doubt, and consequently we get the worst from them. It is always with the best intentions that the worst work is done. And besides, my dear Ernest, when a man reaches the age of forty, or becomes a Royal Academician, or is elected a Member of the Athenaeum Club, or is recognized as a popular novelist, whose books are in great demand at suburban railway stations, one may have the amusement of exposing him, but one cannot have the pleasure of reforming him. And this is, I dare say, very fortunate for him; for I have no doubt that reformation is a much more painful process than punishment, is indeed punishment in its most aggravated and moral form − a fact which accounts for our entire failure as a community to reclaim that interesting phenomenon who is called the confirmed criminal.

ERNEST.   But may it not be that the poet is the best judge of poetry, and the painter of painting? Each art must appeal primarily to the artist who works in it. His judgement will surely be the most valuable?

GILBERT.   The appeal of all art is simply to the artistic temperament. Art does not address herself to the specialist. Her claim is that she is universal, and that in all her manifestations she is one. Indeed, so far from its being true that the artist is the best judge of art, a really great artist can never judge of other people's work at all, and can hardly, in fact, judge of his own. That very concentration of vision that makes a man an artist, limits by its sheer intensity his faculty of fine appreciation. The energy of creation hurries him blindly on to his own goal. The wheels of his chariot raise the dust as a cloud around him. The gods are hidden from each other. They can recognize their worshippers. That is all.

ERNEST.   You say that a great artist cannot recognize the beauty of work different from his own.

GILBERT.   It is impossible for him to do so. Wordsworth saw in *Endymion* merely a pretty piece of Paganism, and Shelley, with his dislike of actuality, was deaf to Wordsworth's message, being repelled by its form, and Byron, that great passionate human incomplete creature, could appreciate neither the poet of the cloud nor the poet of the lake, and the wonder of Keats was hidden from him. The realism of Euripides was hateful to Sophokles. Those droppings of warm tears had no music for him. Milton, with his sense of the grand style, could not understand the method of Shakespeare, any more than could Sir Joshua the method of Gainsborough. Bad artists always admire each other's work. They call it being large-minded and free from prejudice. But a truly great artist cannot conceive of life being shown, or beauty fashioned, under any conditions other than those that he has selected. Creation employs all its critical faculty within its own sphere. It may not use it in the sphere that belongs to others. It is exactly because a man cannot do a thing that he is the proper judge of it.

ERNEST.   Do you really mean that?

GILBERT.   Yes, for creation limits, while contemplation widens, the vision.

ERNEST.   But what about technique? Surely each art has its separate technique?

GILBERT.   Certainly: each art has its grammar and its materials. There is no mystery about either, and the incompetent can always be correct. But, while the laws upon which Art rests may be fixed and certain, to find their true realization they must be touched by the imagination into such beauty that they will seem an exception, each one of them. Technique is really personality. That is the reason why the artist cannot teach it, why the pupil cannot learn it, and why the æsthetic critic can understand it. To the great poet, there is only one method of music – his own. To the great painter, there is only one manner of painting – that which he himself employs. The æsthetic critic, and the æsthetic critic alone, can appreciate all forms and modes. It is to him that Art makes her appeal.

ERNEST.   Well, I think I have put all my questions to you. And now I must admit —

GILBERT.   Ah! don't say that you agree with me. When people agree with me I always feel that I must be wrong.

ERNEST.   In that case I certainly won't tell you whether I agree with you or not. But I will put another question. You have explained to me that criticism is a creative art. What future has it?

GILBERT.   It is to criticism that the future belongs. The subject-matter at the disposal of creation becomes every day more limited in extent and variety. Providence and Mr Walter Besant have exhausted the obvious. If creation is to last at all, it can only do so on the condition of becoming far more critical than it is at present. The old roads and dusty highways have been traversed too often. Their charm has been worn away by plodding feet, and they have lost that element of novelty or surprise which is so essential for romance. He who would stir us now by fiction must either give us an entirely new background, or reveal to us the soul of man in its innermost workings. The first is for the moment being done for us by Mr Rudyard Kipling. As one turns over the pages of his *Plain Tales from the Hills*, one feels as if one were seated under a palm-tree reading life by superb flashes of vulgarity. The bright colours of the bazaars dazzle one's eyes. The jaded, second-rate Anglo-Indians are in exquisite incongruity with their surroundings. The mere lack of style in the storyteller gives an odd journalistic realism to what he tells us. From the point of view of literature Mr Kipling is a genius who drops his aspirates. From the point of view of life, he is a reporter who knows vulgarity better than any one has ever known it. Dickens knew its clothes and its comedy. Mr Kipling knows its essence and its seriousness. He is our first authority on the second-rate, and has seen marvellous things through keyholes, and his backgrounds are real works of art. As for the second condition, we have had Browning, and Meredith is with us. But there is still much to be done in the sphere of introspection. People sometimes say that fiction is getting too morbid. As far as psychology is concerned, it has never been morbid enough. We have merely touched the surface of the soul, that is all. In one single ivory cell of the brain there are stored away things more marvellous and more terrible than even they have dreamed of, who, like the author of *Le Rouge et le Noir*, have sought to track the soul into its most secret places, and to make life confess its dearest sins. Still, there is a limit even to the number of untried backgrounds, and it is possible that a further development of the habit of introspection may prove fatal to that creative faculty to which it seeks to supply fresh material. I myself am inclined to think that creation is doomed. It springs from too primitive, too natural an impulse. However this may be, it is certain that the subject-matter at the disposal of creation is always diminishing, while the subject-matter of criticism increases daily. There are always new attitudes for the mind, and new points of view. The duty of imposing form upon chaos does not grow less as the world advances. There was never a time when Criticism was more needed than it is now. It is only by its means that Humanity can become conscious of the point at which it has arrived.

Hours ago, Ernest, you asked me the use of Criticism. You might just as well have asked me the use of thought. It is Criticism, as Arnold points out, that creates the intellectual atmosphere of the age. It is Criticism, as I hope to point out myself some day, that makes the mind a fine instrument. We, in our educational system, have burdened the memory with a load of unconnected facts, and laboriously striven to impart our laboriously-acquired knowledge. We teach people how to remember, we never teach them how to grow. It has never occurred to us to try and develop in the mind a more subtle quality of apprehension and discernment. The Greeks did this, and when we come in contact with the Greek critical intellect, we cannot but be conscious that, while our subject-matter is in every respect larger and more varied than theirs, theirs is the only method by which this subject-matter can be interpreted. England has done one thing; it has invented and established Public Opinion, which is an attempt to organize the ignorance of the community, and to elevate it to the dignity of physical force. But Wisdom has always been hidden from it. Considered as an instrument of thought, the English mind is coarse and undeveloped. The only thing that can purify it is the growth of the critical instinct.

It is Criticism, again, that, by concentration, makes culture possible. It takes the cumbersome mass of creative work,

and distils it into a finer essence. Who that desires to retain
any sense of form could struggle through the monstrous
multitudinous books that the world has produced, books
in which thought stammers or ignorance brawls? The thread
that is to guide us across the wearisome labyrinth is in the
hands of Criticism. Nay more, where there is no record,
and history is either lost, or was never written, Criticism
can re-create the past for us from the very smallest fragment
of language or art, just as surely as the man of science can
from some tiny bone, or the mere impress of a foot upon
a rock, re-create for us the winged dragon or Titan lizard
that once made the earth shake beneath its tread, can call
Behemoth out of his cave, and make Leviathan swim once
more across the startled sea. Prehistoric history belongs to
the philological and archæological critic. It is to him that
the origins of things are revealed. The self-conscious deposits
of an age are nearly always misleading. Through philological
criticism alone we know more of the centuries of which no
actual record has been preserved, than we do of the centuries
that have left us their scrolls. It can do for us what can be
done neither by physics nor metaphysics. It can give us the
exact science of mind in the process of becoming. It can
do for us what History cannot do. It can tell us what man
thought before he learned how to write. You have asked me
about the influence of Criticism. I think I have answered that
question already; but there is this also to be said. It is Criticism
that makes us cosmopolitan. The Manchester school tried to
make men realize the brotherhood of humanity, by pointing
out the commercial advantages of peace. It sought to degrade
the wonderful world into a common market-place for the
buyer and the seller. It addressed itself to the lowest instincts,
and it failed. War followed upon war, and the tradesman's
creed did not prevent France and Germany from clashing
together in blood-stained battle. There are others of our
own day who seek to appeal to mere emotional sympathies,
or to the shallow dogmas of some vague system of abstract
ethics. They have their Peace Societies, so dear to the
sentimentalists, and their proposals for unarmed International
Arbitration, so popular among those who have never read
history. But mere emotional sympathy will not do. It is

too variable, and too closely connected with the passions; and a board of arbitrators who, for the general welfare of the race, are to be deprived of the power of putting their decisions into execution, will not be of much avail. There is only one thing worse than Injustice, and that is Justice without her sword in her hand. When Right is not Might, it is Evil.

No: the emotions will not make us cosmopolitan, any more than the greed for gain could do so. It is only by the cultivation of the habit of intellectual criticism that we shall be able to rise superior to race-prejudices. Goethe – you will not misunderstand what I say – was a German of the Germans. He loved his country – no man more so. Its people were dear to him; and he led them. Yet, when the iron hoof of Napoleon trampled upon vineyard and cornfield, his lips were silent. 'How can one write songs of hatred without hating?' he said to Eckerman, 'and how could I, to whom culture and barbarism are alone of importance, hate a nation which is among the most cultivated of the earth, and to which I owe so great a part of my own cultivation?' This note, sounded in the modern world by Goethe first, will become, I think, the starting point for the cosmopolitanism of the future. Criticism will annihilate race-prejudices, by insisting upon the unity of the human mind in the variety of its forms. If we are tempted to make war upon another nation, we shall remember that we are seeking to destroy an element of our own culture, and possibly its most important element. As long as war is regarded as wicked, it will always have its fascination. When it is looked upon as vulgar, it will cease to be popular. The change will of course be slow, and people will not be conscious of it. They will not say 'We will not war against France because her prose is perfect', but because the prose of France is perfect, they will not hate the land. Intellectual criticism will bind Europe together in bonds far closer than those that can be forged by shopman or sentimentalist. It will give us the peace that springs from understanding.

Nor is this all. It is Criticism that, recognizing no position as final, and refusing to bind itself by the shallow shibboleths of any sect or school, creates that serene philosophic temper which loves truth for its own sake, and loves it not the less because it knows it to be unattainable. How little we have of this temper in England, and how much we need it! The English mind is always in a rage. The intellect of the race is wasted in the sordid and stupid quarrels of second-rate politicians or third-rate theologians. It was reserved for a man of science to show us the supreme example of that 'sweet reasonableness' of which Arnold spoke so wisely, and, alas! to so little effect. The author of the *Origin of Species* had, at any rate, the philosophic temper. If one contemplates the ordinary pulpits and platforms of England, one can but feel the contempt of Julian, or the indifference of Montaigne. We are dominated by the fanatic, whose worst vice is his sincerity. Anything approaching to the free play of the mind is practically unknown amongst us. People cry out against the sinner, yet it is not the sinful, but the stupid, who are our shame. There is no sin except stupidity.

ERNEST.   Ah! what an antinomian you are!

GILBERT.   The artistic critic, like the mystic, is an antinomian always. To be good, according to the vulgar standard of goodness, is obviously quite easy. It merely requires a certain amount of sordid terror, a certain lack of imaginative thought, and a certain low passion for middle-class respectability. Æsthetics are higher than ethics. They belong to a more spiritual sphere. To discern the beauty of a thing is the finest point to which we can arrive. Even a colour-sense is more important, in the development of the individual, than a sense of right and wrong. Æsthetics, in fact, are to Ethics in the sphere of conscious civilization, what, in the sphere of the external world, sexual is to natural selection. Ethics, like natural selection, make existence possible. Æsthetics, like sexual selection, make life lovely and wonderful, fill it with new forms, and give it progress, and variety and change. And when we reach the true culture that is our aim, we attain to that perfection of which the saints have dreamed, the perfection of those to whom sin is impossible, not because they make the renunciations of the ascetic, but because they can do everything they wish without hurt to the soul, and can wish for nothing that can do the soul harm, the soul being an entity so divine that it is able to transform into elements of a richer experience, or a finer susceptibility, or a newer mode of thought, acts or passions that with the common would be commonplace, or with the uneducated ignoble, or with the shameful vile. Is this dangerous? Yes; it is dangerous – all ideas, as I told you, are so. But the night wearies, and the light flickers in the lamp. One more thing I cannot help saying to you. You have spoken against Criticism as being a sterile thing. The nineteenth century is a turning point in history simply on account of the work of two men, Darwin and Renan, the one the critic of the Book of Nature, the other the critic of the books of God. Not to recognize this is to miss the meaning of one of the most important eras in the progress of the world. Creation is always behind the age. It is Criticism that leads us. The Critical Spirit and the World-Spirit are one.

ERNEST. And he who is in possession of this spirit, or whom this spirit possesses, will, I suppose, do nothing?

GILBERT. Like the Persephone of whom Landor tells us, the sweet pensive Persephone around whose white feet the asphodel and amaranth are blooming, he will sit contented 'in that deep, motionless quiet which mortals pity, and which the gods enjoy'. He will look out upon the world and know its secret. By contact with divine things he will become divine. His will be the perfect life, and his only.

ERNEST. You have told me many strange things to-night, Gilbert. You have told me that it is more difficult to talk about a thing than to do it, and that to do nothing at all is the most difficult thing in the world; you have told me that all Art is immoral, and all thought dangerous; that criticism is more creative than creation, and that the highest criticism is that which reveals in the work of Art what the artist had not put there; that it is exactly because a man cannot do a thing that he is the proper judge of it; and that the true critic is unfair, insincere, and not rational. My friend, you are a dreamer.

GILBERT. Yes: I am a dreamer. For a dreamer is one who can only find his way by moonlight, and his punishment is that he sees the dawn before the rest of the world.

ERNEST. His punishment?

GILBERT.   And his reward. But see, it is dawn already. Draw
    back the curtains and open the windows wide. How cool
    the morning air is! Piccadilly lies at our feet like a long
    riband of silver. A faint purple mist hangs over the Park,
    and the shadows of the white houses are purple. It is too
    late to sleep. Let us go down to Covent Garden and look
    at the roses. Come! I am tired of thought.

The Soul of Man under Socialism

The chief advantage that would result from the establishment of Socialism is, undoubtedly, the fact that Socialism would relieve us from that sordid necessity of living for others which, in the present condition of things, presses so hardly upon almost everybody. In fact, scarcely any one at all escapes.

Now and then, in the course of the century, a great man of science, like Darwin; a great poet, like Keats; a fine critical spirit, like M. Renan; a supreme artist, like Flaubert, has been able to isolate himself, to keep himself out of reach of the clamorous claims of others, to stand 'under the shelter of the wall', as Plato puts it, and so to realize the perfection of what was in him, to his own incomparable gain, and to the incomparable and lasting gain of the whole world. These, however, are exceptions. The majority of people spoil their lives by an unhealthy and exaggerated altruism – are forced, indeed, so to spoil them. They find themselves surrounded by hideous poverty, by hideous ugliness, by hideous starvation. It is inevitable that they should be strongly moved by all this. The emotions of man are stirred more quickly than man's intelligence; and, as I pointed out some time ago in an article on the function of criticism, it is much more easy to have sympathy with suffering than it is to have sympathy with thought. Accordingly, with admirable though misdirected intentions, they very seriously and very sentimentally set themselves to the task of remedying the evils that they see. But their remedies do not cure the disease: they merely prolong it. Indeed, their remedies are part of the disease.

They try to solve the problem of poverty, for instance, by keeping the poor alive; or, in the case of a very advanced school, by amusing the poor.

But this is not a solution: it is an aggravation of the difficulty. *The proper aim is to try and re-construct society on such a basis that poverty will be impossible.* And the altruistic virtues have really prevented the carrying out of this aim. Just as the worst slave-owners were those who were kind to their slaves, and so prevented the horror of the system being realized by those who suffered from it, and understood by those who contemplated it, so, in the present state of things in England, the people who do most harm are the people who try to do most good; and at last we have had the spectacle of men who have really studied the problem and know the life – educated men who live in the East-End – coming forward and imploring the community to restrain its altruistic impulses of charity, benevolence and the like. They do so on the ground that such charity degrades and demoralizes. They are perfectly right. Charity creates a multitude of sins.

There is also this to be said. It is immoral to use private property in order to alleviate the horrible evils that result from the institution of private property. It is both immoral and unfair.

Under Socialism all this will, of course, be altered. There will be no people living in fetid dens and fetid rags, and bringing up unhealthy, hunger-pinched children in the midst of impossible and absolutely repulsive surroundings. The security of society will not depend, as it does now, on the state of the weather. If a frost comes we shall not have a hundred thousand men out of work, tramping about the streets in a state of disgusting misery, or whining to their neighbours for alms, or crowding round the doors of loathsome shelters to try and secure a hunch of bread and a night's unclean lodging. Each member of the society will share in the general prosperity and happiness of the society, and if a frost comes no one will practically be anything the worse.

Upon the other hand, *Socialism itself will be of value simply because it will lead to Individualism.*

Socialism, Communism, or whatever one chooses to call it, by converting private property into public wealth, and substituting co-operation for competition, will restore society to its proper condition of a thoroughly healthy organism, and ensure the material well-being of each member of the community. It will, in fact, give Life its proper basis and its proper environment. But for the full development of Life to its highest mode of perfection something more is needed. What is needed is Individualism. If the Socialism is Authoritarian; if there are Governments armed with economic power as they are now with political power; if, in a word, we are to have Industrial Tyrannies, then the last state of man will be worse than the first. At present, in consequence of the existence of private property, a great many people are enabled to develop a certain very limited amount of Individualism. They are either under no necessity to work for their living, or are enabled to choose the sphere of activity that is really congenial to them and gives them pleasure. These are the poets, the philosophers, the men of science, the men of culture – in a word, the real men, the men who have realized themselves, and in whom all Humanity gains a partial realization. Upon the other hand, there are a great many people who, having no private property of their own, and being always on the brink of sheer starvation, are compelled to do the work of beasts of burden, to do work that is quite uncongenial to them, and to which they are forced by the peremptory, unreasonable, degrading Tyranny of want. These are the poor, and amongst them there is no grace of manner, or charm of speech, or civilization, or culture, or refinement in pleasures, or joy of life. From their collective force Humanity gains much in material prosperity. But it is only the material result that it gains, and the man who is poor is in himself absolutely of no importance. He is merely the infinitesimal atom of a force that, so far from regarding him, crushes him: indeed, prefers him crushed, as in that case he is far more obedient.

Of course, it might be said that the Individualism generated under conditions of private property is not always, or even as a rule, of a fine or wonderful type, and that the poor, if they have not culture and charm, have still many virtues. Both these statements would be quite true. The possession of private property is very often extremely demoralizing, and that is, of course, one of the reasons why Socialism wants to get rid of the institution. In fact, property is really a nuisance. Some years ago people went about the country saying that property has duties. They said it so often and so tediously that, at last, the Church has begun to say it. One hears it now from every pulpit. It is perfectly true. Property not merely has duties, but has so many duties that its possession to any large extent is a bore. It involves endless claims upon one, endless attention to business, endless bother. If property had simply pleasures we could stand it; but its duties make it unbearable. In the interest of the rich we must get rid of it. The virtues of the poor may be readily admitted, and are much to be regretted. We are often told that the poor are grateful for charity. Some of them are, no doubt, *but the best amongst the poor are never grateful.* They are ungrateful, discontented, disobedient and rebellious. They are quite right to be so. Charity they feel to be a ridiculously inadequate mode of partial restitution, or a sentimental dole, usually accompanied by some impertinent attempt on the part of the sentimentalist to tyrannize over their private lives. Why should they be grateful for the crumbs that fall from the rich man's table? They should be seated at the board, and are beginning to know it. As for being discontented, a man who would not be discontented with such surroundings and such a low mode of life would be a perfect brute. Disobedience, in the eyes of any one who has read history, is man's original virtue. It is through disobedience that progress has been made, through disobedience and through rebellion. Sometimes the poor are praised for being thrifty. But to recommend thrift to the poor is both grotesque and insulting. It is like advising a man who is starving to eat less. For a town or country labourer to practise thrift would be absolutely immoral. Man should not be ready to show that he can live like a badly fed animal. He should decline to live like that, and should either steal or go on the rates, which is considered by many to be a form of stealing. As for begging, it is safer to beg than to take, but it is finer to take than to beg. No: a poor man who is ungrateful, unthrifty, discontented and rebellious is probably a real personality, and has much in him. He is at any rate a healthy protest. As for the virtuous poor, one can pity them, of course, but one cannot possibly admire them. They have made private terms with the enemy, and sold their birthright for very bad pottage. They must also be extraordinarily stupid. I can quite understand a man accepting laws that protect private property, and admit of its accumulation, as long as he himself is able under those conditions to realize some form of beautiful and intellectual life. But it is almost incredible to me how a man whose life is marred and made hideous by such laws can possibly acquiesce in their continuance.

However, the explanation is not really difficult to find. It is simply this. Misery and poverty are so absolutely degrading, and exercise such a paralysing effect over the nature of men, that no class is ever really conscious of its own suffering. They have to be told of it by other people, and they often entirely disbelieve them. What is said by great employers of labour against agitators is unquestionably true. Agitators are a set of interfering, meddling people, who come down to some perfectly contented class of the community and sow the seeds of discontent amongst them. That is the reason why agitators are so absolutely necessary. Without them, in our incomplete state, there would be no advance towards civilization. Slavery was put down in America, not in consequence of any action on the part of slaves, or even any express desire on their part that they should be free. It was put down entirely through the grossly illegal conduct of certain agitators in Boston and elsewhere, who were not slaves themselves, nor owners of slaves, nor had anything to do with the question really. It was, undoubtedly, the Abolitionists who set the torch alight, who began the whole thing. And it is curious to note that from the slaves themselves they received, not merely very little assistance, but hardly any sympathy even; and when at the close of the war the slaves found themselves free, found themselves indeed so absolutely free that they were free to starve, many of them bitterly regretted the new state of things. To the thinker, the most tragic fact in the whole of the French Revolution is not that Marie Antoinette was killed for being a queen, but that the starved peasant of the Vendée voluntarily went out to die for the hideous cause of feudalism.

It is clear, then, that no Authoritarian Socialism will do. For, while under the present system a very large number of people can lead lives of a certain amount of freedom and expression and happiness, under an industrial barrack system, or a system of economic tyranny, nobody would be able to have any such freedom at all. It is to be regretted that a portion of our community should be practically in slavery, but to propose to solve the problem by enslaving the entire community is childish. Every man must be left quite free to choose his own work. No form of compulsion must be exercised over him. If there is, his work will not be good for him, will not be good in itself, and will not be good for others. And by work I simply mean activity of any kind.

I hardly think that any Socialist, nowadays, would seriously propose that an inspector should call every morning at each house to see that each citizen rose up and did manual labour for eight hours. Humanity has got beyond that stage, and reserves such a form of life for the people whom, in a very arbitrary manner, it chooses to call criminals. But I confess that many of the Socialistic views that I have come across seem to me to be tainted with ideas of authority, if not of actual compulsion. Of course authority and compulsion are out of the question. All association must be quite voluntary. *It is only in voluntary association that man is fine.*

But it may be asked how Individualism, which is now more or less dependent on the existence of private property for its development, will benefit by the abolition of such private property. The answer is very simple. It is true that, under existing conditions, a few men who have had private means of their own, such as Byron, Shelley, Browning, Victor Hugo, Baudelaire, and others, have been able to realize their personality more or less completely. Not one of these men ever did a single day's work for hire. They were relieved from poverty. They had an immense advantage. The question is whether it would be for the good of Individualism that such an advantage should be taken away. Let us suppose that it is taken away. What happens then to Individualism? How will it benefit?

It will benefit in this way. Under the new conditions Individualism will be far freer, far finer and far more intensified than it is now. I am not talking of the great imaginatively-realized individualism of such poets as I have mentioned, but of the great actual Individualism latent and potential in mankind generally. For the recognition of private property has really harmed Individualism, and obscured it, by confusing a man with what he possesses. It has led Individualism entirely astray. It has made gain not growth its aim. So that man thought that the important thing was to have, and did not know that the important thing is to be. *The true perfection of man lies, not in what man has, but in what man is.* Private property has crushed true Individualism, and set up an Individualism that is false. It has debarred one part of the community from being individual by starving them. It has debarred the other part of the community from being individual, by putting them on the wrong road and encumbering them. Indeed, so completely has man's personality been absorbed by his possessions that the English law has always treated offences against a man's property with far more severity than offences against his person, and property is still the test of complete citizenship. The industry necessary for the making money is also very demoralizing. In a community like ours, where property confers immense distinction, social position, honour, respect, titles, and other pleasant things of the kind, man, being naturally ambitious, makes it his aim to accumulate this property, and goes on wearily and tediously accumulating it long after he has got far more than he wants, or can use, or enjoy, or perhaps even know of. Man will kill himself by over-work in order to secure property, and really, considering the enormous advantages that property brings, one is hardly surprised. One's regret is that society should be constructed on such a basis that man has been forced into a groove in which he cannot freely develop what is wonderful, and fascinating, and delightful in him – in which, in fact, he misses the true pleasure and joy of living. He is also, under existing conditions, very insecure. An enormously wealthy merchant may be – often is – at every moment of his life at the mercy of things that are not under his control. If the wind blows an extra point or so, or the weather suddenly changes, or some trivial thing happens, his ship may go down, his speculations may go wrong, and he finds himself a poor man, with his social position quite gone. Now, nothing should be able to harm a man except himself. Nothing should be able to rob a man at all. What a man really has, is what is in him. What is outside of him should be a matter of no importance.

With the abolition of private property, then, we shall have true beautiful, healthy Individualism. Nobody will waste his life in accumulating things and the symbols for things. One will live. To live is the rarest thing in the world. Most people exist, that is all.

It is a question whether we have ever seen the full expression of a personality, except on the imaginative plane of art. In action, we never have. Cæsar, says Mommsen, was the complete and perfect man. But how tragically insecure was Cæsar! Wherever there is a man who exercises authority, there is a man who resists authority. Cæsar was very perfect, but his perfection travelled by too dangerous a road. Marcus Aurelius was the perfect man, says Renan. Yes; the great emperor was a perfect man. But how intolerable were the endless claims upon him! He staggered under the burden of the empire. He was conscious how inadequate one man was to bear the weight of that Titan and too vast orb. What I mean by a perfect man is one who develops under perfect conditions; one who is not wounded, or worried, or maimed, or in danger. *Most personalities have been obliged to be rebels. Half their strength has been wasted in friction.* Byron's personality, for instance, was terribly wasted in its battle with the stupidity, and hypocrisy, and Philistinism of the English. Such battles do not always intensify strength: they often exaggerate weakness. Byron was never able to give us what he might have given us. Shelley escaped better. Like Byron, he got out of England as soon as possible. But he was not so well known. If the English had had any idea of what a great poet he really was, they would have fallen on him with tooth and nail, and made his life as unbearable to him as they possibly could. But he was not a remarkable figure in society, and consequently he escaped, to a certain degree. Still, even in Shelley the note of rebellion is sometimes too strong. The note of the perfect personality is not rebellion but peace.

It will be a marvellous thing – the true personality of man – when we see it. It will grow naturally and simply, flower-like, or as a tree grows. It will not be at discord. It will never argue or dispute. It will not prove things. It will know everything. And yet it will not busy itself about knowledge. It will have wisdom. Its value will not be measured by material things. It will have nothing. And yet it will have everything, and whatever one takes from it, it will still have, so rich will it be. It will not be always meddling with others, or asking them to be like itself. It will love them because they will be different. And yet while it will not meddle with others it will help all, as a beautiful thing helps us, by being what it is. The personality of man will be very wonderful. It will be as wonderful as the personality of a child.

In its development it will be assisted by Christianity, if men desire that; but if men do not desire that, it will develop none the less surely. For it will not worry itself about the past, nor care whether things happened or did not happen. Nor will it admit any laws but its own laws; nor any authority but its own authority, Yet it will love those who sought to intensify it, and speak often of them. And of these Christ was one.

'Know Thyself' was written over the portal of the antique world. Over the portal of the new world, 'Be Thyself' shall be written. And the message of Christ to man was simply 'Be thyself.' That is the secret of Christ.

When Jesus talks about the poor he simply means personalities, just as when he talks about the rich he simply means people who have not developed their personalities. Jesus moved in a community that allowed the accumulation of private property just as ours does, and the gospel that he preached was not that in such a community it is an advantage for a man to live on scanty, unwholesome food, to wear ragged, unwholesome clothes, to sleep in horrid, unwholesome dwellings, and a disadvantage for a man to live under healthy, pleasant and decent conditions. Such a view would have been wrong there and then, and would of course be still more wrong now and in England; for as man moves northwards the material necessities of life become of more vital importance, and our society is infinitely more complex, and displays far greater extremes of luxury and pauperism than any society of the antique world. What Jesus meant was this. He said to man, 'You have a wonderful personality. Develop it. Be yourself. Don't imagine that your perfection lies in accumulating or possessing external things. Your perfection is inside of you. If only you could realize that, you would not want to be rich. Ordinary riches can be stolen from a man. Real riches cannot. In the treasury-house of your soul, there are infinitely precious things, that may not be taken from you. And so, try so to shape your life that external things will not harm you. And try also to get rid of personal property. It involves sordid preoccupation, endless industry, continual wrong. Personal property hinders Individualism at every step.' It is to be noted that Jesus never says that impoverished people are necessarily good, or wealthy people necessarily bad. That would not have been true. Wealthy people are, as a class, better than impoverished people, more moral, more intellectual, more well-behaved. *There is only one*

class in the community that thinks more about money than the rich,
and that is the poor. The poor can think of nothing else. That is
the misery of being poor. What Jesus does say is that man reaches
his perfection, not through what he has, not even through what
he does, but entirely through what he is. And so the wealthy
young man who comes to Jesus is represented as a thoroughly
good citizen, who has broken none of the laws of his state, none
of the commandments of his religion. He is quite respectable,
in the ordinary sense of that extraordinary word. Jesus says to
him, 'You should give up private property. It hinders you from
realizing your perfection. It is a drag upon you. It is a burden.
Your personality does not need it. It is within you, and not
outside of you, that you will find what you really are, and
what you really want.' To his own friends he says the same
thing. He tells them to be themselves, and not to be always
worrying about other things. What do other things matter?
Man is complete in himself. When they go into the world,
the world will disagree with them. That is inevitable. The world
hates Individualism. But this is not to trouble them. They are to
be calm and self-centred. If a man takes their cloak, they are to
give him their coat, just to show that material things are of no
importance. If people abuse them, they are not to answer back.
What does it signify? The things people say of a man do not alter
a man. He is what he is. Public opinion is of no value whatsoever.
Even if people employ actual violence, they are not to be violent
in turn. That would be to fall to the same low level. After all,
even in prison, a man can be quite free. His soul can be free. His
personality can be untroubled. He can be at peace. And, above
all things, they are not to interfere with other people or judge
them in any way. Personality is a very mysterious thing. A man
cannot always be estimated by what he does. He may keep the
law, and yet be worthless. He may break the law, and yet be
fine. He may be bad, without ever doing anything bad. He may
commit a sin against society, and yet realize through that sin his
true perfection.

There was a woman who was taken in adultery. We are not
told the history of her love, but that love must have been
very great; for Jesus said that her sins were forgiven her, not
because she repented, but because her love was so intense and
wonderful. Later on, a short time before his death, as he sat

at a feast, the woman came in and poured costly perfumes on his hair. His friends tried to interfere with her, and said that it was an extravagance, and that the money that the perfume cost should have been expended on charitable relief of people in want, or something of that kind. Jesus did not accept that view. He pointed out that the material needs of Man were great and very permanent, but that the spiritual needs of Man were greater still, and that in one divine moment, and by selecting its own mode of expression, a personality might make itself perfect. The world worships the woman, even now, as a saint.

Yes; there are suggestive things in Individualism. Socialism annihilates family life, for instance. With the abolition of private property, marriage in its present form must disappear. This is part of the programme. Individualism accepts this and makes it fine. It converts the abolition of legal restraint into a form of freedom that will help the full development of personality, and make the love of man and woman more wonderful, more beautiful, and more ennobling. Jesus knew this. He rejected the claims of family life, although they existed in his day and community in a very marked form. 'Who is my mother? Who are my brothers?' he said, when he was told that they wished to speak to him. When one of his followers asked leave to go and bury his father, 'Let the dead bury the dead', was his terrible answer. He would allow no claim whatsoever to be made on personality.

And so he who would lead a Christlike life is he who is perfectly and absolutely himself. He may be a great poet, or a great man of science; or a young student at a University, or one who watches sheep upon a moor; or a maker of dramas, like Shakespeare, or a thinker about God, like Spinoza; or a child who plays in a garden, or a fisherman who throws his nets into the sea. It does not matter what he is, as long as he realizes the perfection of the soul that is within him. All imitation in morals and in life is wrong. Through the streets of Jerusalem at the present day crawls one who is mad and carries a wooden cross on his shoulders. He is a symbol of the lives that are marred by imitation. Father Damien was Christlike when he went out to live with the lepers, because in such service he realized fully what was best in him. But he was not more Christlike than Wagner, when he realized his soul in music; or than Shelley, when he realized his soul in song. There is no one type for man. There are as many perfections as there are imperfect men. And while to the claims of charity a man may yield and yet be free, to the claims of conformity no man may yield and remain free at all.

Individualism, then, is what through Socialism we are to attain to. As a natural result the State must give up all idea of government. It must give it up because, as a wise man once said many centuries before Christ, there is such a thing as leaving mankind alone; there is no such thing as governing mankind. *All modes of government are failures.* Despotism is unjust to everybody, including the despot, who was probably made for better things. Oligarchies are unjust to the many, and ochlocracies are unjust to the few. High hopes were once formed of democracy; but democracy means simply the bludgeoning of the people by the people for the people. It has been found out. I must say that it was high time, for all authority is quite degrading. It degrades those who exercise it, and degrades those over whom it is exercised. When it is violently, grossly and cruelly used, it produces a good effect, by creating, or at any rate bringing out, the spirit of revolt and individualism that is to kill it. When it is used with a certain amount of kindness, and accompanied by prizes and rewards, it is dreadfully demoralizing. People, in that case, are less conscious of the horrible pressure that is being put on them, and so go through their lives in a sort of coarse comfort, like petted animals, without ever realizing that they are probably thinking other people's thoughts, living by other people's standards, wearing practically what one may call other people's second-hand clothes, and never being themselves for a single moment. 'He who would be free,' says a fine thinker, 'must not conform.' And authority, by bribing people to conform, produces a very gross kind of over-fed barbarism amongst us.

With authority, punishment will pass away. This will be a great gain – a gain, in fact, of incalculable value. As one reads history, not in the expurgated editions written for schoolboys and passmen, but in the original authorities of each time, one is absolutely sickened, not by the crimes that the wicked have committed, but by the punishments that the good have inflicted; *and a community is infinitely more brutalized by the habitual employment of punishment, than it is by the occasional occurrence of crime.* It obviously follows that the more punishment

175

is inflicted the more crime is produced, and most modern legislation has clearly recognized this, and has made it its task to diminish punishment as far as it thinks it can. Wherever it has really diminished it, the results have always been extremely good. The less punishment, the less crime. When there is no punishment at all, crime will either cease to exist, or if it occurs, will be treated by physicians as a very distressing form of dementia, to be cured by care and kindness. For what are called criminals nowadays are not criminals at all. Starvation, and not sin, is the parent of modern crime. That indeed is the reason why our criminals are, as a class, so absolutely uninteresting from any psychological point of view. They are not marvellous Macbeths and terrible Vautrins. They are merely what ordinary, respectable, commonplace people would be if they had not got enough to eat. When private property is abolished there will be no necessity for crime, no demand for it; it will cease to exist. Of course all crimes are not crimes against property, though such are the crimes that the English law, valuing what a man has more than what a man is, punishes with the harshest and most horrible severity, if we except the crime of murder, and regard death as worse than penal servitude, a point on which our criminals, I believe, disagree. But though a crime may not be against property, it may spring from the misery and rage and depression produced by our wrong system of property-holding, and so, when that system is abolished, will disappear. When each member of the community has sufficient for his wants, and is not interfered with by his neighbour, it will not be an object of any interest to him to interfere with any one else. Jealousy, which is an extraordinary source of crime in modern life, is an emotion closely bound up with our conceptions of property, and under Socialism and Individualism will die out. It is remarkable that in communistic tribes jealousy is entirely unknown.

Now as the State is not to govern, it may be asked what the State is to do. The State is to be a voluntary association that will organize labour, and be the manufacturer and distributor of necessary commodities. *The State is to make what is useful. The individual is to make what is beautiful.* And as I have mentioned the word labour, I cannot help saying that a great deal of nonsense is being written and talked nowadays about the dignity of manual labour. There is nothing necessarily dignified about manual labour at all, and most of it is absolutely degrading. It is mentally and morally injurious to man to do anything in which he does not find pleasure, and many forms of labour are quite pleasureless activities, and should be regarded as such. To sweep a slushy crossing for eight hours on a day when the east wind is blowing is a disgusting occupation. To sweep it with mental, moral or physical dignity seems to me to be impossible. To sweep it with joy would be appalling. Man is made for something better than disturbing dirt. All work of that kind should be done by a machine.

And I have no doubt that it will be so. Up to the present, man has been, to a certain extent, the slave of machinery, and there is something tragic in the fact that as soon as man had invented a machine to do his work he began to starve. This, however, is, of course, the result of our property system and our system of competition. One man owns a machine which does the work of five hundred men. Five hundred men are, in consequence, thrown out of employment, and having no work to do, become hungry and take to thieving. The one man secures the produce of the machine and keeps it, and has five hundred times as much as he should have, and probably, which is of much more importance, a great deal more than he really wants. Were that machine the property of all, every one would benefit by it. It would be an immense advantage to the community. All unintellectual labour, all monotonous, dull labour, all labour that deals with dreadful things, and involves unpleasant conditions, must be done by machinery. Machinery must work for us in coal mines, and do all sanitary services, and be the stoker of steamers, and clean the streets, and run messages on wet days, and do anything that is tedious or distressing. *At present machinery competes against man. Under proper conditions machinery will serve man.* There is no doubt at all that this is the future of machinery, and just as trees grow while the country gentleman is asleep, so while Humanity will be amusing itself, or enjoying cultivated leisure – which, and not labour, is the aim of man – or making beautiful things, or reading beautiful things, or simply contemplating the world with admiration and delight, machinery will be doing all the necessary and unpleasant work. The fact is, that civilization requires slaves. The Greeks were quite right there. Unless there are slaves to do the ugly, horrible, uninteresting work, culture and contemplation become almost impossible. Human slavery is wrong, insecure and demoralizing. On mechanical slavery, on the slavery of the machine, the future of the world depends. And when scientific men are no longer called upon to go down to a depressing East-End and distribute bad cocoa and worse blankets to starving people, they will have delightful leisure in which to devise wonderful and marvellous things for their own joy and the joy of every one else. There will be great storages of force for every city, and for every house if required, and this force man will convert into heat, light, or motion, according to his needs. Is this Utopian? A map of the world that does not include Utopia is not worth even glancing at, for it leaves out the one country at which Humanity is always landing. And when Humanity lands there, it looks out, and, seeing a better country, sets sail. Progress is the realization of Utopias.

Now, I have said that the community by means of organization of machinery will supply the useful things, and that the beautiful things will be made by the individual. This is not merely necessary, but it is the only possible way by which we can get either the one or the other. An individual who has to make things for the use of others, and with reference to their wants and their wishes, does not work with interest, and consequently cannot put into his work what is best in him. Upon the other hand, whenever a community or a powerful section of a community, or a government of any kind, attempts to dictate to the artist what he is to do, Art either entirely vanishes, or becomes stereotyped, or degenerates into a low and ignoble form of craft. *A work of art is the unique result of a unique temperament. Its beauty comes from the fact that the author is what he is. It has nothing to do with the fact that other people want what they want.* Indeed, the moment that an artist takes notice of what other people want, and tries to supply the demand, he ceases to be an artist, and becomes a dull or an amusing craftsman, an honest or a dishonest tradesman. He has no further claim to be considered as an artist. *Art is the most intense mode of individualism that the world has known.* I am inclined to say that it is the only real mode of individualism that the world has known. Crime, which, under certain conditions, may seem to have created individualism, must take cognizance of other people and interfere with them. It belongs to the sphere of action. But alone, without any reference to his neighbours, without any interference, the artist can fashion a beautiful thing; and if he does not do it solely for his own pleasure, he is not an artist at all.

And it is to be noted that it is the fact that Art is this intense form of individualism that makes the public try to exercise over it an authority that is as immoral as it is ridiculous, and as corrupting as it is contemptible. It is not quite their fault. The public has always, and in every age, been badly brought up. They are continually asking Art to be popular, to please their want of taste, to flatter their absurd vanity, to tell them what they have been told before, to show them what they ought to be tired of seeing, to amuse them when they feel heavy after eating too much, and to distract their thoughts when they are wearied of their own stupidity. *Now Art should never try to be popular. The public should try to make itself artistic.* There is a very wide difference. If a man of science were told that the results of his experiments, and the conclusions that he arrived at, should be of such a character that they would not upset the received popular notions on the subject, or disturb popular prejudice, or hurt the sensibilities of people who knew nothing about science; if a philosopher were told that he had a perfect right to speculate in the highest spheres of thought, provided that he arrived at the same conclusions as were held by those who had never thought in any sphere at all – well, nowadays the man of science and the philosopher would be considerably amused. Yet it is really a very few years since both philosophy and science were subjected to brutal popular control, to authority in fact – the authority of either the general ignorance of the community, or the terror and greed for power of an ecclesiastical or governmental class. Of course, we have to a very great extent got rid of any attempt on the part of the community, or the Church, or the Government, to interfere with the individualism of speculative thought, but the attempt to interfere with the individualism of imaginative art still lingers. In fact, it does more than linger: it is aggressive, offensive, and brutalizing.

In England, the arts that have escaped best are the arts in which the public takes no interest. Poetry is an instance of what I mean. We have been able to have fine poetry in England because the public does not read it, and consequently does not influence it.

The public likes to insult poets because they are individual, but once they have insulted them they leave them alone. In the case of the novel and the drama, arts in which the public does take an interest, the result of the exercise of popular authority has been absolutely ridiculous. No country produces such badly written fiction, such tedious, common work in the novel-form, such silly, vulgar plays as in England. It must necessarily be so. The popular standard is of such a character that no artist can get to it. It is at once too easy and too difficult to be a popular novelist. It is too easy, because the requirements of the public as far as plot, style, psychology, treatment of life and treatment of literature are concerned, are within the reach of the very meanest capacity and the most uncultivated mind. It is too difficult, because to meet such requirements the artist would have to do violence to his temperament, would have to write not for the artistic joy of writing, but for the amusement of half-educated people, and so would have to suppress his individualism, forget his culture, annihilate his style, and surrender everything that is valuable in him. In the case of the drama, things are a little better: the theatre-going public likes the obvious, it is true, but it does not like the tedious; and burlesque and farcical comedy, the two most popular forms, are distinct forms of art. Delightful work may be produced under burlesque and farcical conditions, and in work of this kind the artist in England is allowed very great freedom. It is when one comes to the higher forms of the drama that the result of popular control is seen. The one thing that the public dislikes is novelty. Any attempt to extend the subject-matter of art is extremely distasteful to the public; and yet the vitality and progress of art depend in a large measure on the continual extension of subject-matter. The public dislikes novelty because it is afraid of it. It represents to them a mode of Individualism, an assertion on the part of the artist that he selects his own subject, and treats it as he chooses. The public is quite right in its attitude. Art is Individualism, and Individualism is a disturbing and disintegrating force. Therein lies its immense value. For what it seeks to disturb is monotony of type, slavery of custom, tyranny of habit, and the reduction of man to the level of a machine. In Art, the public accepts what has been, because they cannot alter it, not because they appreciate it. They swallow their classics whole, and never taste them. They endure them as the inevitable, and, as they cannot mar them, they mouth about them. Strangely enough, or not strangely, according to one's own views, this acceptance of the classics does a great deal of harm. The uncritical admiration of the Bible and Shakespeare in England is an instance of what I mean. With regard to the Bible, considerations of ecclesiastical authority enter into the matter, so that I need not dwell upon the point.

But in the case of Shakespeare it is quite obvious that the public really sees neither the beauties nor the defects of his plays. If they saw the beauties, they would not object to the development of the drama; and if they saw the defects, they would not object to the development of the drama either. *The fact is, the public makes use of the classics of a country as a means of checking the progress of Art.* They degrade the classics into authorities. They use them as bludgeons for preventing the free expression of Beauty in new forms. They are always asking a writer why he does not write like somebody else, or a painter why he does not paint like somebody else, quite oblivious of the fact that if either of them did anything of the kind he would cease to be an artist. A fresh mode of Beauty is absolutely distasteful to them, and whenever it appears they get so angry and bewildered that they always use two stupid expressions – one is that the work of art is grossly unintelligible; the other, that the work of art is grossly immoral. What they mean by these words seems to me to be this. When they say a work is grossly unintelligible, they mean that the artist has said or made a beautiful thing that is new; when they describe a work as grossly immoral, they mean that the artist has said or made a beautiful thing that is true. The former expression has reference to style; the latter to subject-matter. But they probably use the words very vaguely, as an ordinary mob will use ready-made paving-stones. *There is not a single real poet or prose-writer of this century, for instance, on whom the British public has not solemnly conferred diplomas of immorality,* and these diplomas practically take the place, with us, of what in France is the formal recognition of an Academy of Letters, and fortunately make the establishment of such an institution quite unnecessary in England. Of course the public is very reckless in its use of the word. That they should have called Wordsworth an immoral poet, was only to be expected. Wordsworth was a poet. But that they should have called Charles Kingsley an immoral novelist is extraordinary. Kingsley's prose was not of a very fine quality. Still, there is the word, and they use it as best they can. An artist is, of course, not disturbed by it. The true artist is a man who believes absolutely in himself, because he is absolutely himself. But I can fancy that if an artist produced a work of art in England that immediately on its appearance was recognized by the public, through its medium, which is the public press, as a work that was quite intelligible and highly moral, he would begin seriously to question whether in its creation he had really been himself at all, and consequently whether the work was not quite unworthy of him, and either of a thoroughly second-rate order, or of no artistic value whatsoever.

Perhaps, however, I have wronged the public in limiting them to such words as 'immoral', 'unintelligible', 'exotic', and 'unhealthy'. There is one other word that they use. That word is 'morbid'. They do not use it often. The meaning of the word is so simple that they are afraid of using it. Still, they use it sometimes, and, now and then, one comes across it in popular newspapers. It is, of course, a ridiculous word to apply to a work of art. For what is morbidity but a mood of emotion or a mode of thought that one cannot express? The public are all morbid, because the public can never find expression for anything. *The artist is never morbid. He expresses everything.* He stands outside his subject, and through its medium produces incomparable and artistic effects. To call an artist morbid because he deals with morbidity as his subject-matter is as silly as if one called Shakespeare mad because he wrote *King Lear.*

On the whole, an artist in England gains something by being attacked. His individuality is intensified. He becomes more completely himself. Of course the attacks are very gross, very impertinent, and very contemptible. But then no artist expects grace from the vulgar mind, or style from the suburban intellect. Vulgarity and stupidity are two very vivid facts in modern life. One regrets them, naturally. But there they are. They are subjects for study, like everything else. And it is only fair to state, with regard to modern journalists, that they always apologize to one in private for what they have written against one in public.

Within the last few years two other adjectives, it may be mentioned, have been added to the very limited vocabulary of art-abuse that is at the disposal of the public. One is the word 'unhealthy', the other is the word 'exotic'. The latter merely expresses the rage of the momentary mushroom against the immortal, entrancing, and exquisitely-lovely orchid. It is a tribute, but a tribute of no importance. The word 'unhealthy', however, admits of analysis. It is a rather interesting word. In fact, it is so interesting that the people who use it do not know what it means.

What does it mean? What is a healthy, or an unhealthy work of art? All terms that one applies to a work of art, provided that one applies them rationally, have reference to either its style or its subject, or to both together. From the point of view of style, a healthy work of art is one whose style recognizes the beauty of the material it employs, be that material one of words or of bronze, of colour or of ivory and uses that beauty as a factor in producing the aesthetic effect. From the point of view of subject, a healthy work of art is one the choice of whose subject is conditioned by the temperament of the artist, and comes directly out of it. In fine, a healthy work of art is one that has both perfection and personality. Of course, form and substance cannot be separated in a work of art; they are always one. But for purposes of analysis, and setting the wholeness of aesthetic impression aside for a moment, intellectually we can so separate them. An unhealthy work of art, on the other hand, is a work whose style is obvious, old-fashioned, and common, and whose subject is deliberately chosen, not because the artist has any pleasure in it, but because he thinks that the public will pay him for it. *In fact, the popular novel that the public calls healthy is always a thoroughly unhealthy production; and what the public calls an unhealthy novel is always a beautiful and healthy work of art.*

I need hardly say that I am not, for a single moment, complaining that the public and the public press misuse these words. I do not see how, with their lack of comprehension of what Art is, they could possibly use them in the proper sense. I am merely pointing out the misuse; and as for the origin of the misuse and the meaning that lies behind it all, the explanation is very simple. It comes from the barbarous conception of authority. It comes from the natural inability of a community corrupted by authority to understand or appreciate

Individualism. In a word, it comes from that monstrous and ignorant thing that is called Public Opinion, which bad and well-meaning as it is when it tries to control action, is infamous and of evil meaning when it tries to control Thought or Art.

Indeed, there is much more to be said in favour of the physical force of the public than there is in favour of the public's opinion. The former may be fine. The latter must be foolish. It is often said that force is no argument. That, however, entirely depends on what one wants to prove. Many of the most important problems of the last few centuries, such as the continuance of personal government in England, or of feudalism in France, have been solved entirely by means of physical force. The very violence of a revolution may make the public grand and splendid for a moment. It was a fatal day when the public discovered that the pen is mightier than the paving-stone, and can be made as offensive as the brickbat. They at once sought for the journalist, found him, developed him, and made him their industrious and well-paid servant. It is greatly to be regretted, for both their sakes. Behind the barricade there may be much that is noble and heroic. But what is there behind the leading-article but prejudice, stupidity, cant and twaddle? And when these four are joined together they make a terrible force, and constitute the new authority.

In old days men had the rack. Now they have the press. That is an improvement certainly. But still it is very bad, and wrong, and demoralizing. Somebody – was it Burke? – called journalism the fourth estate. That was true at the time, no doubt. But at the present moment it really is the only estate. It has eaten up the other three. The Lords Temporal say nothing, the Lords Spiritual have nothing to say, and the House of Commons has nothing to say and says it. We are dominated by Journalism. In America the President reigns for four years, and Journalism governs for ever and ever. Fortunately in America Journalism has carried its authority to the grossest and most brutal extreme. As a natural consequence it has begun to create a spirit of revolt. People are amused by it, or disgusted by it, according to their temperaments. But it is no longer the real force it was. It is not seriously treated. In England, Journalism, not, except in a few well-known instances, having been carried to such excesses of brutality, is still a great factor, a really remarkable power. The tyranny that it proposes to exercise over people's private lives seems to me to be quite extraordinary. *The fact is, that the public has an insatiable curiosity to know everything, except what is worth knowing.* Journalism, conscious of this, and having tradesmanlike habits, supplies their demands. In centuries before ours the public nailed the ears of journalists to the pump. That was quite hideous. In this century journalists have nailed their own ears to the keyhole. That is much worse. And what aggravates the mischief is that the journalists who are most to blame are not the amusing journalists who write what are called Society papers. The harm is done by the serious, thoughtful, earnest journalists, who solemnly, as they are doing at present, will drag before the eyes of the public some incident in the private life of a great statesman, of a man who is a leader of political thought as he is a creator of political force, and invite the public to discuss the incident, to exercise authority in the matter, to give their views, and not merely to give their views, but to carry them into action, to dictate to the man upon all other points, to dictate to his party, to dictate to his country, in fact to make themselves ridiculous, offensive and harmful. The private lives of men and women should not be told to the public. The public has nothing to do with them at all. In France they manage these things better. There they do not allow the details of the trials that take place in the divorce courts to be published for the amusement or criticism of the public. All that the public is allowed to know is that the divorce has taken place and was granted on petition of one or other or both of the married parties concerned. In France, in fact, they limit the journalist, and allow the artist almost perfect freedom. *Here we allow absolute freedom to the journalist, and entirely limit the artist.* English public opinion, that is to say, tries to constrain and impede and warp the man who makes things that are beautiful in effect, and compels the journalist to retail things that are ugly, or disgusting, or revolting in fact, so that we have the most serious journalists in the world and the most indecent newspapers. It is no exaggeration to talk of compulsion. There are possibly some journalists who take a real pleasure in publishing horrible things, or who, being poor, look to scandals as forming a sort of permanent basis for an income. But there are other journalists, I feel certain, men of education and cultivation, who really dislike publishing these things, who know that it is wrong to do so, and only do it because the unhealthy conditions under which their occupation is carried on oblige them to supply the public with what the public wants, and to compete with other journalists in making that supply as full and satisfying to the gross popular appetite as possible. It is a very degrading position for any body of educated men to be placed in, and I have no doubt that most of them feel it acutely.

However, let us leave what is really a very sordid side of the subject, and return to the question of popular control in the matter of Art, by which I mean Public Opinion dictating to the artist the form which he is to use, the mode in which he is to use it, and the materials with which he is to work. I have pointed out that the arts which have escaped best in England are the arts in which the public has not been interested. They are, however, interested in the drama, and as a certain advance has been made in the drama within the last ten or fifteen years, it is important to point out that this advance is entirely due to a few individual artists refusing to accept the popular want of taste as their standard, and refusing to regard Art as a mere matter of demand and supply. With his marvellous and vivid personality, with a style that has really a true colour-element in it, with his extraordinary power, not over mere mimicry but over imaginative and intellectual creation, Mr Irving, had his sole object been to give the public what it wanted, could have produced the commonest plays in the commonest manner, and made as much success and money as a man could possibly desire. But his object was not that. His object was to realize his own perfection as an artist, under certain conditions, and in certain forms of Art. At first he appealed to the few: now he has educated the many. He has created in the public both taste and temperament. The public appreciates his artistic success immensely. I often wonder, however, whether the public understands that that success is entirely due to the fact that he did not accept their standard, but realized his own. With their standard the Lyceum would have been a sort of second-rate booth, as some of the popular theatres in London are at present. Whether they understand it or not the fact however remains, that taste and temperament have, to a certain extent, been created in the public, and that the public is capable of developing these qualities. The problem then is, why does not the public become more civilized? They have the capacity. What stops them?

The thing that stops them, it must be said again, is their desire to exercise authority over the artist and over works of art. To certain theatres, such as the Lyceum and the Haymarket, the public seems to come in a proper mood. In both of these theatres there have been individual artists, who have succeeded in creating in their audiences – and every theatre in London has its own audience – the temperament to which Art appeals. And what is that temperament? It is the temperament of receptivity. That is all.

If a man approaches a work of art with any desire to exercise authority over it and the artist, he approaches it in such a spirit that he cannot receive any artistic impression from it at all. *The work of art is to dominate the spectator: the spectator is not to dominate the work of art.* The spectator is to be receptive. He is to be the violin on which the master is to play. And the more completely he can suppress his own foolish prejudices, his own absurd ideas of what Art should be or should not be, the more likely he is to understand and appreciate the work of art in question. This is, of course, quite obvious in the case of the vulgar theatre-going public of English men and women. But it is equally true of what are called educated people. For an educated person's ideas of Art are drawn naturally from what Art has been, whereas the new work of art is beautiful by being what Art has never been; and to measure it by the standard of the past is to measure it by a standard on the rejection of which its real perfection depends. A temperament capable of receiving, through an imaginative medium, and under imaginative conditions, new and beautiful impressions is the only temperament that can appreciate a work of art. And true as this is in the case of the appreciation of sculpture and painting, it is still more true of the appreciation of such arts as the drama. For a picture and a statue are not at war with Time. They take no count of its succession. In one moment their unity may be apprehended. In the case of literature it is different. Time must be traversed before the unity of effect is realized. And so, in the drama, there may occur in the first act of the play something whose real artistic value may not be evident to the spectator till the third or fourth act is reached. Is the silly fellow to get angry and call out, and disturb the play, and annoy the artists? No. The honest man is to sit quietly, and know the delightful emotions of wonder, curiosity and suspense. He is not to go to the play to lose a vulgar temper. He is to go to the play to realize an artistic temperament. He is to go to the play to gain an artistic temperament. He is not the arbiter of the work of art. He is one who is admitted to contemplate the work of art, and, if the work be fine, to forget in its contemplation all the egotism that mars him – the egotism of his ignorance, or the egotism of his information. This point about the drama is hardly, I think, sufficiently recognized. I can quite understand that were *Macbeth* produced for the first time before a modern London audience, many of the people present would strongly and vigorously object to the introduction of the witches in the first act, with their grotesque phrases and their ridiculous words. But when the play is over one realizes that the laughter of the witches in *Macbeth* is as terrible as the laughter of madness in *Lear*, more terrible than the laughter of Iago in the tragedy of the Moor. No spectator of art needs a more perfect mood of receptivity than the spectator of a play. The moment he seeks to exercise authority he becomes the avowed enemy of Art and of himself. Art does not mind. It is he who suffers.

With the novel it is the same thing. Popular authority and the recognition of popular authority are fatal. Thackeray's *Esmond* is a beautiful work of art because he wrote it to please himself. In his other novels, in *Pendennis*, in *Philip*, in *Vanity Fair* even, at times, he is too conscious of the public, and spoils his work by appealing directly to the sympathies of the public, or by directly mocking at them. *A true artist takes no notice whatever of the public. The public is to him non-existent.* He has no poppied or honeyed cakes through which to give the monster sleep or sustenance. He leaves that to the popular novelist. One incomparable novelist we have now in England, Mr George Meredith. There are better artists in France, but France has no one whose view of life is so large, so varied, so imaginatively true. There are tellers of stories in Russia who have a more vivid sense of what pain in fiction may be. But to him belongs philosophy in fiction. His people not merely live, but they live in thought. One can see them from myriad points of view. They are suggestive. There is soul in them and around them. They are interpretative and symbolic. And he who made them, those wonderful quickly-moving figures, made them for his own pleasure, and has never asked the public what they wanted, has never cared to know what they wanted, has never allowed the public to dictate to him or influence him in any way, but has gone on intensifying his own personality, and producing his own individual work. At first none came to him. That did not matter. Then the few came to him. That did not change him. The many have come now. He is still the same. He is an incomparable novelist.

With the decorative arts it is not different. The public clung with really pathetic tenacity to what I believe were the direct traditions of the Great Exhibition of international vulgarity, traditions that were so appalling that the houses in which people lived were only fit for blind people to live in. Beautiful things began to be made, beautiful colours came from the dyer's hand, beautiful patterns from the artist's brain, and the use of beautiful things and their value and importance were set forth. The public was really very indignant. They lost their temper. They said silly things. No one minded. No one was a whit the worse. No one accepted the authority of public opinion. And now it is almost impossible to enter any modern house without seeing some recognition of good taste, some recognition of the value of lovely surroundings, some sign of appreciation of beauty. In fact, people's houses are, as a rule, quite charming nowadays. People have been to a very great extent civilized. It is only fair to state, however, that the extraordinary success of the revolution in house-decoration and furniture and the like has not really been due to the majority of the public developing a very fine taste in such matters. It has been chiefly due to the fact that the craftsmen of things so appreciated the pleasure of making what was beautiful, and woke to such a vivid consciousness of the hideousness and vulgarity of what the public had previously wanted, that they simply starved the public out. It would be quite impossible at the present moment to furnish a room as rooms were furnished a few years ago, without going for everything to an auction of second-hand furniture from some third-rate lodging-house. The things are no longer made. However they may object to it, people must nowadays have something charming in their surroundings. Fortunately for them, their assumption of authority in these art-matters came to entire grief.

It is evident, then, that all authority in such things is bad. People sometimes inquire what form of government is most suitable for an artist to live under. To this question there is only one answer. *The form of government that is most suitable to the artist is no government at all.* Authority over him and his art is ridiculous. It has been stated that under despotisms artists have produced lovely work. This is not quite so. Artists have visited despots, not as subjects to be tyrannized over, but as wandering wonder-makers, as fascinating vagrant personalities, to be entertained and charmed and suffered to be at peace, and allowed to create. There is this to be said in favour of the despot, that he, being an individual, may have culture, while the mob, being a monster, has none. One who is an Emperor and King may stoop down to pick up a brush for a painter, but when the democracy stoops down it is merely to throw mud. And yet the democracy have not so far to stoop as the Emperor. In fact, when they want to throw mud they have not to stoop at all. But there is no necessity to separate the monarch from the mob; all authority is equally bad.

There are three kinds of despots. There is the despot who tyrannizes over the body. There is the despot who tyrannizes over the soul. There is the despot who tyrannizes over soul and body alike. The first is called the Prince. The second is called the Pope. The third is called the People. The Prince may be cultivated. Many Princes have been. Yet in the Prince there is danger. One thinks of Dante at the bitter feast in Verona, of Tasso in Ferrara's madman's cell. It is better for the artist not to live with Princes. The Pope may be cultivated. Many Popes have been; the bad Popes have been. The bad Popes loved Beauty, almost as passionately, nay, with as much passion as the good Popes hated Thought. To the wickedness of the Papacy humanity owes much. The goodness of the Papacy owes a terrible debt to humanity. Yet, though the Vatican has kept the rhetoric of its thunders and lost the rod of its lightning, it is better for the artist not to live with Popes. It was a Pope who said of Cellini to a conclave of Cardinals that common laws and common authority were not made for men such as he; but it was a Pope who thrust Cellini into prison, and kept him there till he sickened with rage, and created unreal visions for himself, and saw the gilded sun enter his room, and grew so enamoured of it that he sought to escape, and crept out from tower to tower, and falling through dizzy air at dawn, maimed himself, and was by vine-dresser covered with vine leaves, and carried in a cart to one who, loving beautiful things, had care of him. There is danger in Popes. And as for the People, what of them and their authority? Perhaps of them and their authority one has spoken enough. Their authority is a thing blind, deaf, hideous, grotesque, tragic, amusing, serious and obscene. It is impossible for the artist to live with the People. All despots bribe. The people bribe and brutalize. Who told them to exercise authority? They were made to live, to listen, and to love. Someone has done them a great wrong. They have marred themselves by imitation of their inferiors. They have taken the sceptre of the Prince. How should they use it? They have taken the triple tiara of the Pope. How should they carry its burden? They are as a clown whose heart is broken. They are as a priest whose soul is not yet born. Let all who love Beauty pity them. Though they themselves love not Beauty, yet let them pity themselves. Who taught them the trick of tyranny?

There are many other things that one might point out. One might point out how the Renaissance was great, because it sought to solve no social problem, and busied itself not about such things, but suffered the individual to develop freely, beautifully and naturally, and so had great and individual artists, and great and individual men. One might point out how Louis XIV, by creating the modern state, destroyed the individualism of the artist, and made things monstrous in their monotony of repetition, and contemptible in their conformity to rule, and destroyed throughout all France all those fine freedoms of expression that had made tradition new in beauty, and new modes one with antique form. But the past is of no importance. The present is of no importance. It is with the future that we have to deal. For the past is what man should not have been. The present is what man ought not to be. The future is what artists are.

It will, of course, be said that such a scheme as is set forth here is quite unpractical, and goes against human nature. This is perfectly true. It is unpractical, and it goes against human nature. This is why it is worth carrying out, and that is why one proposes it. For what is a practical scheme? *A practical scheme is either a scheme that is already in existence, or a scheme that could be carried out under existing conditions.* But it is exactly the existing conditions that one objects to; and any scheme that could accept these conditions is wrong and foolish. The conditions will be done away with, and human nature will change. The only thing that one really knows about human nature is that it changes. Change is the one quality we can predicate of it. The systems that fail are those that rely on the permanency of human nature, and not on its growth and development. The error of Louis XIV was that he thought human nature would always be the same. The result of his error was the French Revolution. It was an admirable result. All the results of the mistakes of governments are quite admirable.

It is to be noted also that Individualism does not come to man with any sickly cant about duty, which merely means doing what other people want because they want it; or any hideous cant about self-sacrifice, which is merely a survival of savage mutilation. *In fact, it does not come to man with any claims upon him at all. It comes naturally and inevitably out of man.* It is the point to which all development tends. It is the differentiation to which all organisms grow. It is the perfection that is inherent in every mode of life, and towards which every mode of life quickens. And so Individualism exercises no compulsion over man. On the contrary, it says to man that he should suffer no compulsion to be exercised over him. It does not try to force people to be good. It knows that people are good when they are let alone. Man will develop Individualism out of himself. Man is now so developing Individualism. To ask whether Individualism is practical is like asking whether Evolution is practical. *Evolution is the law of life, and there is no evolution except towards Individualism.* Where this tendency is not expressed, it is a case of artificially arrested growth, or of disease, or of death.

Individualism will also be unselfish and unaffected. It has been pointed out that one of the results of the extraordinary tyranny of authority is that words are absolutely distorted from their proper and simple meaning, and are used to express the obverse of their right signification. What is true about Art is true about Life.

A man is called affected, nowadays, if he dresses as he likes to dress. But in doing that he is acting in a perfectly natural manner. Affectation, in such matters, consists in dressing according to the views of one's neighbour, whose views, as they are the views of the majority, will probably be extremely stupid. Or a man is called selfish if he lives in a manner that seems to him most suitable for the full realization of his own personality; if, in fact, the primary aim of his life is self-development. But this is the way in which everyone should live. *Selfishness is not living as one wishes to live, it is asking others to live as one wishes to live.* And unselfishness is letting other people's lives alone, not interfering with them. Selfishness always aims at creating around it an absolute uniformity of type. Unselfishness recognizes infinite variety of type as a delightful thing, accepts it, acquiesces in it, enjoys it. It is not selfish to think for oneself. A man who does not think for himself does not think at all. It is grossly selfish to require of one's neighbour that he should think in the same way, and hold the same opinions. Why should he? If he can think, he will probably think differently. If he cannot think, it is monstrous to require thought of any kind from him. A red rose is not selfish because it wants to be a red rose. It would be horribly selfish if it wanted all the other flowers in the garden to be both red and roses. Under Individualism people will be quite natural and absolutely unselfish, and will know the meanings of the words, and realize them in their free beautiful lives. Nor will men be egotistic as they are now. For the egotist is he who makes claims upon others, and the Individualist will not desire to do that. It will not give him pleasure. When man has realized Individualism, he will also realize sympathy and exercise it freely and spontaneously. Up to the present man has hardly cultivated sympathy at all. He has merely sympathy with pain, and sympathy with pain is not the highest form of sympathy. *All sympathy is fine, but sympathy with suffering is the least fine mode.* It is tainted with egotism. It is apt to become morbid. There is in it a certain element of terror for our own safety. We become afraid that we ourselves might be as the leper or as the blind, and that no man would have care of us. It is curiously limiting, too. One should sympathize with the entirety of life, not with life's sores and maladies merely, but with life's joy and beauty and energy and health and freedom. The wider sympathy is, of course, the more difficult. It requires more unselfishness. Anybody can sympathize with the sufferings of a friend, but it requires a very fine nature – it requires, in fact, the nature of a true Individualist – to sympathize with a friend's success. In the modern stress of competition and struggle for place, such sympathy is naturally rare, and is also very much stifled by the immoral ideal of uniformity of type and conformity to rule which is so prevalent everywhere, and is perhaps most obnoxious in England.

Sympathy with pain there will, of course, always be. It is one of the first instincts of man. The animals which are individual, the higher animals that is to say, share it with us. But it must be remembered that while sympathy with joy intensifies the sum of joy in the world, sympathy with pain does not really diminish the amount of pain. It may make man better able to endure evil, but the evil remains. Sympathy with consumption does not cure consumption; that is what Science does. And when Socialism has solved the problem of poverty, and Science solved the problem of disease, the area of the sentimentalists will be lessened, and the sympathy of man will be large, healthy, and spontaneous. Man will have joy in the contemplation of the joyous lives of others.

For it is through joy that the Individualism of the future will develop itself. *Christ made no attempt to re-construct society, and consequently the Individualism that he preached to man could be realized only through pain or in solitude.* The ideals that we owe to Christ are the ideals of the man who abandons society entirely, or of the man who resists society absolutely. But man is naturally social. Even the Thebaid became peopled at last. And though the cenobite realizes his personality, it is often an impoverished personality that he so realizes. Upon the other hand, the terrible truth that pain is a mode through which man may realize himself exercised a wonderful fascination over the world. Shallow speakers and shallow thinkers in pulpits and on platforms often talk about the world's worship of pleasure, and whine against it, but it is rarely in the world's history that its ideal has been one of joy and beauty. The worship of pain has far more often dominated the world. Mediævalism, with its saints and martyrs, its love of self-torture, its wild passion for wounding itself, its gashing with knives, and its whipping

with rods – Mediævalism is real Christianity, and the mediæval
Christ is the real Christ. When the Renaissance dawned upon
the world, and brought with it the new ideals of the beauty of
life and the joy of living, men could not understand Christ. Even
Art shows us that. The painters of the Renaissance drew Christ
as a little boy playing with another boy in a palace or a garden, or
lying back in his mother's arms, smiling at her, or at a flower, or
at a bright bird; or as a noble stately figure moving nobly through
the world; or as a wonderful figure rising in a sort of ecstasy from
death to life. Even when they drew him crucified they drew him
as a beautiful God on whom evil men had inflicted suffering. But
he did not preoccupy them much. What delighted them was to
paint the men and women whom they admired, and to show
the loveliness of this lovely earth. They painted many religious
pictures – in fact, they painted far too many, and the monotony
of type and motive is wearisome, and was bad for art. It was
the result of the authority of the public in art-matters, and is
to be deplored. But their soul was not in the subject. Raphael
was a great artist when he painted his portrait of the Pope. When
he painted his Madonnas and infant Christs, he is not a great
artist at all. Christ had no message for the Renaissance, which
was wonderful because it brought an ideal at variance with his,
and to find the presentation of the real Christ we must go to
mediæval art. There, he is one maimed and marred; one who is
not comely to look on, because Beauty is a joy; one who is not
in fair raiment, because that may be a joy also: he is a beggar who
has a marvellous soul; he is a leper whose soul is divine; he needs
neither property nor health; he is a God realizing his perfection
through pain.

The evolution of man is slow. The injustice of men is great.
It was necessary that pain should be put forward as a mode of
self-realization. Even now, in some places in the world, the
message of Christ is necessary. No one who lived in modern
Russia could possibly realize his perfection except by pain. A
few Russian artists have realized themselves in Art, in a fiction
that is mediæval in character, because its dominant note is the
realization of men through suffering. But for those who are not
artists, and to whom there is no mode of life but the actual life
of fact, pain is the only door to perfection. A Russian who
lives happily under the present system of government in Russia

must either believe that man has no soul, or that, if he has, it is not worth developing. A Nihilist who rejects all authority, because he knows authority to be evil, and who welcomes all pain, because through that he realizes his personality, is a real Christian. To him the Christian ideal is a true thing.

And yet, Christ did not revolt against authority. He accepted the imperial authority of the Roman Empire and paid tribute. He endured the ecclesiastical authority of the Jewish Church, and would not repel its violence by any violence of his own. He had, as I said before, no scheme for the re-construction of society. But the modern world has schemes. It proposes to do away with poverty and the suffering that it entails. It desires to get rid of pain and the suffering that pain entails. It trusts to Socialism and to Science as its methods. What it aims at is an Individualism expressing itself through joy. This Individualism will be larger, fuller, lovelier than any Individualism has ever been. Pain is not the ultimate mode of perfection. It is merely provisional and a protest. It has reference to wrong, unhealthy, unjust surroundings. When the wrong, and the disease and the injustice are removed, it will have no further place. It will have done its work. It was great work, but it is almost over. Its sphere lessens every day.

Nor will man miss it. *For what man has sought for is, indeed, neither pain nor pleasure, but simply Life.* Man has sought to live intensely, fully, perfectly. When he can do so without exercising restraint on others, or suffering it ever, and his activities are all pleasurable to him, he will be saner, healthier, more civilized, more himself. Pleasure is Nature's test, her sign of approval. When man is happy, he is in harmony with himself and his environment. The new Individualism, for whose service Socialism, whether it wills it or not, is working, will be perfect harmony. It will be what the Greeks sought for, but could not, except in Thought, realize completely, because they had slaves, and fed them; it will be what the Renaissance sought for, but could not realize completely, except in Art, because they had slaves, and starved them. It will be complete, and through it each man will attain to his perfection. The new Individualism is the new Hellenism.

A Few Maxims for the Instruction of the Over-Educated

Education is an admirable thing. But it is well to remember from time to time that nothing that is worth knowing can be taught.

Public opinion exists only where there are no ideas.

The English are always degrading truths into facts. When a truth becomes a fact it loses all its intellectual value.

It is a very sad thing that nowadays there is so little useless information.

The only link between Literature and the Drama left to us in England at the present moment is the bill of the play.

In old days books were written by men of letters and read by the public. Nowadays books are written by the public and read by nobody.

Most women are so artificial that they have no sense of Art. Most men are so natural that they have no sense of Beauty.

Friendship is far more tragic than love. It lasts longer.

What is abnormal in Life stands in normal relations to Art. It is the only thing in Life that stands in normal relations to Art.

A subject that is beautiful in itself gives no suggestion to the artist. It lacks imperfection.

The only thing that the artist cannot see is the obvious. The only thing that the public can see is the obvious. The result is the Criticism of the Journalist.

Art is the only serious thing in the world. And the artist is the only person who is never serious.

To be really mediaeval one should have no body. To be really modern one should have no soul. To be really Greek one should have no clothes.

Dandyism is the assertion of the absolute modernity of Beauty.

The only thing that can console one for being poor is extravagance. The only thing that can console one for being rich is economy.

One should never listen. To listen is a sign of indifference to one's hearers.

Even the disciple has his uses. He stands behind one's throne, and at the moment of one's triumph whispers in one's ear that, after all, one is immortal.

The criminal classes are so close to us that even the policeman can see them. They are so far away from us that only the poet can understand them.

Those whom the gods love grow young.

Phrases and Philosophies for the Use of the Young

The first duty in life is to be as artificial as possible. What the second duty is no one has as yet discovered.

Wickedness is a myth invented by good people to account for the curious attractiveness of others.

If the poor only had profiles there would be no difficulty in solving the problem of poverty.

Those who see any difference between soul and body have neither.

A really well-made buttonhole is the only link between Art and Nature.

Religions die when they are proved to be true. Science is the record of dead religions.

The well-bred contradict other people. The wise contradict themselves.

Nothing that actually occurs is of the smallest importance.

Dulness is the coming of age of seriousness.

In all unimportant matters, style, not sincerity, is the essential. In all important matters, style, not sincerity, is the essential.

If one tells the truth one is sure, sooner or later, to be found out.

Pleasure is the only thing one should live for. Nothing ages like happiness.

It is only by not paying one's bills that one can hope to live in the memory of the commercial classes.

No crime is vulgar, but all vulgarity is crime. Vulgarity is the conduct of others.

Only the shallow know themselves.

Time is waste of money.

One should always be a little improbable.

There is a fatality about all good resolutions. They are invariably made too soon.

The only way to atone for being occasionally a little overdressed is by being always absolutely over-educated.

To be premature is to be perfect.

Any preoccupation with ideas of what is right or wrong in conduct shows an arrested intellectual development.

Ambition is the last refuge of the failure.

A truth ceases to be true when more than one person believes in it.

In examinations the foolish ask questions that the wise cannot answer.

Greek dress was in its essence inartistic. Nothing should reveal the body but the body.

One should either be a work of art, or wear a work of art.

It is only the superficial qualities that last. Man's deeper nature is soon found out.

Industry is the root of all ugliness.

The ages live in history through their anachronisms.

It is only the gods who taste of death. Apollo has passed away, but Hyacinth, whom men say he slew, lives on. Nero and Narcissus are always with us.

The old believe everything: the middle-aged suspect everything: the young know everything.

The condition of perfection is idleness: the aim of perfection is youth.

Only the great masters of style ever succeed in being obscure.

There is something tragic about the enormous number of young men there are in England at the present moment who start life with perfect profiles, and end by adopting some useful profession.

To love oneself is the beginning of a lifelong romance.

Critical Commentary

THE IMPORTANCE OF BEING EARNEST

Earnest starts and finishes with the hilarious relationship between two young bachelors whose identities, as the play progresses, grow more and more confused. At the outset, it is not entirely clear how and why these young men have come to know one another. In the first act, they meet in Algernon's opulent London flat. They loudly share jokes as if they were the best of friends. Obviously, they are enjoying the pleasures of high Society (the capital letter signalling, as it did in Wilde's day, the most luxurious life to be had). This is, indeed, a world of exceptional privileges: lashings of champagne, lavish parties, and the proprieties of high tea. Social rituals are certainly uppermost in their minds. In fact, among the first of the many ceremonies they lightheartedly discuss is courtship. 'Ernest' will soon be engaged to Algernon's cousin, Gwendolen. The odd thing is, 'Ernest' has been hiding his true identity from Algernon. Why?

This puzzling question is partly answered in the opening scene – with all sorts of implications for what turns into a very complex but perfectly fashioned plot. 'Ernest', it would seem, provides Jack with an excellent alibi: 'My name is Ernest in town and Jack in the country' (p. 32). Jack, posing as 'Ernest', is leading a somewhat precarious double life. In his country seat, he is obviously known to everyone by his real name, Jack Worthing. However, since he finds his life on his estate constraining, and relishes the 'pleasure' of London society, he has had to devise another identity for himself. This, his alter ego, allows him to spend as much time as possible in the city. It is a complex ploy. To maintain these two identities, Jack tells different lies to different people. To his family in Hertfordshire, he claims that he has to go to London to see his irresponsible brother, 'Ernest'. When Jack reaches London and mixes with Algernon, he actually becomes the 'brother' he is supposed to be visiting. The country bores Jack; the city excites 'Ernest'. Only now, it seems, has he been found out. In the first scene, Jack is trying hard to explain to Algernon why he has different names in different places. Jack (alias 'Ernest') anxiously declares: 'I don't know whether you will be able to understand my real motives' (p. 33). Although his motives may be hard to grasp, it becomes clear that this deception is a very careful piece of plotting.

Mistaken identities; subtle deceptions; rapid reversals in relationships: these form the substance of Wilde's agile comedy. Confusions between names and faces, as well as names and places, hereafter proliferate. In each of its three acts, the play turns its attention to all sorts of amusing structures of deceit. Throughout *Earnest*, people are never quite what they seem to be. For a start, they do not even seem to correspond with what we might expect of dramatic characters. If they are not deceiving one another, then they are talking in a way that hardly seems authentic. They quip, joke, and come out with ideas and expressions that would appear to be something other than their own. It is, indeed, difficult to find some kind of psychological insight into either Jack or Algernon or anyone else in the play for that matter. It is *what* they say, rather than *why* they are saying it, that captures our attention. Inventive word-play; brilliant dialogue; sparkling wit: these are the things which drive the drama forward. Their motives vanish behind the brilliant façade of verbal trickery.

Even in the opening scene, the levels of intricate deceit begin to multiply. 'Ernest' is not the only character who adopts a persona to disguise his identity when he goes in search of 'pleasure'. Algernon, too, plays a similar trick upon his own relations. Just as Jack has invented the imaginary 'Ernest', so does Algernon have his fictional alias, 'Bunbury'. Like 'Ernest', 'Bunbury' makes enormous demands upon his inventor. 'Bunbury', according to Algernon, is 'an invaluable permanent invalid' (p. 33) – and so Algernon's endless visits to 'Bunbury' would appear to be the actions of a kind-hearted individual. At least, that is how Algernon wants to be understood. 'Bunbury', with his chronic illnesses and ceaseless calls on Algernon's attentions, enables Algernon to 'go down into the country' whenever he so wishes. For some reason or other, Algernon frequently needs to make a quick escape from London. Again, we are not exactly clear why.

In a sense, Jack's and Algernon's means of deception mirror each other. The country-dweller (Jack) desires to escape to the city, and the city-dweller (Algernon) makes haste for the open country. The country and the city represent completely opposed values. In the country, there is peace, solitude, innocence – and boredom. The city, by contrast, is noisy, sociable, sophisticated – and dangerous. Whenever the country becomes boring, the city is duly entertaining. And when the city becomes too demanding, the country serves as a retreat. Given the extremely deceitful lives both Jack and Algernon indulge in, it is hardly surprising that the play should be punctuated with numerous frantic exits and entrances. People shuttle back and forth between the country and the city with remarkable speed. Practically everyone, for some reason or other, feels the urge to vanish into another world where, it may be inferred, they really ought not to be. And they try to make their escapes as quickly as they can. This impulse to flee from their supposedly proper places certainly gives rise to a great many complications which tie much of the action in entertaining knots.

Jack is the one who seems most keen to escape in the name of 'pleasure', and the more we find out about him, the stranger he seems. He has, to say the least, an unusual family background. Jack is certainly not any ordinary member of the landed gentry. Indeed, his only relation is his ward, Cecily, who is not that much younger than himself. Although heir to an estate, Jack has not inherited his wealth through a line of blood. As we discover in the final scene, Jack was adopted by Sir Thomas Cardew who found him, as an abandoned baby, inside a handbag left in a cloakroom at Victoria Station. He became Sir Thomas's adopted son. Jack, therefore, assumes he is an orphan. But only he, and not Cecily (the late Sir Thomas's daughter), knows the strange circumstances concerning his doubtful origins. Even then, he still does not know what his real identity was before he had the name, Jack Worthing, conferred upon him. In a far from inspired moment, Sir Thomas called him Worthing (a seaside resort in Sussex) because he happened to have a first-class ticket for Worthing in his pocket at the time. By the third and final act, this question of names is resolved. Jack, then, goes through a series of transformations. The man who first of all pretends to have a brother called 'Ernest', and tells his London friends he is 'Ernest', actually discovers, after many sudden reversals in the plot, that he really *is* Ernest. And by becoming truly Ernest in the end, Jack finds out that he is Algernon's brother. In other words, once falsely 'Ernest', Jack is eventually *Ernest* in *earnest*. The drama closes as soon as it has made dramatic sense of this pun.

This comedy, therefore, centres on what might appear a rather laboured play on words – with entirely unexpected consequences. Living a double life has, paradoxically, enabled the revelation of the far-fetched truth that 'Ernest' is, indeed, Ernest. Having sorted out who's who in the furious closing moments, we can see how *Earnest* elegantly turns upon two remarkable ironies. First, a man who has tried to deceive another turns out to be that man's brother. Second, a true identity (Ernest in earnest) is, simultaneously, a linguistic joke (E(a)rnest). Set up first as a manipulative *fiction*, 'Ernest' is ultimately a *fact* – but only through the workings of a most contrived piece of plotting. Given the strenuous lengths to which this piece of word-play on 'E(a)rnest' is taken, it should be abundantly evident that there is some point to it. It is not there just for the sake of fun. Indeed, all the jokes in *Earnest* have serious resonances to them. With this play on 'E(a)rnest' in mind, we can see how this lively and fast-moving comedy raises a number of related questions about who or what a person truly is. What is the difference between an authentic identity and a false one? When is 'Ernest' genuinely in earnest? To put this another way: who or what might be taken in earnest in *Earnest*? The significance of these questions will deepen as we witness the quick turn of dramatic events in detail.

As soon as we discover how 'Ernest' and 'Bunbury' serve as 'covers' for each of the young men, the action swiftly changes, and the imperious Lady Bracknell and her daughter, Gwendolen, sweep on to the stage. Already Algernon has signalled that his aunt is coming to tea. The butler, Lane, has laid the table with suitable things to eat: cucumber sandwiches for Lady Bracknell, and bread and butter for Gwendolen. The trouble is, Algernon finds the cucumber sandwiches irresistible. In fact, he is in danger of eating them all up before his aunt arrives, and indeed he does. The sandwiches are important, for two reasons. Firstly, they are a hallmark of polite society. A proper high tea has to be graced with such delicacies. But secondly, and far less respectably, the sandwiches are among the many edible items suggesting rapacious desires. *Earnest* makes a whole host of rather vulgar allusions to love, romance, and sexuality. At crucial and potentially embarrassing moments, the comedy turns to rituals of eating, and each of the many foods mentioned seems charged with sexual meaning. Cucumber sandwiches; muffins; bread and butter; tea-cake: every single slice points to the hungriest of sexual appetites. Food is where each character's frustrated wishes are indirectly expressed, and most of these wishes concern sex. In this very proper world of courtship, engagements, and sudden bursts of passion, food becomes the focus for all sorts of anxieties that cannot be expressed out loud. 'Gwendolen,' says Algernon, 'is devoted to bread and butter' (p. 30), while he is equally unable to stop eating the sandwiches his aunt expects to be served at tea. Noticeably, Jack's very first words to Algernon closely align 'pleasure' with 'eating' (p. 29). These two things, thereafter, are never sundered. For example, Lady Bracknell reports that she has just eaten crumpets with Lady Harbury 'who seems . . . to be living entirely for pleasure now' (p. 36). The full implications of the play's sexual subtext will be dealt with below.

Stern in her propriety, Lady Bracknell makes a striking impact, and it is her lines that audiences are likely to remember more than any other character's. Her part demands to be played with high-handed grandeur. She is a formidable Society Lady who never deviates from her grave aristocratic bearing. High Society involves a round of meetings and engagements where the rich upper classes lead their lives of leisure: shooting-parties, hunts, balls, and, of course, the 'Season', when young debutantes are ushered into the adult world of courtship and marriage. It is Lady Bracknell's self-appointed mission in life to subject everyone to her unquestionable authority, especially in matters of decorum and etiquette. Pencil in hand, she is ready to take note of Jack's suitability as a potential son-in-law. On practically every count – income, property, land, and politics – he wins her favour, until, that is, the story of the ill-fated handbag unexpectedly drops, like a lead weight, into the conversation. As Lady Bracknell's haughty response signals only too clearly to us, the idea of being born in 'a handbag' (p. 42) represents the ultimate *faux pas* in this ridiculously snobbish world. Under absolutely no circumstances can a daughter of the rich marry the son of a handbag. Who knows where he might have come from? Apart from the farcical element in this exchange between Lady Bracknell and Jack, there is perhaps a more significant point to be taken into consideration here. Lady Bracknell's contemptuous manner clearly demonstrates that the upper classes think of their servants as little more than worthless possessions. A servant, like a handbag, has a menial function. Neither is fit to marry a member of Society. The way this joke is handled would suggest that Wilde disagrees with the principles on which a class-divided society is based. But this is no ordinary society: it would clearly be a mistake to think that the representation of the upper classes here is realistic. Instead, *Earnest* uses the conventions of farce to send up the mannered behaviour and moral hypocrisy that lie at the centre of this privileged world.

This is certainly a rigidly organized society where everyone has to know his or her allotted place. Algernon obviously recognizes where he stands in Lady Bracknell's strictly regulated world of high tea and cucumber sandwiches. He lives in fear of her. This emphasis on female authority is significant, and counts among the many inversions of conventional behaviour to be found in the play. It is typical of Wilde to put a domineering woman – rather than a dominant man – at the centre of his drama. It was an unorthodox move. Victorian society was often claimed to be highly patriarchal. By placing so much emphasis on Lady Bracknell's powerful role, Wilde is once more going against social mores. On the one hand, this Society dame is a figure of fun; her arch mannerisms in all their arrogance are there to be mocked. Yet, on the other, Lady Bracknell has a different function: to demonstrate that, in specific circumstances, women can and do have power over men. Algernon, her nephew, can do nothing but comply with her commands – except when he is 'Bunburying'. But even 'Bunburying' does not entirely escape her omniscient eye.

Early in the play, Lady Bracknell passes her disapproval on 'Mr Bunbury' whose ill-health, she says, is a sign of 'morbidity' (p. 76). Here, at least two carefully coded homosexual allusions can be detected. Once we recognize the importance of these names then it is possible to comprehend exactly why Jack has invented 'Ernest' and Algernon has made up 'Bunbury', and, moreover, how and why they have come to know one another in the first place. To begin with, the name Bunbury suggests sodomy, since it plays on the slang words 'buns' for 'buttocks', and 'bury' implies penetration. Second, the word 'morbid' was frequently used in the 1890s as a euphemism for same-sex desire, which was regarded as an increasingly dangerous and degenerating illness. As we saw earlier (pp. 18–19), 'Ernest' was a code-word for homosexual among a coterie of pederastic writers known to Wilde. At this time, it is important to remember, homosexuality was being discussed with greater intensity by medical writers and sexologists than ever before. It was a type of behaviour that escalated the worries of a society that feared sexual desire in all its multifarious forms. Taken together, then, 'Bunburying' and 'morbid' indicate that Algernon's life of deception has a rather sickening quality about it, and that is why Lady Bracknell would like him to bring it to an end. That said, very few among Wilde's West End theatre audience would have understood the full implications of these words. If they had, they would have been altogether outraged. It is fair to say that there is a lot more provocative sexual innuendo than most critics have been willing to observe in *Earnest*. And, certainly, Wilde's closest associates would have found all sorts of things to laugh about – especially when the majority of the audience could not see that 'the importance of being earnest' meant 'the importance of being homosexual'. The last laugh, then, was to be relished almost by Wilde alone.

In this light, Lady Bracknell seems to know what Algernon is doing when he leaves town to see 'Bunbury'. As she tells Algernon, she insists on the very highest standards of behaviour. Instead of 'Bunburying', Lady Bracknell would prefer Algernon to play the part of the perfect nephew by arranging her music – and he must arrange it according to her specifications. Rather than corrupt Gwendolen with French songs, Lady Bracknell wants the musical performance to take place in German. In this world of amusingly exaggerated propriety, Gwendolen has to be protected from things French; German is thought to be altogether more respectable. Again, Wilde is poking fun at upper-class attitudes to these different European cultures in Britain at this time. In the 1880s and 1890s, French was commonly associated with morally degenerate fiction (such as Emile Zola's *Germinal*, 1885); German, by contrast, was venerated as the language of philosophy (exemplified in the work of such writers as Kant and Hegel). French suggested unleashed sexuality and vulgarity; German represented seriousness and common sense. But a further point comes out from the juxtaposition of these two languages. Once again, it highlights how this upper-class ethos is constructed along a division between healthy and unhealthy, desirable and undesirable things. Wilde, as ever, is laughing at a society based on polarized values, particularly where questions of right and wrong are reduced to absurd prejudices concerning differing nationalities. It is as ridiculous to be ill-disposed to the French language as it is to treat a handbag with contempt. At a deeper level, it is perhaps just as foolish to hold same-sex desire in such disrepute. What does it matter if one was born in a handbag or desires someone of one's own sex? This is certainly one of the questions that emerges from a 'serious' consideration of this supposedly trivial play.

As the play progresses, the matches between the courting couples – Jack and Gwendolen, Algernon and Cecily – are gradually sorted out. The proposal scene between Jack and Gwendolen quickly follows on from Lady Bracknell's pompous moralizing. Here Gwendolen professes her love not for Jack, of course, but for the name she knows him by: 'Ernest'. Yet, by repeatedly attending to how much she likes his name, it seems as if she is more in love with 'Ernest' than with the man himself. 'My ideal has always been to love someone of the name of Ernest. There is something in that name that inspires absolute confidence' (p. 38), she tells Jack. He tries to persuade her that the name is not one he personally likes, and wants to know if she would love him if he had an altogether different one – Jack, for example. Her reply is not encouraging. She is unswervingly committed to 'Ernest':

'It produces vibrations' (p. 39), she adds. This statement appears bizarre until we learn that Gwendolen is not the only young woman enamoured of the exciting resonances produced by the name of 'Ernest'. In the second act, Cecily, too, will confess her love for 'Ernest', but she is referring to the man she *imagines* to be 'Ernest', who is actually Algernon, himself mistaken for Jack's invented younger brother. Again there is a symmetry to the plot, enabling the play to reiterate its serious points about love and romance. By way of this dramatic structure of repetition, *Earnest* encourages the audience to examine the nature of romantic love, and how it may be simply an infatuation with names, rather than people. After all, the question of names and naming is one of the central preoccupations of the play. 'Ernest', of course, connotes different meanings for Gwendolen and Cecily. Gwendolen, like Samuel Butler in *The Way of All Flesh*, finds the name bold and upstanding. Cecily, by contrast, associates it with naughtiness, and she has every reason to think that is so since 'Ernest' is supposed to be such an antithesis to the man she views as her virtuous guardian: her seemingly proper Uncle Jack.

It is up to Lady Bracknell to find out who or what Jack Worthing truly is. In the first act, when Jack is caught proposing marriage to Gwendolen by Lady Bracknell, and the sudden and unexpected disclosure of the handbag ensues, Lady Bracknell informs him, in the most condescending tone imaginable, that he had better 'make a definite effort to produce at any rate one parent, of either sex, before the season is quite over' (p. 43). Only family ties will turn Jack into a worthy suitor, no matter how much money or land he has to his name. To Jack, understandably, Lady Bracknell is a 'gorgon'. However, this exchange paves the way for one of the most profound statements embedded in the script. All the way through, it is obvious that *Earnest* is deriding upper-class affectations. Just as the comedy implicitly attacks a class-divided world, it also questions the sexual divisions that cut through society. At this point, Jack wonders whether Gwendolen will turn out to be as monstrous as her mother. And Algernon gives this significant reply: 'All women become like their mothers. That is their tragedy. No man does. That's his' (p. 44). Here is a classic piece of Wildean dialectic in action. On the one hand, the idea that young women will be schooled into the restrictive behaviour of their mothers' generation is tragic. On the other, the fact that sons will grow up without having any of the positive attributes of women is fatal. The way society constructs differences between men and women is clearly problematic.

The second act, like the third, shifts the action to the Manor House, Woolton, in the county of Hertfordshire, a short train journey from London. And there, to say the least, the plot thickens. Algernon has secretly taken note of Jack's address, writing it on his shirt-cuff in the closing moments of Act I when Gwendolen returns to profess her undying love for 'Ernest'. Algernon, disguised as 'Ernest', seizes the opportunity to track Jack down to this country estate. At the start of Act II we meet Cecily for the first time. She is learning German from her tutor Miss Prism. There are several things worth noting in the conversation that passes between the teacher and her pupil. Cecily finds her academic work boring; Miss Prism instructs Cecily to apply herself to it. Cecily is more interested in her diary; Miss Prism, reprovingly, reminds Cecily that 'memory . . . is the diary that we all carry about with us' (p. 49). Again, in this incident, Wilde's dialectic is in play, and here it takes an important turn. Cecily claims that memory 'usually chronicles the things that have never happened' (p. 49), and that its wild imaginings are the stuff of novels. Miss Prism might be expected to oppose this view. But she does not. Instead, Miss Prism admits to once having written a 'three-volume' novel: the kind of fiction that was popular in the Victorian 'circulating libraries'. These long novels were notoriously sentimental affairs, and that is how Wilde's audience would have understood this reference. Gilbert, in 'The Critic as Artist', roundly condemns this kind of writing, which particularly found favour with women readers: 'Anybody can write a three-volumed novel. It merely requires a complete ignorance of both life and literature' (p. 113). So what is it that the comedy is driving at here? Again it concerns identity, and how people are never exactly what they appear to be. This episode shows that Miss Prism has much more in common with Cecily than she is willing to admit. A great deal more will be heard about the manuscript of Prism's novel towards the end of the third act.

Algernon, pretending to be 'Ernest', shortly arrives. Cecily, at first, is taken aback: the last person she would expect to meet unannounced is the disreputable 'Ernest'. Algernon's plan is to seduce her. But, strangely, she is already infatuated with 'Ernest', even though she has never met him before. Cecily, with her lively imagination, has fallen in love with 'Ernest' through the terrible stories she has heard about his wickedness. Love, therefore, could not come about in a more artificial context, since it is the stuff of pure make-believe. 'Ernest' is simply an imaginary hero in a romantic story that Cecily would like to think is true. Once more, an incident such as this is saying something important about social ideals. Here it appears that love is a fiction, not something based upon those cherished Victorian values of sincerity and truth. The Victorians certainly believed in true love yet they had cloyingly sentimental ways of expressing it. Wilde's point is to show that the conventional portrayal of true love was really a sham. True love is far from true when it the main preoccupation of a young woman's overactive fancy. Cecily has taken her imaginary love affair with 'Ernest' to ridiculous extremes. She tells 'Ernest' that she has been engaged to him since 14 February, and she shows him the correspondence they have supposedly written to each other. These love letters, of course, are ones which Cecily herself has made up. Yet the date on which their engagement began is, in an entirely different way, significant. Not only is it St Valentine's Day (celebrating love), it also marks the first night of Wilde's comedy in London. The date of a fictional love affair, then, also commemorates a truth about the play. This small but significant detail is entirely consistent with the ambiguous value of what seems real and what is artificial in the comedy as a whole.

This encounter between Cecily and Algernon has an amusing parallel in the relationship established between the prim Miss Prism and the seemingly upright Rector, Dr Chasuble, who have earlier passed across the stage. Both of these characters present an image that is outwardly sexless, remote from passion, and somewhat narrow-minded. Yet this is only one side to their split personalities. They, too, are not what they seem. Already we have witnessed Miss Prism's admission that she is the author of a now forgotten three-volume novel. And Dr Chasuble, slightly later, makes a very careless and telling slip of the tongue which reveals him to be somewhat more sexual than he might care to admit. Reproving Cecily for her unwillingness to take her education seriously, he chooses his words very badly indeed: 'Were I fortunate enough to be Miss Prism's pupil, I would hang upon her lips' (p. 50). He should, of course, have used the phrase 'upon her every word'. All the way through the second and third acts, Chasuble uses a highly inappropriate style of speech for a man of the church. But that does not stop him from boasting about the high quality of his sermons. The Bishop, he claims, has been struck by Chasuble's 'analogies' (p. 55). Yet his 'analogies' are altogether inapposite. There is a critical point at issue here. Wilde is clearly sending up the mannered rhetoric of the priesthood. Paired together, these supposedly respectable characters, a celibate vicar and a spinster governess, have sex lurking somewhere in their minds. Prism upholds decent middle-class values: thrift, duty, and hard work; and Chasuble pontificates about his religious virtues. Yet this unlikely couple will eventually discover their love for one another at the end of the play.

Hereafter, the number of exits and entrances rapidly increases and *Earnest* becomes more and more like a bedroom farce. On his return to the Manor, Jack is horrified to see Algernon posing as 'Ernest' – the persona whom Jack had formerly adopted when living his life of 'pleasure' in the city. Soon afterwards, Gwendolen arrives, in search of her beloved (who still, to her, is 'Ernest'). Both men, problematically, are temporarily 'Ernest' at one and the same time. They are both using the same mask in an attempt to outwit one another with competing forms of deception. By now, the most intricate knot of this contorted drama has been tied. A tense scene follows, where Gwendolen and Cecily sit down to tea alone. They quickly infer that they are rivals in love, and verge on insulting one another, placing maximum strain on their stuffy upper-class etiquette. Since both are in love with 'Ernest', they assume they are talking about the same man. Of course they are speaking at cross purposes, since the 'Ernest' they are in love with is not 'Ernest' at all. It takes a few minutes for them to realize that their 'Ernests' are, in fact, different men. And when they do they become the best of friends. Jack dispenses with 'Ernest', and 'Ernest' reveals himself as Algernon. These overturnings and reversals take place at lightning speed. All would seem to be well; but these young men know they will be called to account by Gwendolen and

Cecily. It is still not entirely clear why Algernon and Jack have gone to such lengths in posing as 'Ernest'. It is up to the third act to set the record straight.

However, the third act adds more layers of complexity to the plot, and so heightens the excitement. Lady Bracknell enters abruptly. She has come to retrieve her daughter, and once more catches the young lovers unawares. But she is in for a further surprise. Almost immediately, Lady Bracknell discovers that she has not one but *two* engagements of marriage to countenance. Algernon and Cecily; Jack and Gwendolen: these are the happy couples set before her. She is very far from pleased: Gwendolen cannot marry the son of a handbag; and her nephew can in no circumstances be engaged to the ward of one. Yet just as she is about to depart, the infuriated Lady Bracknell is stopped in her tracks when she learns of Cecily's sizeable fortune. Jack tells her it amounts to 'about a hundred and thirty thousand pounds' (p. 78). Suddenly, Lady Bracknell's mood changes.

Money is music to her ears. She now insists that Cecily may, after a little guidance and training, fit into Society. The play is clearly poking fun at Lady Bracknell's double standards. For the rich, money is supposed not to be a problem. Money is simply something you have, rather than labour to earn. The upper classes were not expected to concern themselves with finance. Jobs, wages, income – these were the obsessions of middle-class employers and working people, not the idle rich. But, as this scene shows, money is clearly what matters to Lady Bracknell more than anything else in life.

Humour does not stop there. Once again, there is another potentially shocking joke to be found in the midst of these proceedings. Looking Cecily up and down, Lady Bracknell suggests a way of instantly improving the girl's appearance: 'A thoroughly experienced French maid produces a really marvellous result in a very brief space of time. I remember recommending one to young Lady Lancing, and after three months her own husband did not know her' (p. 78). On the face of it, she means that a well-trained servant will enhance a woman's attractiveness to the degree that her husband would no longer recognize her. But since all things French have been associated so far with harmful influences, there is some reason to believe this is an allusion to something that would have been thought sexually corrupt – like lesbianism. The French maid seemed to satisfy Lady Lancing to an extreme degree. Certainly, this implication is even more strongly accentuated when we hear Jack's prompt aside: 'And after six months nobody knew her' (p. 78). The 'marvellous result' seems to have excluded Lady Lancing from Society.

Earnest, as has already been shown, is peppered with risk-taking comments about same-sex desire, and these fall from the lips not just of Algernon, Jack, and Lady Bracknell but of almost every other character. In Act II it is Cecily who notes that 'Ernest' (on this occasion, Algernon) has probably been leading a 'double life', and that such an activity is 'wicked' (p. 52). And Gwendolen, in her conversation over tea with Cecily, remarks: 'men of the noblest possible moral character are extremely susceptible to the influence of the physical charms of others. Modern, no less than ancient history, supplies us with many most painful examples of what I refer to' (pp. 65–6). Gwendolen, either by design or default, is alluding to the cult of homosexuality in Ancient Greece, which was proving an increasing problem in the teaching of Plato to public schoolboys. Classical literature was, at one and the same time, considered the highest form of learning for young men, and yet it uncomfortably referred to the lowest form of vice. No wonder men of 'noble character' were 'susceptible' to undesirable activities.

The comedy allows Gwendolen another remark of this kind. Again when conversing with Cecily over tea, Gwendolen expresses her views on men's role in life: 'The home seems to me to be the proper sphere for the man. And certainly once a man begins to neglect his domestic duties he becomes painfully effeminate, does he not? And I don't like that. It makes men so very attractive' (p. 65). These comments, as usual, cut in two directions. Firstly, Victorians often stated that women had a 'proper sphere', and that was the home. Gwendolen, therefore, is turning this idea on its head. To her, men are best kept indoors. Outside the home, she implies, they may run into trouble. One implication is that husbands were often unfaithful to their wives, and so it is vital for men to attend to their 'domestic duties', namely their families. 'Domestic duties', however, are things generally ascribed to women. Yet there is a second, and somewhat more subtle, reading that may emerge from these lines. The notion that men become 'effeminate' once they stray from their 'proper sphere', and in so doing grow 'attractive', suggests that they are sexually active outside the home, not just with prostitutes, but with other men: 'effeminate' is a word closely connected with homosexuality. Gwendolen's statement, then, is complex and contradictory. Inside the home, men are both wifely (in women's 'proper sphere') and husbandly (attending to their families). Outside the home, men are 'attractive' (free from family constraints) and 'effeminate' (homosexual). However we choose to interpret these lines, we can see that the play is suggesting that there is something wrong with the way people are supposed to lead their lives. Everything that makes people 'attractive' or gives them 'pleasure' involves transgressing the limits laid down by society. A society run on narrow-minded morals that sets unfair limits on 'pleasure' can make for disaster. And it is on this note that the play rushes to its end.

Pleasure, it seems, leads the whole cast into temptation – whether that means eating someone else's sandwiches or going 'Bunburying' in the country. Miss Prism, as she admitted to Cecily earlier, indulged her pleasures when writing a three-volume novel. It was an activity that got her into considerable trouble. Little might we anticipate that her former novel-writing is responsible for Jack's abandonment as a baby on the Brighton line. Once Lady Bracknell hears Prism's name, the whole humilating story of the handbag is revealed. Lady Bracknell, when referring to Prism harshly as 'a female of repellent aspect, remotely connected with education', is airing an old upper-class prejudice against governesses, who were often thought untrustworthy. Governesses were seen as impostors from the lower ranks of the educated middle classes who were allowed into the homes of the rich to teach their children. For many members of the landed classes, it was important to ensure that young women teachers did not ingratiate themselves into the household. They were employees who should have no ambition to rise above their station – by, for example, trying to marry into a wealthy family. Wilde takes this demeaning attitude against middle-class educators such as Prism to new extremes to highlight the snobbery and ignorance of the rich. 'In a moment of mental abstraction, for which I never can forgive myself,' says

Prism, 'I deposited the manuscript in the bassinette, and placed the baby in the handbag' (p. 83). Presented with the bag, Prism confirms that it was hers. Jack instantly – and most mistakenly – assumes Prism is his mother. Assured this is not the case, Jack then demands to know exactly who he is. After a quick turning of the pages of the Army Lists, his first name is revealed. Jack is told he is Algernon's brother. And so he discovers – in all its multifarious ways – the importance of being E(a)rnest.

If playful with its plotting and punning, *Earnest* remains a witty piece of social commentary, noting throughout how society is riven with prejudices and snobbery. There are, we may infer, pointless divisions between the classes, between the country and the city, and between men and women. As we have seen, Wilde never misses an opportunity to challenge conventional values, and it is through this dialectical principle that his energetic critique proceeds. Everything that might be taken for granted is turned upside-down so that fiction becomes fact, and fact an unlikely kind of fiction. This activity – of swapping or alternating real and imagined worlds – may make us wonder to what degree a play such as *Earnest* is any more or less authentic than the world it represents. What is the play suggesting about the real world? That our lives are the stuff of farce? That comedy is more serious than real life? It is hard to tell the difference between the sincere and the artificial. Perhaps we should not try to make any distinction between them at all? It is this point – and it is a profoundly philosophical point – that Wilde probes in 'The Critic as Artist'. There, Gilbert reminds his interlocutor, Ernest, that Plato's criticism attends to, among several other things, 'the æsthetic value of appearances, the relation of the visible arts to the external world, and the relation of fiction to fact' (p. 107). This long essay, therefore, can be viewed as an extended meditation on the ideas about reality and artificiality brought to our attention in the quick-fire wit of *Earnest*.

THE CRITIC AS ARTIST: PART I

'The Critic as Artist' largely takes the form of a Socratic dialogue. This is the form in which Plato wrote his philosophical works. In a dialogue such as this, a teacher responds to the questions of his pupil. An argument, therefore, unfolds dialectically. Questions wait in turn upon answers, and thus the ideas at issue change shape and direction by degrees. Throughout, Wilde's essay juxtaposes differing points of view, and attempts to synthesize them. The setting is a gentleman's library situated in one of the finest parts of London. It is an appropriately learned environment. Gilbert (the teacher) and Ernest (the pupil) are discussing a much-debated topic among the cultured elite: the purpose and function of criticism. To well-educated late nineteenth-century readers, the frame of reference of their erudite conversation would have been an entirely familiar one. Every allusion – whether to classical literature or the poetry of their own time – would have posed no problems of understanding for Wilde's audience. A century later, to those of us with a different education, this essay may seem difficult to approach, especially where many of the names and references are obscure. However, even if 'The Critic as Artist' assumes a considerable amount of foreknowledge of Victorian intellectual life, there is a clear line of thinking that new readers can follow. The present critical commentary does not labour to explain every single allusion (which can, in any case, be located in the notes that follow); instead, this commentary focuses on the key points of debate about the role of criticism, and how and why Wilde's views by and large went against the grain of contemporary Victorian thought.

At the centre of the first part of this essay are two conflicting views of art. Ernest asserts what might be termed a Romantic estimation of art:

> It seems to me that the imagination spreads, or should spread, a solitude around it, and works best in silence and in isolation. Why should the artist be troubled by the shrill clamour of criticism? Why should those who cannot create take upon themselves to estimate the value of creative work? What can they know about it? (pp. 98–9)

In Ernest's opinion, like the Romantic thinkers of the late eighteenth century, art exists independently from the world around it. Many Romantics subscribed to this belief. Keats, the poet, and Kant, the philosopher, are good examples. Beneath his assertions and rhetorical questions, Ernest is suggesting that the art-work, like the artist, stands both above and apart from the everyday life of society. According to him, the artist is a solitary figure – often thought of as a genius – who has the sole authority to declare the meaning of his or her work. Criticism, therefore, is the product of inferior minds, and so it should not pretend to assess or illuminate the work of art. The painter, Whistler, would no doubt gladly support Ernest's pronouncements, as Whistler's infamous 'Ten O'Clock Lecture' shows. Gilbert strongly disagrees. But Ernest is keen to impress his point. After a short disquisition on Ancient Greece, he firmly asserts: 'The Greeks had no art-critics' (p. 103). He claims that this is so because classical culture was entirely founded on principles of beauty. In Ancient Greece, art reigned supreme, and artists and craftsmen were highly respected figures. No critics dictated standards of taste to them.

Gilbert, who may be thought of as Wilde's mouthpiece here, explains that the example of Ancient Greece shows how the distinction Ernest is making between art and criticism is, in fact, false. Rather than declare that the Greeks were a nation of artists, Gilbert states that it is more appropriate to think of them as a 'nation of art-critics' (p. 104). Ernest is slightly baffled by this view: 'You have said that the Greeks were a nation of art-critics. What art-criticism have they left us?' (p. 104). Gilbert points out that Greek society was shaped by 'the critical spirit' (p. 105), and that it is misleading to say that Ancient Greece was without criticism. Plato's philosophy debated 'the ethical effect of art, its importance to culture, and its place in the formation of character' (p. 107). Furthermore, Aristotle provided an enduring theory of tragedy. Gilbert notes that all modern concepts of genre – lyric, epic, and drama in all its forms – have been inherited from Ancient Greece. Finally, Gilbert assures Ernest that the Greeks doubtless discussed art in the same lively and informed manner as well-educated Victorians. But Ernest remains unpersuaded. He sticks to his earlier point: 'the creative faculty is higher than the critical' (p. 110). Gilbert must now argue at greater length to show Ernest that this is an erroneous view.

The problem for Ernest is that he puts criticism and creativity at opposite poles. They need not be seen that way, advises Gilbert: 'The antithesis between them is entirely arbitrary' (p. 110). It is, Gilbert says, more helpful to understand that criticism is in itself a creative act. Criticism, for him, involves 'self-consciousness', rather than the direct expression of emotions. Again, Gilbert's ideas run in complete opposition to those of the Romantics who, in Wordsworth's famous phrase, aimed at 'the spontaneous overflow of powerful feelings'.[1] As Gilbert states in the second part of this essay: 'All bad poetry springs from genuine feeling' (p. 153). Similarly, Gilbert observes that 'the work that seems to us to be the most natural and simple product of its time is always the result of the most self-conscious effort' (p. 110). Art, then, is underpinned by critical reflection, not immediate expression. It is this reflective, as opposed to expressive, turn of mind that 'invents fresh forms' (p. 111). By contrast, 'The mere creative instinct does not innovate, but reproduces' (p. 112). In other words, creativity can mean unthinking spontaneity. This latter point is borne out by Gilbert's example of the three-volume novel, which he believes can be created by anybody with the ability to read and write.

Gilbert's commitment to the 'critical spirit' is made even clearer when he discusses the practice of reviewing other people's work. He refers to the 'sixpenny papers' (p. 113), namely those periodicals which the educated classes read. In them, Gilbert tells Ernest, 'the critics . . . are far more cultured than the people whose work they are called upon to review' (p. 113). This may sound very snobbish. It may also reveal Wilde, the self-appointed art critic, defending his own line of work. (Wilde established his reputation in the 1880s as an art critic. Only in the early 1890s did he become known as a famous playwright.) Yet we need not be so cynical in our response to Gilbert's words. In his capacities as both an editor and a regular reviewer for these periodicals, Wilde was writing at a time when the arts were more commercialized than ever before. He certainly felt that the term 'literature' was under threat, and subject to degradation by inadequate criticism. It was, he felt, his role in life to bring about revolutions in culture. Gilbert deplores the vulgarizing influence of 'modern journalism', which simply vitiates the quality of everyday life. Like the three-volume novel, modern journalism shows only the ability to reproduce given material. It cannot innovate.

It follows that Gilbert sees the critical spirit as a vital force that keeps culture alive by extending and modifying old forms. These are forms which have their genesis in classical times; it is up to the present to revise and reanimate this cultural heritage. History will ossify if we do not. 'The one duty we owe to history,' he says, 'is to re-write it' (p. 114). If we ignore this charge, then we will be hamstrung by narrow-minded ideas, ones guided by 'conscience' (p. 115), by which he means that brooding sense of guilt that made so many Victorians nervous about voicing unorthodox opinions and seeking change. The last thing Gilbert would like to see is the future duplicating the past. He emphasizes how it is essential to question the values we have inherited, to build on them and transform them. In order to revolutionize our lives we should embrace, rather than fear, 'Sin': 'Without it [Sin] the world would stagnate, or grow old, or become colourless' (p. 115). Thus criticism 'treats the work of art simply as a starting-point for a new creation' (p. 122), and that 'new creation' involves taking risks (committing 'sins'). Gilbert adds that the critical spirit is not restricted by subject-matter. Critics are not obliged to conform with 'verisimilitude' (p. 120), or truth to life. Instead, any topic will serve the critic. What does matter is the 'treatment' (p. 119) of that topic. The treatment should not be frightened of harbouring dangerous thoughts, ones that a prurient general public might find shocking or absurd. It is on this point that Wilde's disagreements with the prescriptions of Matthew Arnold have their greatest force.

Arnold had very high standing in the late Victorian world of letters, and Wilde saw Arnold's view of criticism as extremely damaging. In his well-known essay 'The Function of Criticism at the Present Time' (1864), Arnold insisted that it was the work of the critic to 'see the object in itself as it really is'.[2] Gilbert negates this view, and so Ernest comes to see that 'the primary aim of the critic is to see the object as in itself it really is not' (p. 123). Through Gilbert, Wilde is arguing that the art-work is recreated by the critic, regardless of the artist's primary intentions. This he sees as the positive force of criticism. The critic has the opportunity to bring new interpretations to bear on painting, sculpture, poetry, and drama. Wilde does not see criticism acting in some high-handed and morally judgemental manner telling people timeless truths about the unchanging beauty of art, as Arnold did. Rather, criticism renders art forever anew through the careful application of what he called self-consciousness. Wilde reached these conclusions because he felt that art was not the sole possession of its creator. No art for him held an exclusive meaning. Arnold, by contrast, counted among the many critics who wished to see art comprehended as a reflection of its author's attitudes. Gilbert asserts that art is independent of the creator's 'intentions' (p. 122); 'it is rather the beholder who lends to the beautiful thing its myriad meanings' (p. 122), and these are meanings that will alter from one historical moment to another. Art, then, is a living, mutable entity. Bound to the vicissitudes of history, it is inevitably subject to the changes in the moods and tastes of each period that examines it. Criticism does not distort the art-work by applying new interpretations to it. Instead it enriches art from one era to another.

In these respects, Wilde was using Gilbert to put forward a very advanced theory about the critical interpretation of art, one that anticipated mid-twentieth-century debates about artists and their intentions. A main strand in modern literary criticism concerns whether art should be analysed in terms of an author's intentions or judged from a dispassionate point of view, free from biographical and other circumstantial information. One essay in particular is worth consulting in this respect: Monroe C. Beardsley and W.K. Wimsatt's 'The Intentional Fallacy', first published in 1946.[3] Wilde's avant-garde approach to art was informed by his close reading of Hegel's aesthetics, and, once more, this involved a dialectical interplay between the art-work and its beholder, its form and the historical context in which it was being analysed. In Hegelian terms, the beholder constantly remakes the art-work according to the historical conditions in which that art-work is beheld.

Gilbert's final words focus on 'the æsthetic sense' (p. 125), and how this faculty, which must be distinguished from reason and recognition, builds on the primary impression made by the art-work, and culminates in a richer synthesis. Criticism, therefore, does not trade in simple meanings or directly communicated messages. Nor is it tied to mechanistic reasoning or straightforward processes of cognition. It is interested instead in a principle of changeability where 'no interpretation' is 'final' (p. 125). The meaning of the art-work is open to anyone who brings a reflective turn of mind and an enhanced aesthetic sense to bear upon it. Ultimately, Wilde is positing a subjective theory of art, not a scientifically objective one. It is this question of changing interpretations, based on a subjective viewpoint, that preoccupies the second part of Wilde's essay.

Ernest quickly identifies what he imagines to be a problem in Gilbert's reasoning. Surely, he asks, if the highest criticism is purely 'impressive', and thereby subjective, 'will not the critic be sometimes a real interpreter' (p. 127)? In other words, Ernest wants to know how to discriminate between valid (true) and invalid (false) interpretations. Somewhere amid these varying interpretations there must, he feels, be a 'real' one. In response, Gilbert notes that there are different levels of interpretation, each with its merits. At the top of the scale there is the 'synthetic impression of the work of art', and at the bottom there is 'analysis' and 'exposition'. (The present commentary is both an 'analysis' and an 'exposition' of Wilde's essay.) That is, analysis and exposition attempt to provide a clear outline of the key ideas articulated in a piece of work. These terms are drawn from, and modify, those used in Arnold's essay on 'The Function of Criticism at the Present Time', where the 'grand work of literary genius' is said to be 'a work of synthesis and exposition, not of analysis and discovery'.[4] For Arnold, literature is at its finest when it unites disparate elements and then explains them. The best criticism, Gilbert argues, emerges not from the 'exposition' that Arnold prizes in literature but from considerable learning which informs a 'critical spirit'. To maximize the use of the 'critical spirit', the critic must not strive to explain the works under examination. Rather, criticism must intensify the complex mystery of the work.

Yet how can the critic intensify the mystery of the art-work? Gilbert provides the formula:

> it is only by intensifying his own personality that the critic can interpret the personality and work of others, and the more strongly this personality enters into the interpretation the more real the interpretation becomes, the more satisfying, the more convincing, the more true. (p. 128)

The subjective impulse, then, must govern criticism. And the most 'real' or powerful criticism is that which bears the stamp of a developed individual with a unique 'critical spirit'. Personality is the most strongly marked word in this context; it is a quality

223

that can be discerned in the finest actor who breathes life into a playscript. Criticism, likewise, should exhibit a remarkable, perhaps idiosyncratic, personality, since personality – in Wilde's specific sense – refers to the expression of original thoughts informed by a fine aesthetic sensibility. And it is in the aesthetic sense that Gilbert, towards the end of the essay, believes the future of the world to lie.

The remainder of 'The Critic as Artist' amplifies Gilbert's devotion to the radical possibilities of art which it is the duty of criticism to understand and develop. One of his main points is that art enables everybody to enter into a world which is more perfect than reality. 'Art does not hurt us' (p. 134), claims Gilbert, and he adds: 'through Art . . . we can shield ourselves from the sordid perils of actual existence' (p. 135). Ernest questions this idealized notion of art, and wonders whether such a view renders art 'immoral' (p. 135). Gilbert's answer is that art elicits hostile responses from people because of the emotions it excites. Art is dangerous, he states, because it involves 'Contemplation' (p. 136), an activity which Victorian society holds in contempt since 'Contemplation' apparently does not involve hard work and useful toil, qualities upheld by middle-class people with little taste for culture. As Gilbert insists, it is only through acts of 'Contemplation', self-consciousness, and self-reflection that the critical spirit can be developed to a sufficient degree for changes in culture to come about. Late nineteenth-century society, it seems, places far too much emphasis on mindless '*doing*', rather than '*being*'. In fact, Gilbert says, there is one stage better than '*being*', and that is '*becoming*' (p. 139). It is this process of '*becoming*' – with all its connotations of changefulness – that is the outcome of critical thought. This stress on '*becoming*' owes much to Hegelian thinking, a point made apparent in one of Gilbert's closing phrases: 'The Critical Spirit and the World-Spirit are one' (p. 162). The concept of 'spirit' here is a translation of Hegel's *Geist*, which defines the force that constantly changes the shape of history. Art, then, will be best served by critics who have the finest abilities to 'contemplate' and thus produce a 'synthesis' of the relationship between the work they are examining and the 'spirit' of their age. It is worth reiterating that different ages will necessarily produce different kinds of criticism – and thus create completely new interpretations of art. Just as history changes, so too will the understanding of the art-work in question.

Gilbert elaborates his theory of history by making several references to heredity. Heredity became a dominant force in Victorian intellectual circles from the 1870s onwards. (It should be noted that heredity was not a theory that concerned Hegel. The interest in heredity gathered strength at the same time that Hegel was introduced into Britain.) Wilde was not unusual among the learned elite in appealing to hereditarian ideas to advance a progressive concept of historical change. Such notions were entirely in keeping with the increasingly dominant place of Darwinian thought in critical debates about the historical development of societies. Noting the importance of the word 'modernity' (p. 137), Gilbert declares that the Victorian age can only come to appreciate its modernity by taking into account 'every century that has preceded it' (p. 137). The labours of those past ages are handed on from one generation to another, he argues, by heredity, and so history is imprinted in the body and soul of human beings. Gilbert goes so far as to argue that 'the imagination is the result of heredity' (p. 138). Twentieth-century critics are more than likely to disagree with Wilde on this point, particularly when Darwinian ideas have been put to racialist ends during the course of imperialism and fascism. Besides, few today would take on trust claims that 'race-experience' (p. 138) is transmitted through human genes. In reaching out to heredity, Wilde was attempting to endorse his concept of history as something which was handed down through time, and yet which would take many different forms.

Two further points in the final pages of Wilde's essay are worth noting. Ernest now understands that the act of criticism, at its best, is strongly subjective. But he wonders whether Gilbert's promotion of a subjective theory loses sight of the objectivity of the art-work. The terms subjective and objective had been deployed by many different writers throughout the nineteenth century, and some thought they were, in the final analysis, rather meaningless. John Ruskin, for one, declared that they displayed 'German dulness, and English affectation'.[5] Gilbert makes playful use of them. In a typical Wildean inversion, he notes that 'the more objective a creation appears to be, the more subjective it really is' (p. 144). In other words, a critically informed creation, which gives a good sense of its power of imagination, is the product of a mind at its most subjective or aesthetic. Ernest remains somewhat doubtful. He suggests, slightly later, that the 'true critic' is always 'rational' (p. 147). Again, Gilbert disabuses him. He states that art exists outside the bounds of the rational intellect; there is nothing 'sane' (p. 147) about it. Ernest then ventures that the critic must at least be 'sincere' (p. 148) when discussing art. But this, too, is a mistaken assumption. 'A little sincerity is a dangerous thing' (p. 148), argues Gilbert, since sincerity inhibits the growth and development of the aesthetic sense. Sincerity is a virtue that may prevent the critical mind from taking risks.

The second part of this essay, then, is generally an extension of the founding principles of the first. This commentary has not provided a detailed résumé of the many artists and art-works mentioned in the course of the dialogue. The main point that needs to be made here about this impressively wide range of reference is that while the allusions to classical literature are well-informed if standard ones (of the kind to be found in Arnold's and Walter Pater's essays), the Victorian authors chosen for discussion are somewhat eccentric, especially as Gilbert refers to popular and sentimental authors such as Georges Ohnet in almost the same breath as the master of realist fiction, Gustave Flaubert. Gilbert's point is that the critic can produce artistic criticism no matter what materials are to hand. Classical literature and popular culture can both serve the critic well. This was an unorthodox position to maintain, and it might be said it was altogether more democratic and open to changing currents of taste than the writings of Ruskin, Arnold, and Pater. Likewise, Wilde could have taken up the poetry of the distinguished Poet Laureate, Alfred Tennyson, whose work was seen as the finest of its day, but he chose to concentrate instead on Robert Browning. In some respects, Browning is an understandable choice for Wilde. His reputation was still high after his death in 1889. Yet, as Gilbert's remarks demonstrate, Browning was an idiosyncratic writer, one who was notoriously difficult to interpret. Browning went completely against the lyrical style favoured by Victorian readers, and this made him an object of some derision. It is for these things that Wilde admires Browning. He had cultivated, to use Gilbert's word, 'individualism' – a word that, incidentally, Arnold despised.[6] For Wilde, Browning's was a unique talent in his own day. That, too, was Wilde's project – to be an individual, an independent thinker, someone who defied conventions. No one else in Wilde's own time would put forward views that turned practically every piece of received wisdom about the role and function of criticism on its head. 'The Critic as Artist', therefore, practises exactly what it preaches. In its dialogic form, the essay appropriately keeps shifting its focus, opening itself out to new ways of thinking about criticism and art. And its elegance of phrase is almost perfect testimony to the power of the 'critical spirit' at its most inquiring. Never for one moment could we doubt that 'The Critic as Artist' is the work of anyone other than Oscar Wilde. His ideas did have their origins in the work of writers with whom he was acquainted at Oxford (notably Pater); but his subversive style was unmatched by any of his rivals.

THE SOUL OF MAN UNDER SOCIALISM

'The Soul of Man under Socialism' is Wilde's most explicitly political work. Read alongside *Earnest*, it demonstrates his considerable discontent with a class-divided society. The essay has been printed separately on a number of occasions by socialist groups, and many thousands of copies were distributed in the Soviet Union. Yet in many respects this essay does not seem to conform with socialist discourse. For a start, like 'The Critic as Artist', 'The Soul of Man under Socialism' makes a strong appeal to 'individualism'. What exactly does Wilde mean by this term? It is not a word that usually appears in a socialist context, since it may suggest that the individual is more important than the community, and socialism always places emphasis on communal rather than individual values. Let us not be confused. For Wilde, individualism represents the highest state of human development; it is an ideal that every person should aim towards. It is a form of self-care and self-respect. It should not, then, be muddled with mean-minded egotism or anti-social behaviour. Rather, as a socialist, Wilde seeks to do away with inequalities by giving priority to people's basic needs and rights.

Wilde's chief complaint is that society places a higher price on property than people; he was writing in an age when male suffrage had until recently been based on income: 'so completely has man's personality been absorbed by his possessions that the English law has always treated offences against a man's property with far more severity than offences against his person, and property is still the test of complete citizenship' (p. 170). Again, as in the previous essay, 'personality' is a key word. It connotes uniqueness, to which everyone is entitled. In Wilde's socialist utopia, each and every human being will work together with a common aim in mind: that men and women can and must realize that they are free to become whoever they want to be. The cultivation of 'personality' implies a complete state of ethical and aesthetic perfection. Wilde says that the growth of 'personality' will lead to the acceptance of difference, since everybody will have a personality of his or her own. This is a far cry from the usual conceptions of socialism and communism, which in practice have sometimes meant inhibiting freedom of individual expression at the behest of the state. That said, it is often claimed that capitalism encourages people to be self-seeking and individualistic, in a sense very different from Wilde's concept of individualism. Wilde, then, voices socialist principles that are familiar but the terminology he uses is not one shared by other socialists of his day.

Under the banner of socialism, Wilde praises ideas that go completely against the moral order of late Victorian Britain. Not only will a world founded on a love of individualism and personality dispense with property, it will also rid itself of marriage (p. 174). Moreover, its aim is to remove any controlling government (p. 175). At points such as these Wilde sounds wildly anarchic. But his thinking on such issues is systematic, and generally in keeping with the social critique to be found in his comedies. His idealistic plans fall into a clear order. Once property has been outlawed, he argues, then crime will disappear because there will be nothing left to steal. Everything will belong to everybody. He claims that Jesus Christ espoused a similar doctrine, since the Saviour believed that a spiritual life was far more important than a material one. It has to be said here that Christianity has been appropriated by many different sects for different political ends. In his socialist appeal to Christ's teaching, Wilde was making an unorthodox move, particularly in a world where the life of the upper classes was strongly connected with the Church of England, itself a major owner of property. To this end, Wilde praises the virtues of art in elevating the spirituality of men and women to a higher plane, above a materialistic world based on ownership and profiteering. In this, Wilde is not so distinct from Arnold, the ideologue of culture as an improving force, whom Wilde took such pains to challenge in 'The Critic as Artist'. For Arnold, culture was a spiritually uplifting force that would lead the middle classes forward to a morally better world of 'sweetness and light'. Arnold's ideas are expounded at greatest length in his best-known work, *Culture and Anarchy* (1869). However, Wilde diverged from Arnold when it came to the revolutionary power of culture, which Wilde located, not in 'sweetness and light', but in such dangerous forces as 'sin' and 'crime' (see p. 178).

Art, for Wilde, always had the capacity to transform given values and meanings. Yet he emphasizes that its transgressive potential can barely be witnessed in Victorian society. Wilde despairs of the kinds of art which have become popular, and deplores modern fiction in particular; it is altogether predictable. In general, he says, the 'public has always, and in every age, been badly brought up' (p. 179). It is the duty of artists not to succumb to the public's lack of education and want of taste, even if the pressure to do so may be enormous: 'The one thing that the public dislikes is novelty' (p. 180). It is only in those arts which are unpopular, Wilde claims, that artistic progress has been made. The most unpopular of these arts is poetry. Since the public takes no notice of poets, their work is free to develop of its own accord. Similarly, an artist is likely to become more of an individual once his or her work is attacked by popular prejudice. He points out that the public have devised a rather pathological vocabulary for describing works of art that do not lower themselves to acceptable standards. Avant-garde and risk-taking art is called 'unhealthy' or 'exotic' (p. 182). Moreover, public opinion is guided by the prejudices of vulgar journalism that exploits scandal to sell its wares. How, then, can art have a civilizing influence in society on a popular scale? 'Why does not the public become more civilized? They have the capacity. What stops them?' (p. 187).

Wilde turns to drama to point to one area of culture where the educated public approaches art with an open mind. At the

Lyceum or Haymarket Theatres, he claims, the public show considerable 'receptivity' (p. 187). These sentiments explain, in part, why Wilde concentrated his mind on comedy in the early to mid-1890s; it is clear that the West End theatres were where he felt the transformative powers of art could have an appreciable impact. Another related aspect of culture where art has had a desired effect is in home decoration. Wilde does not name, but implicitly notes, the remarkable influence of the Arts and Crafts movement initiated by the socialist artist, William Morris, and which Wilde embodied in his aesthetic exhibitionism of the 1880s. Improvement in furnishing – such as the use of designs adapted from nature – has come about because 'the craftsmen of things so appreciated the pleasure of making what was beautiful, and woke to such a vivid consciousness of the hideousness and vulgarity of what the public had previously wanted'. Consequently, these craftsmen 'simply starved the public out' (p. 189). In the right conditions, therefore, the beautiful and edifying force of art can be released and so alter human lives. The trouble is, Wilde does not explain how and why art has achieved its goal in interior design and not in the writing of fiction. Instead, he turns once more to individualism and how it is inhibited by the state, religion, and public opinion. He adds that his 'scheme' is likely to be regarded as 'unpractical' (p. 192). All he can affirm is that socialism will do away with tyranny and enable each and every human being to be exactly what he or she wants to be in an 'unselfish and unaffected' (p. 192) manner.

It is, of course, in this 'unselfish and unaffected' spirit that Wilde sought to live his own life, although many viewed him purely as an exhibitionist with no philosophy guiding him towards challenging public opinion. When Wilde's writings are read closely it can be seen how he remained faithful to his principles, making the critic into an artist, and vice versa, in a dynamic way. And by courting the dangers he espoused, he had to suffer the most appalling kinds of humiliation. For many years after the trials that went against him, it was practically impossible for anybody to mention his name in public. So for all its political idealism, his essay on socialism points to many truths about the ferocious intolerance towards art and artists in his own time.

1 William Wordsworth, 'Preface' to *Lyrical Ballads* (1800, 1802), ed. R.L. Brett and A.R. Jones (London, Methuen, 1965), p. 246.

2 Matthew Arnold, 'The Function of Criticism at the Present Time' (1864), in *Lectures and Essays in Criticism*, ed. R.H. Super (Ann Arbor, Michigan, University of Michigan Press, 1962), p. 258. Arnold, in fact, is quoting from one of his earlier essays here. The phrase 'to see the object itself as it really is' first appeared in the second of three lectures entitled *On Translating Homer* (1861).

3 W.K. Wimsatt Jr and Monroe C. Beardsley, 'The Intentional Fallacy' (1946), in David Lodge (ed.), *Twentieth-Century Literary Criticism: A Reader* (London, Longman, 1972), pp. 334–45.

4 Arnold, 'The Function of Criticism,' p. 261.

5 John Ruskin, *The Works of John Ruskin*, ed. E.T. Cook and Alexander Wedderburn (London: Allen, 1903–12), vol. 5, p. 201. These are the opening words of Ruskin's influential article, 'Of the Pathetic Fallacy', in *Modern Painters III* (1856).

6 Arnold wrote disparagingly of those aristocrats and middle-class proponents of personal freedom who have a 'passion for doing as one likes'. This he calls 'individualism': *Culture and Anarchy* (1869), ed. John Dover Wilson (Cambridge, Cambridge University Press, 1935), p. 102.

Select Bibliography

EDITIONS

Jackson, Russell (ed.) (1980) *The Importance of Being Earnest*, New Mermaids, London: Benn. (A sound edition with clear and very thorough explanatory notes.)

Murray, Isobel (ed.) (1989) *Oscar Wilde*, The Oxford Authors, Oxford: Oxford University Press. (Includes most of Wilde's best-known writings, apart from 'The Soul of Man under Socialism', with detailed notes.)

CRITICISM AND COMMENTARY

Bartlett, Neil (1988) *Who Was that Man? A Present for Mr Oscar Wilde*, London: Serpent's Tail. (A scholarly meditation in an experimental form on Wilde's exploits in the sexual underworld of London. Throws new light on the 'double life' at stake in *The Importance of Being Earnest.*)

Beckson, Karl (ed.) (1970) *Oscar Wilde: The Critical Heritage*, London, Routledge & Kegan Paul. (Collects reviews of Wilde's writings at the time of their original publication.)

Booth, Michael (ed.) (n.d.) *Prefaces to English Nineteenth-Century Theatre*, Manchester: Manchester University Press. (See chapters 2, 3, and 4, on drama 1850–1900, comedies, and farces, respectively.)

Craft, Christopher (1990) 'Alias Bunbury: Desire and Termination in *The Importance of Being Earnest*', *Representations*, 31, pp. 19–46. (Analyses the complexities of homosexual and heterosexual desire in the play.)

Denvir, Bernard (1986) *A Documentary History of Taste in Britain: The Late Victorians: Art, Design, and Society 1852–1910*, London: Longman. (A very useful anthology of major writings on art and design during the late Victorian period. Provides a wide-ranging context in which to consider Wilde's theories of art and criticism.)

Dollimore, Jonathan (1987) 'Different Desires: Subjectivity and Transgression in Wilde and Gide', *Textual Practice*, 1, 1, pp. 48–67. (Examines the different strategies used by Wilde and Gide to articulate homosexual desire.)

Ellmann, Richard (1987) *Oscar Wilde*, London: Hamish Hamilton. (The definitive biography including a wealth of contextual material for comprehending Wilde's writings.)

Gagnier, Regenia (1987) *Idylls of the Marketplace: Oscar Wilde and the Victorian Reading Public*, Aldershot: The Scolar Press. (Ambitious study that looks at Wilde's work in relation to the fashions and tastes of the 1880s and 1890s.)

Goodman, Jonathan (ed.) (1988) *The Oscar Wilde File*, London: Allison & Busby. (An assemblage of critical comments on Wilde's writings during the 1890s. Contains illuminating materials from newspaper reports of the three trials which led to Wilde's imprisonment in 1895.)

Hyde, H. Montgomery (ed.) (1962) *The Trials of Oscar Wilde*, New York: Dover Books. (A transcript of the proceedings of the trials, including a useful introduction and commentary.)

Jackson, Russell (ed.) (1989) *Victorian Theatre: A New Mermaid Background Book*, London: Benn. (Lively collection of Victorian materials covering all aspects of mid- and late nineteenth-century theatre. Chapters illuminate such issues as the actor's life, theatre management, and the process of directing and producing plays.)

Pierson, Stanley (1973) *Marxism and the Origins of British Socialism*, Ithaca, NY: Cornell University Press. (Not strictly connected with Wilde but provides a fine introduction to the major strands of late Victorian socialism.)

Powell, Kerry (1990) *Oscar Wilde and the Theatre of the 1890s*, Cambridge: Cambridge University Press. (Sets Wilde's dramas within a very broad theatrical context.)

Showalter, Elaine (1991) *Sexual Anarchy: Gender and Culture at the Fin de Siècle*, London: Bloomsbury. (Ranges widely over aspects of the *fin de siècle*, including questions of degeneration, the New Woman, and homosexuality. Plentiful references to Wilde.)

Small, Ian (ed.) (1979) *The Aesthetes: A Sourcebook*, London: Routledge & Kegan Paul. (A helpful collection of major writings about the 'aesthetic movement' of the 1880s. Includes works by Wilde, Pater, Whistler, and Swinburne.)

Smith, Philip E. II, and Helfand, Michael S. (eds) (1989) *Wilde's Oxford Notebooks*, New York: Oxford University Press. (The editors' long introductory essay gives a highly attentive, if somewhat narrowly focused, account of Wilde's intellectual heritage, especially in relation to his years studying classics at Oxford.)

Smith, Timothy d'Arch (1970) *Love in Earnest: Some Notes from the Lives and Writings of English 'Uranian' Poets from 1889 to 1930*, London: Routledge & Kegan Paul. (Scholarly study of male writings about boy-love. Explains how and why the pun on 'earnest' arose in Wilde's play.)

Stokes, John (1989) *In the Nineties*, Hemel Hempstead: Harvester-Wheatsheaf. (Elegant study of major cultural controversies during the 'naughty nineties', when Wilde was a key figure.)

Tydeman, William (ed.) (1982) *Wilde: Comedies: A Selection of Critical Essays*, Casebook Series, London: Macmillan.

Von Eckhart, Wolf, Gilman, Sander L., and Chamberlin, J. Edward (1988) *Oscar Wilde's London*, London: Michael O'Mara Books. (Exceptionally well-illustrated analysis of Wilde's London life during the 1880s and 1890s. Also serves as a good basic introduction to this period of British social history.)

Notes

Act I

27 *The cast* Several of the names in *Earnest* are significant, not least of all Ernest itself. John Worthing's surname refers to one of four towns in Sussex mentioned in the play. It is worth noting that he is a magistrate: a suitable role for a country squire. The letters after Canon Chasuble's name mean that he is a doctor of divinity. Lady Bracknell's surname refers to the town where the mother of Wilde's lover, Alfred Douglas, resided. The title held by Gwendolen Fairfax shows that she is the daughter of either a Baron or a Viscount. The name of the butler, Lane, is taken from the publisher, John Lane, who brought out many of the most avant-garde literary works of the 1890s, including Wilde's.

27 *Half-Moon Street* A fashionable street in central London running between Curzon Street and Piccadilly.

28 *Lord Shoreham* A fictional character whose name is taken from a Sussex seaside town.

29 *customary in good society to take some slight refreshment at five o'clock* It was appropriate to serve a light tea at five o'clock to people who called as part of their routine visits to each other's homes.

30 *Divorce Court* This was established in 1857, after much parliamentary debate, to make obtaining a divorce easier. Before 1857, divorces were rare and could only be procured by an act of parliament; few could afford the expense of going through this process.

31 *Scotland Yard* The headquarters of the London Metropolitan Police Force.

31 *Tunbridge Wells* A fashionable spa town in Kent.

32 *The Albany* The residence of the homosexual emancipationist, George Ives, an acquaintance of Wilde's.

33 *Bunburyist* A deceiver, one who uses an alibi like 'Bunbury' to escape from social obligations. Wilde did have an old school friend called Bunbury.

34 *Willis's* A well-known restaurant in King's Street, St James's, London where artistic and aesthetic people went.

34 *sent down* As a matter of etiquette, each gentleman was expected to act as an escort to a lady at dinner.

35 *the corrupt French Drama* Wilde may be calling to mind the work of Alexander Dumas the younger, whose *Lady of the Camellias* (adapted by Verdi in the opera, *La Traviata*) was considered a controversial work in the 1850s.

35 *Wagnerian* Richard Wagner's epic operas were favoured by the educated artistic elite.

41 *Grosvenor Square* The central square in Mayfair, the most expensive residential area in London.

41 *Belgrave Square* At the centre of Belgravia, which is to this day another select residential area in London.

41 *Lady Bloxham* Her surname is taken from the editor of the *Chameleon*, the magazine in which Wilde's 'Phrases and Philosophies for the Use of the Young' appeared. Bloxam was the author of a story about pederasty called 'The Priest and the Acoloyte'. Both Wilde's 'Phrases' and Bloxam's story would be used as evidence against Wilde during the trials of 1895.

42 *Liberal Unionist* The group of liberals who voted against Gladstone's Home Rule for Ireland bill of 1886. They stand for the conservative side of liberal politics, and hence are acceptable to Lady Bracknell's Society. Radicals among the ranks of the liberals would certainly not be to her taste.

43 *Wedding March*   Probably by Mendelssohn (1842), a well-known piece.

44 *as right as a trivet*   A trivet is a three-legged stand for a teapot. The phrase roughly means that everything is perfectly safe or steady.

45 *she is only just eighteen*   Eighteen marked the age when a young woman could 'come out' as a debutante in Society. It was the most suitable age for becoming engaged to an appropriate young gentleman.

46 *the club*   Referring to a gentlemen's club, an exclusive gathering place for the male members of Society.

46 *the Empire*   A variety theatre in Leicester Square, London, which had been severely criticized by Mrs Ormiston Chant, who found the 'promenade' by 'ladies of the town' (namely, prostitutes) highly offensive. The 'promenade' was an open area adjacent to the theatre where for a few shillings spectators could get a distant view of the performance on stage while taking drinks and meeting people. This 'promenading' area was shut off from the rest of the theatre in 1894, and commentators claimed that 'prudes' like Mrs Chant held full sway over public opinion. The Empire Theatre was, then, a very topical reference.

47 *Woolton, Hertfordshire*   Woolton is a fictional place; the county of Hertfordshire lies to the north of London.

47 *smoking jacket*   An essential item of gentlemen's clothing made of velvet or silk and worn on informal occasions, such as for smoking in the drawing-room.

Act II

48 *Basket chairs*   Wickerwork chairs.

48 *Moulton*   The name of a gardener who never appears in the play.

49 *As a man sows so let him reap*   A biblical motto: 'whatsoever a man soweth, that shall he also reap' (Galatians 6:7).

49 *three-volume novels that Mudie sends us*   Mudie's was a lending library which traded in three-volume novels. By circulating novels in three volumes, it meant that three

readers could borrow different parts of the same work of fiction. Three-volume novels went out of fashion in the late nineteenth century because of advances in publishing technology.

50 *Egeria . . . Lætetia* The names veer between entirely different meanings. Egeria was the nymph who dictated wise laws to Numa Pompilius, the second King of Rome, which were then embodied in the Vestal Virgins; the name, therefore, connotes chastity. Laetitia means happiness, a quality hardly apposite to Miss Prism.

51 *Evensong* A church service that takes place on Sunday evening.

51 *Political Economy . . . the Fall of the Rupee* Cecily is studying academic subjects still not thought fit for young women. Political economy, drawing on the work of Adam Smith, David Ricardo, and John Stuart Mill, examined the principles upon which capital was produced. This reference glances at the growth of women's colleges at Oxford and Cambridge, for which, it might seem, Cecily is being trained. 'The Fall of the Rupee' is a topical reference. Indian currency had been severely devalued in the 1890s.

52 *Uncle Jack is sending you to Australia* Exile in the colonies was frequently seen as a way of reforming a recalcitrant young gentleman's manners and thus building up his character. It would be an appropriate fate for Jack's naughty brother 'Ernest'.

53 *A Maréchal Niel* A yellow noisette rose, fashionable in Britain after the 1860s.

53 *misanthrope . . . womanthrope* Misanthrope, of course, means a hater of humanity; 'womanthrope' is a neologism, and means a misogynist, or hater of women.

54 *the Primitive Church was distinctly against matrimony* Chasuble's name comes from the vestment worn by Roman Catholic priests and which was also donned by priests in the High Anglican church. Chasuble is trying to point out that Anglicanism should be closely related to the Catholic (or so-called 'Primitive', pre-Reformation) church which did not allow priests to marry. Much is made of Chasuble's celibacy throughout the comedy.

55 *Grand Hotel* The Grand Hotel, in the Boulevard des Capucines, was among the most luxurious in Paris. Like the Savoy in London, it was a hotel favoured by Wilde.

55 *manna* An allusion to the Old Testament where, during their pilgrimage from Egypt to the Holy Land, God miraculously provided the Israelites with this food, a white substance that fell with the dew.

55 *Society for the Prevention of Discontent among the Upper Orders* A fictional society whose name humorously parodies the many charitable societies established in the Victorian period to do good works, such as the Society for Bettering the Condition of the Poor and the Society for the Relief of the Destitute Sick.

56 *the immersion of adults . . . canonical practice* Chasuble is pointing out that both methods of christening, either sprinkling of water on the forehead or complete immersion of the body, are acceptable to the law of the church. Baptists favour the latter method. However, in the Church of England, baptism by full immersion is extremely rare, and Wilde is surely being ironical here.

58 *dog-cart* A two-wheeled horse-drawn carriage; the modern equivalent would be a small hatchback.

64 *philanthropic work in London* Charitable work was one of the few activities that upper-class women were allowed to perform in society. Cecily does not want to follow in their footsteps.

65 *once a man begins to neglect his domestic duties* An inversion of the norm; women, not men, were supposed to attend to 'domestic duties'.

65 *men of the noblest possible moral character . . . physical charms of others* A coded allusion to homosexuality.

66 *Morning Post* The newspaper most popular among Society people for gossip and news of engagements and marriages.

68 *agricultural depression* Since the 1870s, British farming had been in decline, mainly because of the effect of cheap foreign imports.

Act III

74 *German scepticism* A form of philosophy that examines appearances not essences; Immanuel Kant (1724–1804) is one of its major exponents.

76 *luggage train* A train designed for carrying freight rather than passengers.

76 *University Extension Scheme* Extramural courses mounted by the University of London. These courses were among the most significant developments in adult education.

77 *Court Guides* The Court Guide was published annually. It contained the names and addresses of members of the aristocracy and upper classes.

78 *one of the Mr Markbys is occasionally to be seen at dinner parties* Lady Bracknell notes that at times people of a lower class, such as solicitors, are allowed into the company of the aristocracy.

78 *the Funds* Sometimes known as gilts, these were government stocks which were regarded as a safe form of investment; they yielded a low but reliable rate of interest.

80 *an Oxonian* A graduate of the University of Oxford.

80 *Perrier-Jouet, Brut, '89* One of Wilde's favourite kinds of champagne.

82 *the Anabaptists* The Evangelicals who contested the precepts of Protestantism at the time of the Reformation. Anabaptists believed in the complete immersion of the body in water as the only form of baptism.

82 *the pew-opener* A person employed in church to open the private pews of eminent persons.

83 *Upper Grosvenor Street* A fashionable street in west London.

83 *Bayswater* Another fashionable district of west London.

83 *bassinette* A hooded perambulator or pram.

84 *Brighton* A major seaside resort in Sussex made fashionable during the time of the Regency.

84 *Gower Street omnibus* A horse-drawn bus travelling along a street in the Bloomsbury district of central London.

84 *Leamington* Leamington Spa, Warwickshire, was a well-known watering place. It had been patronized by royalty.

85 *who has the right to cast a stone against one who has suffered?* In the Gospel according to St John, Christ said: 'He that is without sin among you, let him first cast a stone at her' (John 8:7). Death by stoning was the punishment under Jewish law for adultery.

86 *Army Lists* Lists of all the commissioned officers in the British Army.

86 *Mallam, Maxbohm, Magley* 'Maxbohm' is a contract of Max Beerbohm, the celebrated illustrator, novelist, and satirist. Beerbohm was a friend of Wilde's.

THE GRIBSBY EPISODE

90 *fly* A small horse-drawn carriage.

90 *House of Lords* Sometimes called the Upper House, this house of parliament comprises hereditary peers, life peers, law lords, archbishops, and bishops.

91 *Wordsworth* One of the major Romantic poets, William Wordsworth (1770–1850) is remembered for his highly reflective, philosophical poetry. He was made Poet Laureate in 1843.

92 *Holloway* A prison in north London; Wilde was sent there after his arrest in 1895.

93 *don't cross the cheque* Gribsby wants the cheque left uncrossed so that monies can be passed on directly to the Savoy Hotel.

THE CRITIC AS ARTIST

Part I

95 *Cicero* Marcus Tullius Cicero (106–43 BC), Roman orator and statesman.

95 *Balzac* Honoré de Balzac (1799–1850), novelist, famous for his *Comédie humaine* (*The Human Comedy*) (1842–8), a series of realist novels; among the best-known of these are *Eugénie Grandet* (1833) and *Le Père Goriot* (1834).

95 *Flaubert* Gustave Flaubert (1821–80), author of several highly innovative novels, including *Madame Bovary* (1856–7).

95 *Berlioz* Louis-Hector Berlioz (1803–69), French composer, who brilliantly combines classical and Romantic influences. He is perhaps best known for his *Symphonie Fantastique* (1830). His memoirs are remarkable for their romantic self-absorption and sardonic humour.

95 *Byron* George Gordon, sixth baron Byron (1788–1824), poet, whose name was associated with sexual scandal; one of his most exciting works, in this respect, is *Don Juan* (1819–24).

95 *Madame de Sévigné* Marie de Rabutin Chantal de Sévigné (1626–96), famous letter writer; her correspondence is noted for its moments of high drama.

96 *Rousseau* Jean-Jacques Rousseau (1712–78), philosopher, economist, and novelist. Among his most widely read works are *Emile* (1762) and *The Social Contract* (1762). His ideas anticipated those of the French Revolution in 1789.

96 *Cellini* Benvenuto Cellini (1500–71), Italian goldsmith, sculptor, and writer; his life and crimes are recorded in his *Autobiography* (published 1728).

96 *King Francis* King Francis I of France (1494–1547); patron of major Renaissance artists such as Andrea del Sarto.

96 *Perseus* A great hero in Greek myth, the son of Zeus and Danaë, celebrated for obtaining the head of the Medusa, and for breaking Andromeda free from the chains that bound her to a rock.

96 *the dead terror* The Medusa, sometimes known as Gorgo(n), was one of three monstrous sisters in early Greek mythology. Snakes grew like hairs on her head, and it was said that anyone who looked directly at her face would be turned to stone. Perseus managed to slay her by looking into a reflective shield.

96 *Montaigne* Michel Eyquem Montaigne (1533–92), renowned for his *Essays* (1580), first translated into English by John Florio, tutor to Shakespeare's patron, the Earl of Southampton, in 1625. The *Essays* explicated his sceptical attitude towards the permanence of social customs and institutions.

96 *a saint like the bitter son of Monica* Saint Augustine of Hippo (354–430), a Latin father of the Church of Rome,

was the son of St Monica. He spent much of his life as a follower of Manichaeanism (which was regarded by the Roman Catholic church as heretical) before returning to Christianity.

96 *Cardinal Newman* John Henry Newman (1801–90), a controversial figure in the 1840s, whose life and writings were a constant source of fascination to Wilde. His *Tract XC* (1841) discussed the compatibility of the 39 Articles of the Church of England with the teachings of Roman Catholicism. A figurehead in the Oxford Movement, he left the Church of England in 1845 for the Roman Catholic Church (Wilde converted to Rome on his deathbed). The Oxford Movement comprised the followers of John Keble, who in 1833 initiated a return to High Church principles. Gilbert is here quoting from Newman's autobiography, *Apologia pro Vita Sua* (1864).

96 *The lonely church at Littlemore* The church to which Newman retired in 1842. He was received into the Roman Catholic Church there in 1845.

96 *Benign Mother* The Virgin Mary, whose iconography is central to the Roman Catholic Church.

96 *Mr Secretary Pepys* Samuel Pepys (1633–1703), famous diarist. His diary begins on 1 January 1660. It is written in code, which was first deciphered in 1825. An edition of his *Diary* appeared in 1875–9.

96 *indiscretion is the better part of valour* An inversion of the proverb 'discretion is the better part of valour'.

97 *Touchstone* The clown in Shakespeare's festive comedy, *As You Like It.*

97 *Boswell* James Boswell (1740–95), whose widely read biography of the great eighteenth-century critic, Samuel Johnson, was published in 1791.

97 *Chopin* Frédéric François Chopin (1810–49), Franco-Polish composer, celebrated especially for his piano music.

97 *Dvořák* Antonin Dvořák (1841–1904), Czech composer. His works include nine popular symphonies, written between 1865 and 1893.

98 *Academician* A reference to William Powell Frith (1819–1909), one of the most prominent and popular members

of the Royal Academy, the bastion of British art. Frith painted spectacularly large canvases featuring highly detailed crowd scenes, such as *Derby Day* (1858) and *The Railway Station* (1862).

99 *Browning Society* A society established in 1881 to discuss Robert Browning's notoriously difficult poetry. Browning jokingly referred to it as the 'Me Society'.

99 *Broad Church Party* The group of Oxford intellectuals who contributed to *Essays and Reviews*, a controversial volume published in 1860. This book advocated a more liberal attitude towards the historical truth of the Bible.

99 *Mr Walter Scott's Great Writers Series* Walter Scott, not to be confused with the early nineteenth-century Scottish writer of that name, was a publisher who brought out popular studies of well-known 'canonical' writers such as Dickens and Keats.

99 *Olympians . . . the Titans* In ancient Greek myth, Olympia is the main sanctuary of the great god, Zeus. It was there that the Olympic games began in 776 BC. Twelve gods resided at Olympus after seizing power from the Titans (also twelve in number). Both groups signify tremendous strength.

99 *the Muse's hollow hill* The Muses were nine goddesses who inspired the creation of poetry. Each presided over one of the arts or sciences. They were born at Pieria at the foot of Mount Olympus.

100 *Pegasus* The winged horse born of the Medusa when she was slain by Perseus.

100 *tettix* A cicada: an insect known for its discordant, chirping sound.

100 *men and women that live* An allusion to Robert Browning's best-known volume of poetry, *Men and Women* (1855).

100 *Fra Lippo Lippi* The title of a dramatic monologue by Browning, first published in *Men and Women*.

100 *Saul* Another dramatic monologue by Browning, published in two versions, first in *Dramatic Romances and Lyrics* (1845) and then in *Men and Women*.

100 *Mildred Tresham* The tragic heroine of Browning's play, *A Blot in the 'Scutcheon* (1843).

100   *the Spanish monk*   The speaker in Browning's poem, 'Soliloquy of the Spanish Cloister', in *Dramatic Lyrics* (1842).

100   *Blougram*   The speaker in Browning's monologue, 'Bishop Blougram's Apology', in *Men and Women*.

100   *Ben Ezra*   One of the best-known poems in Browning's *Dramatis Personae* (1864).

100   *Bishop of St Praxed's*   The speaker in Browning's poem, 'The Bishop Orders his Tomb at St Praxed's Church', in *Dramatic Romances and Lyrics*.

100   *Setebos*   The pagan god mentioned in the title of Browning's poem, 'Caliban upon Setebos', in *Dramatis Personae*.

100   *Sebald . . . Pippa . . . Ottima*   The main characters in Browning's verse-drama, *Pippa Passes* (1841).

100   *Strafford*   The protagonist in Browning's stage play named after him (1837), which concerns the politics of the English Civil War.

100   *Andrea*   The speaker of Browning's poem named after the Mannerist painter, 'Andrea del Sarto', in *Men and Women*.

100   *George Meredith*   Meredith (1828–1909) was highly regarded as a novelist in his own day. His difficult style is comparable to Browning's. Perhaps his most celebrated novel is *The Egoist* (1879).

101   *old friend*   James Abbott McNeill Whistler (1834–1903), innovative artist, and, in some ways, a model for Wilde's outlandish behaviour. This is an ironic remark since Wilde and Whistler had become arch-rivals in the 1880s. Whistler frequently accused Wilde of plagiarizing his phrases and philosophies.

101   *Hermes*   Son of Zeus and Maia, Hermes was a messenger of the gods. He was supposed to have invented the lyre.

101   *child of Leto*   Apollo was the son of Leto, a goddess and one of the Titans. Leto was also the mother of Artemis (see p. 246).

101   διὰ λαμπροτάτου βαίνοντες ἁβρῶς αἰθέρος, treading delicately through the brilliant air.

101   *Phædrus*   Plato's *Phædrus* is a Socratic dialogue that examines questions of aesthetics and rhetoric. It also looks at the origins of writing.

101 *agnus castus* Tree belonging to the Vitex genus. The *agnus castus* was associated with chastity.

101 *Tanagra* A city in Boeotia where small terracotta statues were unearthed from tombs.

101 *sandyx* Red pigment.

101 *asphodel* Daffodil; in ancient Greek myth representing death. In the underworld, the dead lie upon the plain of asphodel.

102 *Priam* Priam was the last king of Troy.

102 *Odysseus* A prominent figure in Homer's epics, the *Iliad* and, of course, the *Odyssey*. He is perhaps the most famous and daring of adventurers in classical myth.

102 *Sirens* The Sirens appear in the *Odyssey*. Their sweet but lethal song drew sailors to their destruction. Odysseus managed to resist the powerful lure of their song.

102 *Marathon* Marathon is where the Athenians defeated the Persians, for the first time, in 490 BC.

102 *Salaminian bay* Another scene of battle, this time where the Greeks defeated the Persians in 480 BC.

102 *sardonyx* A type of onyx.

102 *Artemis* The daughter of Zeus and Leto; also the twin sister of Apollo. In ancient Greek myth, Artemis is often pictured as the virgin huntress who brings sudden death. The Romans associated her with fertility.

102 *palmates* A hand-shaped ornament.

102 *Nereids* Sea-maidens, the daughters of Nereus (a sea-god). Nereids often featured as decorations on vases and wall-paintings of the fourth century AD.

102 *Phædra* The daughter of Minos, king of Crete. Phaedra loved her stepson, Hippolytus, who rejected her, and was driven to his death. She then hanged herself. Her story is recorded in Euripides' tragedy, *Hippolytus.*

102 *Persephone* The daughter of Zeus and Demeter, Persephone was snatched by Hades, the god of the underworld, and forced to spend half of every year there.

103 *Eros* The Greek god of love.

103 *Donatello's angels* Donatello (*c.* 1386–1466) is regarded as the finest Florentine artist before Michelangelo.

103 ΚΑΛΟΣ ΑΛΚΙΒΙΑΔΗΣ or ΚΑΛΟΣ ΧΑΡΜΙΔΗΣ: Noble Alcibiades or noble Charmides.

103 *Mænads* Women stirred into a frenzy by Dionysus.

103 *Dionysus* Greek god of wine and ecstasy.

103 *must-stained* Stained with wine that is still being fermented.

103 *Silenus* The spirit of wildlife in ancient Greek myth. He is represented as half-man, half-beast.

103 *Ilyssus . . . Higginbotham* Ilyssus is the name of one of the two streams watering the Athenian plain from Mount Hymettus. It is celebrated in Plato's *Phædrus*. In 'The Function of Criticism at the Present Time' (1864), Arnold wrote: 'If we are to talk of ideal perfection, of the "the best in the whole world", has one reflected what a touch of grossness in our race, what an original shortcoming in the more delicate spiritual perceptions, is shown by the natural growth amongst us of such names, – Higginbottom, Stiggins, Bugg! In Ionia and Attica they were luckier in this respect than "the best race in the world"; by the Ilissus there was no Wragg, poor thing!' Ostensibly, Wilde is indicating that in classical times culture had not been vulgarized by commercial instititions such as the Royal Academy. But he is, no doubt, treating Arnold's notorious (because high-minded) phrase with oblique irony. Elizabeth Wragg, a young woman in a workhouse, murdered her illegitimate child in 1864; after her arrest, she attracted a good deal of attention in newspapers. Arnold objected to the singularly blunt manner in which the press noted the event: 'The child was only afterwards found dead on Mapperly Hills, having been strangled. Wragg is in custody.' Arnold considers this style a defining feature of an uncritical mind, and says that both conservative and radical politicians share this fault. In criticizing this kind of writing, Arnold is requesting a more sensitive way of reporting events such as this. The trouble is, Arnold seems to be more interested in the question of journalistic style than the horror of child-murder; and this would seem to be the point Wilde is indirectly making here.

103 *art congresses* Festivals promoting, as Wilde saw it, second-rate art among the masses.

103 *Darwinian principle of the survival of the vulgarest*   Charles
Darwin's theory of evolution was based on the idea of
'natural selection'; Darwin is often credited with the
concept of the 'survival of the fittest', which Wilde is
inverting here. The phrase was coined, in fact, by Herbert
Spencer (1820–1903).

104 *Narcissus*   The ancient Greek god who fell in love with
his own reflection.

104 *Prince Florizel of Bohemia*   One of the main characters
in Shakespeare's tragi-comedy, *The Winter's Tale*, a play
renowned for its debates about the relationships between
art and nature. In relation to the reference to the 'fair
Cuban' (below), Wilde has Robert Louis Stevenson's *New
Arabian Nights* (1882) and *More New Arabian Nights* (1885)
in mind. Prince Florizel is the name of one of Stevenson's
protagonists.

104 *fair Cuban*   One of the storytellers in *More New Arabian
Nights* by Stevenson.

104 *Hellenic or Hellenistic*   Ancient Greek or in the ancient
Greek mode. Strictly speaking, Hellenistic refers to the
extended influence of Greek power after the death of
Alexander (323 BC) until Greece was absorbed by Rome
(86 BC).

105 *Mr Pater*   Walter Pater (1839–94), a distinguished and
somewhat controversial art critic at Oxford University.
His best-known work is *Studies in the History of the
Renaissance* (1873). Wilde's writings are strongly indebted
to Pater's belief in 'art for art's sake'.

106 *Homer*   (Perhaps eighth century BC.) Supposedly the
author of the *Iliad* and the *Odyssey*.

106 *Milton . . . Paradise . . . Regained*   All the major works of
the English poet, John Milton (1608–74), are mentioned
here.

106 *Augustan age*   In the arts in Britain, the late seventeenth
and early eighteenth centuries became known as the
Augustan age. This was a time of neoclassical revival
emulating the glories of the first emperor of Rome,
Augustus (27 BC–AD 14).

106 *Hegesias*   Hegesias of Magnesia (third century BC), orator
and historian; his style was routinely attacked by followers

of Cicero.

106   *conduct is three-fourths of life*   This is the view put forward by Arnold in *Literature and Dogma* (1873).

106   *pæons*   A metrical foot of four syllables, any one long, and three short.

107   *Plato to Plotinus*   Plotinus (*c.* AD 205–70) was the chief exponent of 'Neoplatonism'.

107   *Aristotle's Treatise on Poetry*   Aristotle (384–322 BC) lays down the basic principles of comedy and tragedy in his *Poetics*.

107   *Kosmos*   Cosmos, universe.

107   *Goethe*   Johann Wolfgang von Goethe (1749–1832), German poet. Perhaps his greatest achievement is *Faust* (1808, 1832).

108   κάθαρσις: Catharsis; purgation. The term originates in Aristotle's *Poetics*. Although its exact meaning has been disputed, critics generally agree that catharsis defines the feeling of exaltation experienced by the audience at the moment when the tragic hero has been defeated.

108   *'perilous stuff'*   From Shakespeare's tragedy, *Macbeth*, Act V, scene iii.

108   *Alexandria*   The northern Egyptian city founded by Alexander the Great in 331 BC. In classical times, it was regarded as the intellectual centre of the world.

108   *Sicyon*   Hero of Greek comedy, *Sicionus*, by Menander (341–290 BC).

109   *Arts and Crafts guilds, and Pre-Raphaelite movements*   These were the major movements in Victorian art which adhered to John Ruskin's belief in remaining true to nature. The Pre-Raphaelites included Dante Gabriel Rossetti and John Millais among their company, and they rose to fame in the 1850s. The Arts and Crafts movement emerged in the 1870s and 1880s. Its most distinguished artist was the writer and designer, William Morris.

109   *Lucian*   (AD 115–80). Writer of comedies, satires, and parodies.

109   *Longinus*   Writer of first century AD. He is renowned for his tract on the 'sublime' in art.

109   *Quinctilian*   Marcus Fabius Quintilian (AD 35–95?) was a famous teacher of rhetoric at Rome.

109   *Pliny* Gaius Plinius Caecilius Secundus ('Pliny the Younger') (*c.* AD 61–112) was taught by Quintilian; he was a major exponent of the 'literary letter'.

109   *Fronto* Marcus Cornelius Fronto (*c.* AD 100–176) was one of the foremost orators of his day.

109   *Pausanias* (Second century AD). Greek traveller and geographer, author of a 'Description of Greece'.

109   μονόχρονος ἡδονή: Undivided pleasure.

110   *the creative faculty is higher than the critical* This is the opposite of the view espoused by Arnold in 'The Function of Criticism at the Present Time': 'Everybody, too, would be willing to admit, as a general proposition, that the critical faculty is lower than the inventive . . . The critical power is of lower rank than the creative. It is undeniable that the exercise of a creative power, that a free creative activity, is the highest function of man.'

110   *Arnold's definition of literature as a criticism of life* In his essay on 'Joubert' (1865, in *Essays in Criticism, First Series*), Arnold writes: '*a criticism of life*. The end of all literature . . . is, in truth, nothing but that'.

110   *'wiser than they knew'* . . . *Emerson* Ralph Waldo Emerson (1803–82), American poet, essayist, and transcendentalist philosopher. In 'The Over-Soul' (*Essays: First Series*, 1841), Emerson states: 'We are wiser than we know.'

110   *Apollo* One of the twelve Olympians, Apollo is the god of light, youthful male beauty, and reason.

111   *'And so not built at all . . .'* Adapted from several well-known lines in Alfred Tennyson's *Idylls of the King* (1859) where Camelot is described as a 'city built/ To music, therefore never built at all,/ And therefore built for ever.'

112   *Anthology* Meleager's *Greek Anthology*, compiled in the first century AD.

112   *sham Scotch dialect* A reference to the popular Scotch dialect poems of Fiona Macleod. This was in fact the pseudonym of a distinguished man of letters, William Sharp. Macleod's 'true' identity was only discovered after Sharp's death in 1905.

113   *three-volumed novel* Three-volume novels were popular in the mid-Victorian period, when the circulating libraries

gave middle-class readers access to modern fiction. New methods of binding and printing meant that the three-volume novel was superseded by a single volume. The circulating libraries were increasingly a thing of the past at the time when Wilde was writing.

113 *Newnham* Newnham College, Cambridge, was among the first of several university colleges for women opened in the 1870s and 1880s.

114 *the fig-tree . . . thistle* In the Gospel according to Matthew (7:16), Jesus notes that false prophets can be known by the strange fruits they bear: 'Do men gather grapes of thorns, or figs of thistles?'

115 *Materialism* Belief that only worldly, rather than religious, things matter in life.

115 *M. Renan . . . chastity . . . Magdalen . . . Lucretias* Ernest Renan (1823–92), French historian whose *Life of Jesus* (1863) counted among several of the most important works of the period to throw doubt on the veracity of the Bible. In his essay, 'Numbers of the Majority and the Remnant' (1884), Arnold cites Renan's remark 'Nature cares nothing for chastity' on several occasions. Renan first made this comment in *Souvenirs d'enfance et de jeunesse* (1883). Mary Magdalene was saved from evil by Jesus; she was transformed from a prostitute into a model of chastity. The story of Lucretia is recounted by Livy and Ovid. Married to Tarquinius Collatinus, she was raped by Sextus; after confessing her shame to her husband, she killed herself. Her story has been retold by Chaucer and Shakespeare, among others.

116 *Ilion* Another name for Troy.

116 *Aulis* Town in Boeotia where the Greek fleet assembled before sailing in battle against Troy.

116 *Antigone* One of the four children of Jocasta and Oedipus. She was walled up alive in a tomb by her uncle (Creon) because she had buried her own brother, Polyneices, without permission. Her story is recorded by Sophocles in the tragedy named after her.

116 *Hector* The eldest son of Priam, the king of Troy, Hector is a key figure in the *Iliad*. He was among the greatest Trojan fighters.

116 *Lucian . . . Menippus . . . Helen* Menippus was a cynic philosopher of the third century BC. He satirized human folly. Helen was the queen of Troy, known for her beauty. Both feature in Lucian's *Dialogues*.

116 *Leda* Mother of Helen of Troy. Zeus transformed her into a swan to seduce Leda. Helen was thus said to have been born from an egg.

116 *Andromache* Wife of Hector, heroine of the tragedy by Euripides named after her (*c.* 426 BC).

116 *Achilles . . . Lord of the Myrmidons* Achilles was the chief warrior in the Trojan War. The Myrmidons were his followers who filled the fifty ships which he led into battle.

116 *Dodona* The most ancient oracle known to the Greeks.

117 *Troy, Panthous' son, Euphorbus . . . the Priamid . . . Patroklus* Euphorbus, a Trojan warrior, wounded Patroclus, Achilles' devoted friend. Hector, the son of Priam, put Euphorbus to death for this act.

117 οἶνοψ πόντος: Wine-dark sea. A standard Homeric description.

117 *Danaoi* The Greeks.

117 *St Helena . . . Veronese* Paolo Veronese (1528–88), major painter of the sixteenth-century Venetian school; his *Vision of St Helen* dates from about 1572.

117 *Giorgione . . . idly upon the chords* Giorgione (*c.* 1476–1510), Venetian painter. The painting in question is *The Concert of the Fête Champêtre*.

118 *dancing nymphs . . . Corot* Jean-Baptiste-Camille Corot (1796–1875), distinguished landscape painter.

118 *Green-tressed Goddess . . . Coleridge* Samuel Taylor Coleridge (1772–1834) refers to the 'Green-haired goddess' in 'Hymn to the Earth' (1834).

119 *Gustave Flaubert . . . masterpiece of style* Wilde undoubtedly means Flaubert's great realist novel, *Madame Bovary* (1857).

119 *Mr Lewis Morris's poems* Lewis Morris (1833–1907), a minor Welsh poet who wrote in the style of Tennyson.

119 *M. Ohnet's novels* Georges Ohnet (1848–1918), highly popular sentimental French novelist.

119 *plays of Mr Henry Arthur Jones* (1851–1929). Popular

writer for the stage in Wilde's day. Along with Arthur Wing Pinero, Jones was respected for his controversial Society dramas.

119 *Bestia Trionfans* 'The Triumphant Beast', properly known as *Spaccio della bestia Trionfante* [*The Expulsion of the Triumphant Beast*] (1584), a work by the Italian hermetic philosopher, Giordano Bruno. 'The Triumphant Beast' represents the sum of all human vices.

120 *Æschylus* (*c*. 524–456 BC). Great Athenian dramatist.

120 *His sole aim is to chronicle his own impressions* Here Gilbert is following Pater's beliefs as laid out in the Preface to *The Renaissance*. There Pater slightly modifies Arnold's desire 'To see the object as in itself it really is'; he argues: 'in aesthetic criticism the first step towards seeing one's object as it really is, is to know one's impression as it really is, to discriminate it, to realize it distinctly.'

121 *Proserpina* The Roman name for Persephone (see p. 246).

121 *Cumnor cowslips* An allusion to one of Arnold's well-known poems, the elegy entitled 'Thyrsis' (1866). Arnold's speaker laments that Proserpina (Persephone) never knew the beauty of the 'Cumner [*sic*] cowslips' on the hills near Oxford.

121 *Pater . . . Monna Lisa . . . Lionardo* The *Mona Lisa* is the most famous painting by Leonardo da Vinci (1452–1519), and the best-known exhibit in the Louvre Gallery, Paris. Here Wilde adopts several of Pater's best-known phrases eulogizing the *Mona Lisa* in *The Renaissance*.

122 ' "*the ends of the world are come*" ' A quotation of a quotation. Here Gilbert is citing Pater's allusion to 1 Corinthians 10:11 in Pater's essay on Leonardo da Vinci.

122 *La Gioconda* An alternative title for the *Mona Lisa*. It means 'the smiling one'.

122 *the sins of the Borgias* Cesare Borgia (*c*. 1475–1507) was an infamous Italian duke who arrogated more and more power to himself through various dastardly deeds. Machiavelli referred to him as a model politician in *The Prince* (written 1513).

123 *Tannhäuser* The full title is *Tannhäuser und der Sängerkrieg auf der Wartburg*, an opera by Richard Wagner (1813–83)

first performed in 1845. It draws on legends in the Middle High German poem, *Der Wartenburgkrieg* (*c.* 1250). Tannhäuser (*c.* 1200–*c.* 1270) was a German poet of legendary fame.

123   *Venus*   Wagner's opera adapts the medieval German legend of Tannhäuser's visit to the grotto of Venus. Her beauty tempted gallant young knights to their damnation.

123   ΕΡΩΣ ΤΩΝ ΑΔΥΝΑΤΩΝ: Love of the impossible.

123   *Dorian*   In the ancient world, one who spoke the Doric dialect. Dorian culture was regarded as inferior to that of the Greeks.

123   *'bring the soul into harmony with all right things'*   In the third book of *The Republic*, Plato argues that music should have a spiritually uplifting effect on the soul. Wilde makes a similar statement in his poem, 'Humanitad' (1881).

124   *Othello . . . Lear*   Heroes of two of Shakespeare's most famous tragedies.

126   *Chambertin and a few ortolans*   Fine wine and poultry; in other words, a luxurious repast.

Part II

126   *The Survival of Thersites*   In the *Iliad*, Thersites is the only low-born character in the company of the Greeks. He was notorious for his abusive and recalcitrant behaviour.

127   *'terribly at ease in Zion'*   Another implicit attack on Arnold, who wrote in *Culture and Anarchy* that 'Socrates is terribly *at ease in Zion*'. In other words, Socrates, a Greek, would have had no problems living in a Judaeo-Christian (or Hebraic) world.

127   *the late Rector of Lincoln*   The Rector of Lincoln College, University of Oxford, here is Mark Pattison (1813–84), who contributed to *Essays and Reviews* (see p. 244).

127   *Sidney . . . Daniel . . . Jonson . . . Marlowe . . . Marlowe's greater son*   Renaissance poets and dramatists: Sir Philip Sidney (1554–86); Samuel Daniel (*c.* 1562–1619); Ben Jonson (1572–1637); and Christopher Marlowe (1564–93). 'Marlowe's greater son' is presumably Shakespeare.

127   *Agamemnon*   The king of Mycenae, he led the Greek forces in the Trojan War. On his return, he was killed

by his wife, Clytemnestra, and her lover, Aesgisthus, both of whom were avenged by Agamemnon's son, Orestes. He is celebrated in both the *Iliad* and in Aeschylus' trilogy, the *Oresteia*.

127 *Athens of Pericles* Pericles was an Athenian statesman who controlled the affairs of state from about 460 BC until his death in 429. Under his rule, some of the most imposing buildings in Athens were constructed, including the Acropolis.

127 *riddling Sphinx . . . feet are wounded . . . knows not his name* This concerns the tragedy of Oedipus. He answered the riddle of the Sphinx (a female monster). Warned by the oracle that his son would kill him, Oedipus' father, Laius, wounded and abandoned him as a baby. Brought up unaware of his true parentage, Oedipus would marry his mother and murder his father.

128 *Mantegna* Andrea Mantegna (*c.* 1431–1506), Italian Renaissance artist influenced by Donatello (see p. 246).

129 *Rubinstein* Anton Rubinstein (1829–94), Russian composer and performer, highly regarded for his technical accomplishments as a pianist.

129 *Sonata Appassionata of Beethoven* Ludwig van Beethoven (1770–1827), German composer, the most distinguished successor to Mozart.

129 *Obiter Dicta* The essays of Augustine Birrell (1850–1933) published in 1884.

130 *tears . . . Roman poet* An allusion to the *Aeneid* by the Roman poet, Virgil (70–19 BC).

130 *Divine Comedy* The major work of the Italian poet, Dante Alighieri (1265–1321). It is divided into three books, *Hell*, *Purgatory*, and *Paradise*. Each one is composed of cantos in *terza rima*, a verse form made up of sets of three-line stanzas with an interlocking rhyme scheme: *aba*, *bcb*, *cdc*, *ded* and so on.

131 *Harpies* Another name for Sirens (see p. 246). They appear in Dante's *Hell*, canto 13.

131 *Ghibelline* The Italy of Dante's time was divided by two factions, the Guelfs and the Ghibellines. The Guelfs, by reputation, were a democratic people. Dante belonged to this group. The Ghibellines, in

contrast, were a feudal aristocracy who notoriously abused their power.

131 *Casentine hills* The Casentino is a beautiful hill district of the Upper Arno in Italy; alluded to in *Hell*, canto 30.

131 *Sinon, the false Greek of Troy* Pretending he was a deserter from the Greek Army, Sinon led a giant wooden horse into the city of Troy. Once inside the city walls, Greek soldiers jumped out of the horse and attacked the Trojans; mentioned in *Hell*, canto 30.

131 *Nimrod* According to Genesis 10: 8–10, Nimrod founded the Assyrian empire where the Tower of Babel was built. He appears as a giant in *Hell*, canto 31.

131 *Styx* In classical mythology, one of the rivers of the underworld. The gods swore their most solemn oaths by the Styx.

131 *Argenti* A proud Florentine knight who shod his horse with silver (hence his name). His faction opposed Dante. He makes an appearance in *Hell*, canto 7.

131 *Cocytus* One of the rivers of the underworld. The frozen lake of Cocytus appears in *Hell*, canto 32.

131 *Bocca* Bocca degli Abati, a traitor to the Ghibellines. He appears in *Hell*, canto 32.

131 *Alberigo* Fra Alberigo is among the many unfeeling characters who inhabit one of the rings encircling hell. See *Hell*, canto 33.

131 *Lucifer* The devil; appears in *Hell*, canto 34.

131 *Cæsar* Gaius Julius Caesar (*c.* 100–44 BC), Roman emperor. Those who betrayed him appear in *Hell*, canto 34.

132 *poison of the Maremma . . . Madonna Pia* 'The Lady of Piety' married Nello, a Guelf leader, lord of Castello della Pietra in the Maremma – a region on the coast of Tuscany known for its poisonous, malarious airs. La Pia was murdered by Nello. Her story is referred to in *Purgatory*, canto 5.

132 *Ismene* River in Boeotia mentioned in *Purgatory*, canto 18.

132 *Nella* Giovanella Donati, wife of Forese Donati (a close friend of Dante). In *Purgatory*, canto 23, Dante records Forese's neglect of Nella.

132 *Buonconte* Buonconte de Montefeltro, the Ghibelline leader, mentioned in *Purgatory*, canto 5.

132 *Sordello* Troubadour (*c.* 1200–69), regarded by many as one of Dante's major precursors. He first appears in *Purgatory*, canto 6.

132 *Mantua* Sordello was born in Goito, near Mantua, the city most closely associated with his name.

132 *Rudolph of Hapsburg* (1218–92). Holy Roman Emperor, noted for his neglect of his duties. He is discovered in *Purgatory*, canto 8.

132 *Henry of England* Henry III (1207–72). In his most famous poem, *The Lament for Blacatz*, Sordello accuses him of sloth and cowardice.

132 *Beatrice* Dante's beloved. She is addressed throughout his poetry.

132 *Lethe* Another of the rivers of the underworld. Those who crossed it forgot everything they had left behind. In Dante's *Inferno*, canto 14, Lethe is the river that flows to the centre of the Earthly Paradise from Mount Purgatory to the other side of the world.

132 *Eunoe* This mythological river restores memories of good things. In Dante's Earthly Paradise the soul must drink first from Lethe and then from Eunoe to regain its lost innocence.

132 *Piccarda Donati* A young nun who was forcibly married to a man to whom she was formerly betrothed. She is mentioned in *Purgatory*, canto 24.

132 *Cunizza . . . Ezzelin* Cunizza was the sister of Ezzelino da Romano (1194–1259). According to legend, she married Count Richard de Saint-Boniface but held a lifelong passion for Sordello, with whom she eloped. Ezzelino, a notorious tyrant of Northern Italy, led his Ghibelline party into violent wars against the rival Guelfs. His bloody massacre at Padua is recorded in *Inferno*, canto 12.

132 *Folco . . . Provence . . . Azalais* Folco was a famous troubadour (1180–1255), writing in Provençal. Azalais was his beloved.

132 *Canaanitish harlot* Mary Magdalene, a figure who represents the redemptive power of God's love, turns away

from her life of prostitution to one of piety. She is first mentioned in Luke 8:2 as the woman from whom Christ cast out 'seven devils'. She reappears as one of the women who accompanied Christ as he carried his cross to Calvary, and was among the followers present at the Resurrection.

133 *Joachim of Flora* Abbot of Calabria (*c.* 1130–1202), preacher and visionary. He appears in *Paradise*, canto 12.

133 *Aquinas . . . St Francis . . . Bonaventure . . . St Dominic* All fathers of the Christian Church. Dominic (*c.* 1170–1221), founder of the Order of Friars Preachers; Aquinas (*c.* 1225–74), Dominican philosopher; Francis (*c.* 1181–1226), founder of the Franciscan Order; and Bonaventure (1221–74), Franciscan theologian. All are mentioned in *Paradise*, canto 12.

133 *Mars, Cacciaguida* Cacciaguida was the great-great-grandfather of Dante. Dante encounters him in Mars, the fifth heaven of *Paradise*, cantos 15–17.

133 *Saturn* The seventh heaven of *Paradise*.

133 *Mystical Rose* Celebrated in *Paradise*, canto 30, where it is an elaborate symbol of divine love.

133 *the great Florentine* Dante.

133 *Gautier . . . Baudelaire* Théophile Gautier (1811–72) and Charles Baudelaire (1821–67), French poets who worked closely together. Baudelaire dedicated his *Les Fleurs du mal* (1857, 1861, 1868) to Gautier.

133 *'Que m'importe que tu sois sage? / Sois belle! et sois triste!'* 'What does it matter to me that you are wise? / Be beautiful! and be sad!' from Baudelaire's 'Madrigal Triste', in *Les Fleurs du mal* (third edition, 1868).

133 *poisonous honey* In 1 Samuel 14:43 Jonathan reveals to his father, Saul, the King of Israel, that he has eaten the honey that Saul forbade the Israelites after a successful battle against the Philistines. Saul had declared that his people should make a sacrifice to God. Jonathan, a prize warrior, did not hear this instruction, and criticized Saul's commandment, since it came at a time when the Israelites were famishing. There ensued a power struggle between father and son, with the support of the people behind Jonathan. In other words, Jonathan was accused of a crime of which he was in fact guiltless.

133 *the flowers that grow in the garden of Perdita*   In Shakespeare's *The Winter's Tale*, Perdita is the daughter lost at birth because of the brutal banishment by her father, King Polixenes of Bohemia, who wrongly suspected her mother of adultery. Abandoned in Sicilia, she was found by shepherds. In Act IV scene iv, at the age of sixteen, Perdita is garlanded in flowers. She is the centre of attention at a rustic sheep-shearing festival where her father, still unknown to her, is present. Much of this scene is given over to a complex philosophical debate between father and daughter about the cultivation of flowers, and whether 'hybrids' are the products of 'art' or 'nature'.

134 *Meleager*   Greek poet of the *Anthology* (see p. 250).

134 *the lover of Heliodore*   King Seleucus IV Philopator of Syria was murdered by one of his ministers, Heliodorus.

134 *Fantine*   The unfortunate woman in *Les Misérables* (1862) by Victor Hugo (1802–85). Her illegitimate child, Cosette, is saved from the clutches of foster parents by Jean Valjean, a kindly criminal.

134 *Manon Lescaut*   Heroine of *Histoire du chevalier des Grieux et de Manon Lescaut* (1731), a tempestuous romance, by Antoine-François (L'Abbé de) Prévost (1697–1763).

134 *Tyrian*   Adonis, beautiful boy who was the mortal lover the goddess, Venus.

134 *Orestes*   Son of Agamemnon who avenged his father's death (see p. 254).

135 *Spinoza*   Baruch (Benedictus) de Spinoza (1632–77), Dutch philosopher, proponent of pantheism, the belief that God lives in everything.

135 *the great art-critic of the Greeks*   Aristotle.

135 *Cordelia and the daughter of Brabantio*   Tragic heroines in Shakespeare's *King Lear* and *Othello* respectively. Brabantio's daughter is Desdemona. Both daughters disappoint their fathers.

135 *Private Views*   Occasions when vistors are allowed into art galleries by invitation only.

136 *città divina*   In *The Renaissance*, Pater refers to a poem by Matteo Palmieri entitled *La Città Divina*. This poem, says Pater, 'represented the human race as an incarnation of those angels who, in revolt of Lucifer, were neither for

Jehovah nor for His enemies'. The poem was condemned for its heretical views. Its proper title is 'La città di Vita'.

136 *fruitio Dei*   Pleasure in God.

136 *the Academic philosopher*   Plato.

137 *Pater . . . intangible Being*   In his essay on 'Coleridge' in *Appreciations* (1889), Pater writes: 'Who would change the colour or curve of a rose-leaf for that . . . colourless, formless, intangible, being – Plato put so high?'

137 *Illumination of Philo*   Philon Judaeus (*c.* 30 BC–45 AD), head of the Jewish community in Alexandria; he interpreted Judaism in the light of Greek philosophy.

137 *Abyss of Eckhart*   Johannes (Meister) Eckhart (*c.* 1260–1327), German mystic. His works were deemed heretical.

137 *Vision of Böhme*   Jakob Böhme (1575–1624), German mystic.

137 *Swedenborg's blinded eyes*   Emanuel Swedenborg (1688–1772), Swedish mystic.

137 *Kant*   Immanuel Kant (1724–1804), German philosopher.

137 *written upon the wall the prophecy of our doom*   See Daniel 5, where King Belshazzar sees the strange words MENE, MENE, TEKEL, UPHARSIN written upon a wall. Translated, these words mean 'God hath numbered thy kingdom, and finished it; thou art weighed in the balances, and art found wanting'. This inscription reveals his doom.

137 *Nemesis*   Greek goddess of retribution.

137 *Fates*   In classical mythology, the Fates wove a web around each and every human life. There were three of them: Lachesis (who assigned one's lot at birth); Clotho (who spun the thread of life); and Atropos (who cut the thread at the moment of death).

138 *Leopardi*   Giacomo Leopardi (1798–1837), regarded as Italy's greatest Romantic poet.

138 *Theocritus*   (*c.* 300–*c.* 260? BC) Sicilian pastoral poet.

138 *Pierre Vidal*   Twelfth-century Provençal troubadour.

138 *Lancelot*   In Arthurian myth, Lancelot enjoyed a secret love for Arthur's queen, Guinevere.

138 *Abelard*   Pierre Abelard (1079–1142); priest who was the fated lover of Héloïse (1101–64). He was castrated at the order of her uncle, a canon of Notre Dame.

138 *Villon* François Villon (1431–?), French poet, infamous for his criminal life.

138 *Endymion* In ancient Greek myth, a beautiful young man loved by the Moon. John Keats (1795–1821) published his poem, *Endymion*, in 1818.

138 *Atys* Another beautiful young man celebrated in classical mythology; remembered for his brutal self-castration.

138 *the Dane* Hamlet.

139 *'the best that is known and thought in the world'* From Arnold's 'The Function of Criticism at the Present Time', where he claims that English literature in the Victorian period manifests very little striving towards artistic perfection.

139 *Epicurus* (341–271 BC), Greek philosopher, proponent of hedonism.

139 ΒΙΟΣ ΘΕΩΡΗΤΙΚΟΣ: Life of contemplation.

140 *joints of his harness* See 1 Kings 22:34, where Ahab, King of Israel, receives a fatal wound at the hands of the Philistines in the battle of Ramoth-gilead.

140 *Philistine* Arnold complained that English culture was vitiated by the narrow-minded attitudes of those middle-class people he jokingly referred to as Philistines. Historically speaking, the Philistines were the most educated people of their time.

140 *disinterested intellectual judgement* In 'The Function of Criticism at the Present Time', Arnold writes: 'I am bound by my own definition of criticism: *a disinterested endeavour to learn and propagate the best that is known and thought in the world.*'

140 *the survival of the failure* Another play on the Spencerian notion of 'the survival of the fittest'. After reading Darwin's *The Origin of Species*, Spencer (1820–1903) developed a theory of social Darwinism. This theory is extrapolated in *First Principles* (1862).

141 *Fabianists* The Fabian Society, founded in 1883–4, was a powerful intellectual group of socialists.

141 *Utopia* Published in 1516, *Utopia* is a satirical work by Sir Thomas More (1478–1535). The title names an imaginary and ideal island in the New World.

141   *the voice of one crying in the wilderness*   See Matthew 3:3,
      where St John the Baptist goes out into the wilderness to
      preach God's word. This was in preparation for his supreme
      task: the baptizing of Jesus Christ.

142   *People say that the schoolmaster is abroad*   A well-known
      quotation by Lord Brougham (1778–1868): 'Look out
      gentlemen, the schoolmaster is abroad' (from a speech
      delivered in 1825).

142   *self-culture . . . Goethe*   An allusion to Pater's chapter on
      'Winckelmann' in *The Renaissance*.

142   *Renaissance . . . Humanism*   Renaissance humanists were
      engaged in the *studia humanitatis* – the study of the
      'humanities': grammar, rhetoric, history, poetry, and
      moral philosophy. This type of education was fostered
      in sixteenth-century England. Study of the humanities
      was distinct from mathematics, natural philosophy, and
      theology. The word 'humanism' came into its own in
      the nineteenth century, and was applied to questions
      of human nature, particularly in relation to the areas of
      inquiry covered by Renaissance humanists.

143   *Chuang Tsŭ*   Taoist philosopher (fourth century BC);
      Wilde reviewed a translation of his works in 1890.
      Chuang Tsŭ advocated releasing oneself to the ebb and
      flow of life.

144   *Rosencrantz and Guildenstern*   Minor characters in *Hamlet*.
      Their marginal role in the play has been a source of
      comment by a number of writers.

145   *ever be looking for fresh impressions*   Pater wrote in the
      controversial 'Conclusion' to *The Renaissance*: 'What we
      have to do is to be for ever curiously testing new opinions
      and courting new impressions, never acquiescing in a facile
      orthodoxy.'

145   *nouveau frisson*   New sensation.

145   *Luministe*   Type of painting exploiting lighting effects.

145   *Symboliste*   School of experimental French poetry evolv-
      ing from the work of Charles Baudelaire; its main
      exponents are Paul Verlaine (1842–98), Arthur Rimbaud
      (1854–91), and Stéphane Mallarmé (1842–98).

145   *Marvel . . . Sidney . . . Lord Brooke . . . Penshurst oaks
      . . . Imaginary Portraits*   In his *Imaginary Conversations*

of Literary Men and Statesmen (1824–9), Walter Savage Landor (1775–1864) includes three dialogues between John Milton (1608–74) and Andrew Marvell (1621–78), and one between Sir Philip Sidney (1554–86) and Sir Fulke Greville (1st Baron Brooke) (1554–1628) at Sidney's Home, Penshurst, in Kent. Greville's *Life* of Sidney was published in 1652.

145 *Watteau* Jean-Antoine (1684–1721), French painter, whose landscapes created an idealized picture of life.

145 *Aufklärung* German word meaning 'enlightenment'. The rise of rationalist and empiricist philosophies in Europe during the seventeenth and eighteenth centuries is referred to as the Enlightenment.

146 *old Pagan . . . Carlyle* The 'old Pagan' is Landor (see note on 'Marvel . . . ' on this page). Thomas Carlyle (1795–1881), was a Scottish essayist and polemicist, one of the most influential figures in Victorian letters.

146 *Ruskin* John Ruskin (1819–1900) distinguished critic who was committed to the representation of truth to nature in art. His influence on Wilde is inestimable.

146 *Browning . . . painter and poet* Browning wrote many poems about Italian grand masters (see p. 244).

146 *M. Renan . . . dialogue* Renan's *Dialogues et Fragments Philosophiques* were published in 1876.

146 *Rossetti . . . sonnet-music . . . Giorgione . . . Ingres* Dante Gabriel Rossetti (1828–82), English poet and painter. He wrote many 'Sonnets for Pictures', including 'For a Venetian Pastoral, by Giorgione' and 'For "Ruggiero and Angelica", by Ingres' (both 1881).

147 *Art . . . Plato . . . divine madness* Art, for Plato, is dangerous. In *The Republic*, all artists are exiled from his city.

148 *Chaos has come again* An echo of Shakespeare's *Othello* Act III, scene iii, where Othello, the black lieutenant of the Venetian Army, is in the process of being tricked into believing that his wife, Desdemona, is committing adultery by the seemingly 'honest' Iago. Finding it hard to think of Desdemona's infidelity, Othello says to her: 'Excellent wretch! Perdition catch my soul / But I do love thee! And when I love thee not, / Chaos is come again.'

148 *Tartuffe* Comedy by Jean-Baptise Poquelin (pseudonym Molière) (1622–73).

148 *Chadband* The hypocritical cleric in *Bleak House* (1852–3) by Charles Dickens (1812–70).

149 *new Journalism . . . old vulgarity 'writ large'* The New Journalism refers to the sensationalizing papers of the 1880s and 1890s such as the *Pall Mall Gazette* and the *Daily Chronicle*. These papers traded in exposing scandals.

149 *Temperament* Pater, in his Preface to *The Renaissance*, writes: 'What is important, then, is not that the critic should possess a correct abstract definition of beauty for the intellect, but a certain kind of temperament, the power of being moved by the presence of beautiful objects.'

150 *lovely passage in . . . Plato . . . young Greek* See Book 3 of *The Republic*.

150 *Waynfleete's chapel* Magdalen College, Oxford, which Wilde attended from 1874 to 1878, was founded by William of Waynflete (*c.* 1395–1486), Bishop of Winchester and Lord Chancellor.

151 *Christ Church* One of the Oxford colleges.

151 *Laud's building in the College of St John* William Laud (1573–1645) became president of St John's College, Oxford, in 1611, and later Archbishop of Canterbury.

151 *Caliban* The 'savage' represented in Shakespeare's late romance, *The Tempest*. His name is almost an anagram of 'cannibal'.

151 *the creative instinct is strong in the Celt* See Introduction (pp. 13–14). Wilde is implicitly attacking Arnold's anti-Celtic prejudices in 'On the Study of Celtic Literature' (1866).

151 *Impressionist painters of Paris and London* 'Impressionist' originally referred to a loose association of French painters who were experimenting with colour and line, including Claude Monet (1840–1926) and Pierre-August Renoir (1841–1919).

152 *Gautier's immortal Symphonie en Blanc Majeur* Gautier's poem, 'Symphonie en Blanc Majeur', appeared in his collection, *Emaux et camées* (1852).

152 *'moment's monument', as Rossetti phrased it* In his prefatory sonnet to 'The House of Life' sonnet sequence (1881),

Dante Gabriel Rossetti wrote: '*A Sonnet is a moment's monument*'.

152   *the Archaicistes*   Group of painters who followed Gustave Moreau (1826–98) in their use of erotic subject-matter drawn from mythology.

154   *Plato tells us . . . rhythm and harmony into the mind*   See Book 3, chapter 9 of *The Republic* where Socrates discusses the rules affecting musical accompaniment, harmony, and rhythm as inseparable parts of song.

154   *Forms are the food of faith, cried Newman*   See Newman's *Apologia pro Vita Sua*.

154   *Queen Constance*   The Mother of Arthur, Duke of Brittany, in Shakespeare's *King John*. In Act III, scene iii, she makes a poignant speech mourning the death of her son.

155   *Royal Academician*   Membership of the Royal Academy of Arts was a mark of considerable distinction. The Royal Academy was the most influential body in determining artistic taste and judgement in the nineteenth century.

155   *Athenaeum Club*   Gentleman's club in central London. Founded in 1824, its membership drew on distinguished persons from the arts and sciences.

156   *Wordsworth . . . Endymion . . . Shelley . . . deaf to Wordsworth's message . . . Byron . . . could appreciate neither poet . . . wonder of Keats*   When Wordsworth visited London in 1817, he was introduced to Keats by the painter, Benjamin Haydon (1786–1846). Haydon reports that after Keats had read out his hymn to Pan from *Endymion* (1818), Wordsworth drily said it was 'a very pretty piece of Paganism'. This remark understandably wounded Keats. Shelley's 'Peter Bell the Third' (1819) is a cruel parody of Wordsworth's 'Peter Bell' (1798). In canto 2 of *Don Juan*, Byron attacks Wordsworth, and in canto 9 he mocks Keats. In later life, Byron said: 'When I was in Switzerland, Shelley used to dose me with Wordsworth physic even to the point of nausea.'

156   *Euripides . . . Sophokles*   These famous Greek tragedians were arch-rivals.

156   *Sir Joshua . . . Gainsborough*   Sir Joshua Reynolds (1723–92), painter and essayist. His fourteenth *Discourse* (1788)

on art discusses the work of the landscape painter, Thomas Gainsborough (1727–88). Gainsborough's work stood for much that Reynolds disliked.

157 *Mr Walter Besant* (1836–1901). Novelist, essayist, and historian.

157 *Mr Rudyard Kipling . . . Plain Tales from the Hills* Rudyard Kipling (1865–1936), Anglo-Indian poet, novelist, and essayist, published his collection of stories, *Plain Tales from the Hills*, in 1888. Subtly evoking the tense atmosphere of Anglo-Indian life, this volume was an immediate success.

158 *Le Rouge et le Noir* Published in 1830, this is one of the best-known novels of Stendhal, the pseudonym of Marie Henri Beyle (1783–1842).

158 *Criticism, as Arnold points out* A further reference to 'The Function of Criticism at the Present Time' where Arnold, unlike Wilde, ranks the creative faculty above the critical. However, in the course of his argument, Arnold would seem to betray his principles, since great 'creative' genius seems to be borne out by a fine 'critical' turn of mind, as this extract indicates: 'The grand work of literary genius is a work of synthesis and exposition, not of analysis and discovery; its gift lies in the faculty of being happily inspired by a certain intellectual and spritual atmosphere, by a certain order of ideas, when it finds itself in them; of dealing divinely with these ideas, presenting them in the most effective and attractive combinations, – making beautiful works with them, in short. But it must have the atmosphere, it must find itself amidst the order of ideas, in order to work freely; and these it is not so easy to command.' Wilde, then, would appear to be reading Arnold's essay against itself.

159 *Titan lizard . . . Behemoth . . . Leviathan* The 'Titan lizard' is Behemoth the crocodile, and Leviathan the whale, mentioned in Job, 40–1.

159 *Manchester school . . . Peace Societies* The Manchester School was a grouping of radical political economists committed to the principle of *laissez-faire*. Among their leading lights were Richard Cobden (1804–65) and John Bright (1811–89).

160 *Napoleon . . . Eckerman* Johann Peter Eckermann (1792–1854) fought in the Napoleonic Wars and assisted Goethe in the publication of his work.

160 *peace that springs from understanding* 'And the peace of God, which passeth all understanding, shall keep your hearts and minds, through Christ Jesus' (Philippians 4:7).

161 *'sweet reasonableness'* In the twelfth chapter of *Literature and Dogma* (1873), Matthew Arnold declares that readers of the Bible should be in search of 'righteousness', and take their example from 'the method and secret and sweet reasonableness' of Jesus Christ. 'Sweet reasonableness' is Arnold's translation of the Greek *epieikeia*.

161 *The Origin of Species* Darwin's famous work, which put forward the theory of 'natural selection', was published in 1859.

161 *Julian* Flavius Claudius Julianus ('Julian the Apostate') (AD 332–63) was raised as a Christian but renounced his religion in favour of the old pagan gods.

161 *antinomian* Antinomians were a sect of Christians who believed that they were not bound by God to any moral law. They claimed that human beings had a natural inner impulse towards good.

THE SOUL OF MAN UNDER SOCIALISM

164 *Darwin* Charles Darwin (1809–82), theorist of evolution. His best-known work, *The Origin of Species*, was published in 1859.

164 *Keats* John Keats (1795–1821), one of the most highly regarded Romantic poets. Among his most famous works are his odes.

164 *Renan* Joseph Ernest Renan (1823–92) gained notoriety in Europe with his *Life of Jesus* (1863), which contested the religious authority of the Bible.

164 *article on the function of criticism* 'The Critic as Artist', parts 1 and 2, reprinted in this edition.

168 *Slavery was put down in America* Slavery and the slave trade were brought to an end in the American South at the time of American Civil War in 1862.

168 *the Abolitionists* Anti-slavery campaigners.

168 *Marie Antoinette ... Vendée* The French Revolution exploded in 1789, leaving its mark on political debate for the next hundred years. Marie Antoinette, the queen, was sentenced to death by the revolutionaries. The Vendée was one of the areas of France where counter-revolutionary forces gathered in 1793. The name suggests pro-monarchist feelings.

169 *Shelley* Percy Bysshe Shelley (1792–1822), radical Romantic poet, whose work was frequently subject to political controversy.

169 *Victor Hugo* (1802–85). French novelist. Among his most famous works is *Les Misérables* (1862).

170 *Cæsar ... Mommsen* Theodor Mommsen (1817–1903) wrote a *History of Rome* (1856). Caesar, one of the greatest emperors of Rome, seized power from Pompey, and was then toppled by Brutus and Cassius. Shakespeare's *Julius Caesar* dramatizes these events.

171 *Marcus Aurelius* Roman emperor (AD 121–80), who was also a stoic philosopher and author of *Meditations*.

172 *'Know Thyself!'* This maxim comes from the Athenian law-giver, Solon (*c.* 628–*c.* 559 BC). In its Latin form ('*Nosce teipsum*'), it stood as a central tenet of Renaissance moral wisdom: see, for example, Sir John Davies's poem, *Nosce Teipsum* (1599).

172 *Jesus ... the accumulation of private property* Wilde is drawing on the authority of the Gospels to underline Christ's 'socialist' teaching, notably the sermon on the Mount (Matthew, 5 and Mark, 10:21): 'Sell whatsoever thou hast and give to the poor.'

173 *a woman who was taken in adultery* Wilde's biblical reference seems to be confused. Although he is alluding to Mary Magdalene, out of whom Christ cast 'seven devils' (see Luke 8:2), the words Wilde uses pertain to the woman committed for adultery in John, 8:3–14.

174 *'Let the dead bury the dead'* Strictly speaking, this should read 'Let the dead bury their dead'. The quotation is from Matthew, 8:22.

174 *Father Damien ... lepers* Joseph Damien de Veuster (1840–89) was a Belgian Roman Catholic missionary celebrated for his work among lepers in Hawaii.

175 *Oligarchies . . . ochlocracies* Oligarchy is a form of government by a powerful elite; ochlocracy is the opposite, namely government by the uneducated masses.

175 *the bludgeoning of the people by the people for the people* In his famous Gettysburg Address of 1863, the American President, Abraham Lincoln said that 'government of the people, by the people, and for the people, shall not perish from the earth'. Wilde is casting doubt on this supposedly democratic claim.

175 *'He who would be free . . . must not conform'* These thoughts come from the Greek Stoic philosopher, Epictetus (of the first century AD).

176 *the Macbeths and terrible Vautrins* The popular image of the eleventh-century Macbeth family is recorded in Shakespeare's tragedy, *Macbeth*, Vautrin is a criminal who appears on many occasions in Honoré de Balzac's popular nineteenth-century novels, collected together under the title of *The Human Comedy*.

180 *France . . . Academy of Letters* The French Academy of Letters was established in 1634 by Cardinal de Richelieu to promote all aspects of the arts and to maintain standards in the use of the French language. Membership of the Académie Française is limited to forty persons of distinction. Britain established no similar institution until the Arts Council was founded in 1946.

181 *Charles Kingsley* novelist (1819–75), best known for his moral tale for children, *The Water Babies* (1863), and his novels of Christian Socialism, notably *Alton Locke* (1850).

182 *the public press* Wilde is noting how new kinds of sensationalizing journalism were reaching a mass readership of working- and lower middle-class people. The *Daily Mail*, for example, was established in 1896 as a paper dedicated to the popular spirit of empire.

182 *'morbid'* The word literally means sickening or unhealthy; here, however, it also has a homosexual implication.

184 *the pen is mightier than the paving-stone* A play on the idiomatic phrase 'the pen is mightier than the sword', first used by Edward Bulwer-Lytton.

184 *Burke* Edmund Burke (1729–97) Tory politician and author, best known for his *Reflections on the Revolution*

in *France* (1790). The 'three estates' of the realm were traditionally the Lords Spiritual (men of the church), the Lords Temporal (hereditary peers), and the Commons (Members of Parliament). Burke is often credited with the term 'fourth estate' as applied, by way of a joke, to the press. The term, in fact, comes from the *Historical Essays* (1828) of Thomas Babington Macaulay (1800–59).

185 *some incident in the private life of a great statesman* Divorce cases brought against or by famous politicians were blown out of all proportion by the press. Many political careers were consequently ruined. In 1889, Charles Stewart Parnell, the champion of Home Rule, was destroyed in this way.

186 *Mr Irving* Sir Henry Irving (1838–1905), famous actor, renowned for his leading roles in Shakespearean plays. He was established at the Lyceum Theatre from 1871.

187 *Lyceum . . . Haymarket* The finest theatres of the West End of London. Wilde's *A Woman of No Importance* opened at the Haymarket Theatre in 1893.

188 Thackeray's *Esmond . . . Pendennis . . . Philip . . . Vanity Fair* William Makepeace Thackeray (1811–63) was a very popular novelist and editor. Novels referred to here are *The History of Henry Esmond* (1852), *The History of Pendennis* (1848–50) *The Adventures of Philip* (1861–2) and *Vanity Fair* (1847–8).

188 *George Meredith* Novelist (1818–1909), regarded as a challenging, unorthodox writer, whose well-known novels include *The Egoist* (1879). Wilde clearly thought highly of him.

189 *the Great Exhibition* Installed in the Crystal Palace in Hyde Park, London, in 1851. It was a popular exhibition of modern technology and design, displaying wares from all over the British Empire.

190 *Dante . . . Verona* The Italian poet Dante Alighieri (1265– 1321) had been sentenced to death in 1321. He fled to Verona where he sought refuge with the ruler of that city, Can Grande.

190 *Tasso . . . Ferrara's madman's cell* Torquato Tasso (1544–95), Italian poet, author of the famous epic, *Jerusalem Delivered* (1580–1). Legend says he lived at the court of

Ferrara. He fell in love with the Duke of Ferrara's sister and because of this passion was confined to a madman's cell for seven years.

190 *Pope . . . Cellini* The pope in question is Clement VII (1478–1534), who is best remembered in Britain for refusing to annul the marriage of Henry VIII to Catherine of Aragon, an event which brought about the establishment of the Church of England. Benvenuto Cellini (1500–71), was an Italian goldsmith, sculptor, and writer, whose *Autobiography* was published in 1728. He was a notorious criminal, pardoned for murder by Clement VII but then imprisoned by the same Pope until he escaped in 1537.

191 *Louis XIV* (1638–1715). The most powerful monarch who ever reigned in France. He is remembered for the endless wars he waged in Northern Europe and for his extraordinary profligacy. The Palace of Versailles was built at his behest.

194 *Thebaid* Early Christian hermits settled in this area located around Thebes in Egypt.

195 *Raphael* (1483–1520). Master painter of the Italian Renaissance.

196 *Nihilist* A name for a Russian revolutionary; the Nihilists assassinated Czar Alexander II in 1881. Wilde's first play, *Vera; or the Nihilists* (1880), examines their politics.

196 *Hellenism* Classical Greek culture; an ideal model of life. The term was used most influentially in Victorian period by Matthew Arnold.